I0867933

KRISTER AMONG THE JEWS AND GENTILES

Studies in Judaism and Christianity

Exploration of Issues in the Contemporary Dialogue between Christians and Jews

EDITORS

Michael McGarry, CSP

Mark-David Janus, CSP, PhD

Yehezkel Landau, DMin

Peter Pettit, PhD

Elena Procario-Foley, PhD

Ellen M. Umansky, PhD

Rabbi Stephen Wylen

A STIMULUS BOOK

KRISTER AMONG THE JEWS AND GENTILES

Essays in Appreciation of the Life and Work of Krister Stendahl

Edited by Paula Fredriksen
and Jesper Svartvik

A STIMULUS BOOK

PAULIST PRESS • NEW YORK • MAHWAH, NJ

Frontispiece by Lennart Boberg

Cover image by Denver Post via Getty Images
Cover and book design by Lynn Else

Library of Congress Control Number: 2018948417

ISBN: 978-0-8091-5401-2 (paperback)
ISBN: 978-1-58768-779-2 (e-book)

Published by Paulist Press
997 Macarthur Boulevard
Mahwah, New Jersey 07430

www.paulistpress.com

Printed and bound in the
United States of America

CONTENTS

IV. THE FRIENDSHIP

CONTRIBUTORS

George J. Brooke is now Rylands Professor of Biblical Criticism and Exegesis Emeritus at the University of Manchester, where he taught from 1984 until 2016. He has been president of the British Association of Jewish Studies (1999) and of the Society for Old Testament Study (2012). He has written extensively on the Dead Sea Scrolls, and some of his essays are available in collections: *The Dead Sea Scrolls and the New Testament* (2005) and *Reading the Dead Sea Scrolls: Essays on Method* (2013). He is currently editor of the Brill Series Studies on the Texts of the Desert of Judah.

James Carroll is the author of eight works of nonfiction, most recently *Christ Actually*, a book about Jesus seen in light of the Holocaust; and twelve novels, most recently *The Cloister*, a story about the twelfth-century fork in the road that led to the twentieth-century nightmare. His work has received the Scripps-Howard Journalism Award, the National Book Award, the National Jewish Book Award, the PEN-John Kenneth Galbraith Award, the Thomas Merton Award, and the Peace Now Award. He is an Associate of the Mahindras Humanities Center at Harvard University. He lives in Boston with his wife, the writer Alexandra Marshall.

Paula Fredriksen, Aurelio Professor of Scripture Emerita at Boston University, since 2009 has been Distinguished Visiting Professor of Comparative Religion at the Hebrew University, Jerusalem. A fellow of the American Academy of Arts and Sciences, she also holds three honorary doctorates in theology and religious studies. Author of *Augustine on Romans* (1982) and *From Jesus to Christ* (1988; 2000), her *Jesus of Nazareth, King of the Jews* won a 1999 National Jewish Book Award. In *Augustine and the Jews* (2010), she explored the development of Christian anti-Judaism; in *Sin: The Early History of an Idea* (2012), the shifting conceptions of God and of humanity in the period from Jesus to Augustine. Her two latest studies, *Paul: The Pagans' Apostle* (2017), and *When Christians Were Jews: The First Generation* (2018), explore the interactions of radical Jewish apocalyptic expectations and Roman political order within first-century Mediterranean culture.

Amy-Jill Levine is University Professor of New Testament and Jewish Studies, Mary Jane Werthan Professor of Jewish Studies, and professor of New Testament studies at Vanderbilt Divinity School and College of Arts and Science; she is also affiliated professor, Centre for the Study of Jewish-Christian Relations, Cambridge, UK. Her books include *The Misunderstood Jew: The Church and the Scandal of the Jewish Jesus; The Meaning of the Bible: What the Jewish Scriptures and the Christian Old Testament Can Teach Us* (with Douglas Knight); *The New Testament: Methods and Meanings* (with Warren Carter); and *Short Stories by Jesus: The Enigmatic Parables of a Controversial Rabbi*. With Sandy Eisenberg Sasso, she coauthored the children's books *Who Counts? 100 Sheep, 10 Coins, and 2 Sons* and *The Marvelous Mustard Seed*. With Marc Z. Brettler, she coedited the *Jewish Annotated New Testament*. Holding a BA from Smith College and an MA and a PhD from Duke University, as well as six honorary doctorates, Professor Levine is a self-described Yankee Jewish feminist who teaches New Testament in Nashville, Tennessee, the buckle of the Bible Belt.

John W. Marshall is associate professor in the Department for the Study of Religion at the University of Toronto and holds graduate cross-appointments in Jewish studies and classics. He is the author of *Parables of War: Reading John's Jewish Apocalypse*, and, with John Kloppenborg, the coeditor of *Apocalypticism, Anti-Semitism and the Historical Jesus: Subtexts in Criticism*. His publications treat Paul within Judaism, postcolonial analyses of early Christianity, apocalyptic movements in early Christianity, and their relations to Judaism. He is currently a member of the editorial board of the *Journal of Biblical Literature*, and vice principal of University College at the University of Toronto.

Laura Salah Nasrallah is professor of New Testament and early Christianity at Harvard University: The Divinity School. She is author of *An Ecstasy of Folly: Prophecy and Authority in Early Christianity* (2004) and *Christian Responses to Roman Art and Architecture: The Second-Century Church amid the Spaces of Empire* (2010). She is also coeditor, with Elisabeth Schüssler Fiorenza, of *Prejudice and Christian Beginnings: Investigating Race, Gender, and Ethnicity in Early Christian Studies* (2009), and, with Charalambos Bakirtzis and Steven J. Friesen, of *From Roman to Early Christian Thessalonikē: Studies in Religion and Archaeology* (2010). She has recently completed a book entitled *Archaeology and the Letters of Paul.*

Jesper Svartvik holds the Krister Stendahl Chair of Theology of Religions at Lund University and at the Swedish Theological Institute in Jerusalem. His teaching and research include interreligious studies, especially Jewish-Christian relations, and biblical studies, especially the New Testament in its contemporary Jewish contexts. He has authored nine books: *Mark and Mission* (2000); a commentary in Swedish on the Gospel of Thomas (2002, 2nd ed. 2004); *Skriftens ansikten* (The Visages of Scripture, 2001, 2nd ed. 2005); *Ordet* (The Word, 2004); *Bibeltolkningens bakgator* (The Back Alleys of Biblical Interpretation, 2006); *Textens tilltal* (The Address of the Text, 2009); and also a trilogy on three key concepts in Christian theology (creation, reconciliation, and grace) in the light of Jewish-Christian relations: *Förundran och förväntan* (Amazement and Expectation, 2012), *Försoning och förvandling* (Reconciliation and Transformation, 2014; English and Spanish translations 2018) and *Förunderligt förtroende* (Amazing Trust, 2016). He has coedited several other books, among them *Christ Jesus and the Jewish People Today* (2011; Italian translation 2012); *Religious Stereotyping and Interreligious Relations* (2013); and *Enabling Dialogue about the Land* (2018).

PREFACE

Professor of biblical studies and dean of Harvard Divinity School, bishop in his native Stockholm and pathbreaking participant in interreligious dialogue, scholar and pastor: Krister Stendahl served—with grace, humility, and humor—in all these roles. 2018 marks ten years since his death, *aetate* eighty-six, on April 15, 2008. This book, in honor of his memory, provides its readers in seven succinct chapters with discussions, analyses, and appreciations of Stendahl's contributions in various arenas: institutional formation, both of university and of church; interreligious dialogue and relations; biblical and historical research. Its authors not only sketch the contours of Stendahl's service and scholarship, but also reflect upon his legacy. How can Krister Stendahl's insights—moral, theological, historical, professional—guide us as we face the challenges of today?

Paula Fredriksen	*Jesper Svartvik*
Jerusalem, Israel	Lund, Sweden
6 Tevet 5778	Fourth Sunday in Advent
	December 24, 2017

All proceeds from this publication go to support the Krister Stendahl Scholarship Fund of the Swedish Theological Institute in Jerusalem.

INTRODUCTION
THE WORD AND THE WORLD

Two prime foci organized Krister Stendahl's work: the word—that is, the Bible—and the world. *The word*: Stendahl was, foremost, a biblical scholar. These texts were the fountain of his faith, the foundation of his theology, and the source for his scholarly curiosity. *The world*: profoundly social, and no less profoundly socially conscious, Stendahl was always concerned about the implications of his scholarly endeavors for the world that, in the spirit of *tikkun 'olam*, he endlessly sought to repair and improve. The collection of essays that follow trace the ways in which Stendahl lived out these twin concerns both privately and publicly.

In the first chapter, "A Towering Presence, Bent Like Grass," *Jesper Svartvik* offers a biographical study of Stendahl's professional life. Drawing on hundreds of journal articles in Swedish, as well as on still-unpublished materials from Stendahl's archived papers at Harvard Divinity School, Svartvik surveys Stendahl's important years in Sweden, both when he trained as a doctoral student under Anton Fridrichsen in Uppsala in the 1950s, and when he served as bishop in the diocese of Stockholm in the 1980s. Svartvik also investigates and analyzes the impact that Stendahl had on Sweden between these two formative periods in his life. The Swedish theological landscape changed drastically between 1954 and 1984, and Stendahl played his part in these changes: although teaching in those years at Harvard Divinity School, he was often consulted in Sweden on both ecclesiastical and academic matters. Working with both published and unpublished materials, Svartvik particularly addresses one of the metaquestions of this volume: How did Stendahl form the age, and how did the age form Stendahl?

In her chapter "Saying No: Krister Stendahl on Scripture and on Leadership," *Laura Nasrallah* explores how Krister Stendahl's act of saying no during his time as a professor and especially during his deanship at Harvard Divinity School was paradoxically connected to an abundance in his impact. The chapter explores Stendahl's list of noes in biblical studies—how *not* to approach a text you love, his decision to rescind an agreement to write a commentary on the Letter to the Romans due to his heavy leadership schedule, and an interview in which Stendahl himself wonders when he should have said no. Using archival materials, including letters and handwritten sermon notes, the chapter shows how these noes opened up significant areas for scholarship and theological leadership, including charismatic Christians, members of the Latter Day Saints, sustained support and encouragement of feminist students at Harvard Divinity School, and sustained dialogue with Jewish scholars and practitioners. He "redeemed the time" by saying no to some tasks and turning to what was urgent, whether interfaith work, support of the feminist struggle, or preaching against the racist violence of the 1960s.

In "From Holy Envy to Holy Criticism," *Amy-Jill Levine* argues synthetically from Stendahl's legacy that Jewish-Christian interfaith dialogue needs to move past the stage of show-and-tell to genuine and mature mutual respect. Identifying the settings where Jewish-Christian dialogues take place—among professionals appointed by church bodies or by Jewish organizations, in academic symposia on college campuses, and in local gatherings of interested laity—she shows how each group can contribute to correcting negative stereotypes of Jews and Judaism promoted to this day in various Christian websites, publications, sermons, and study guides. On the Jewish side, Levine considers the impact of Jewish ambivalence—and even aversion—toward Messianic Jews on interfaith dialogue. Finally, she urges that even long-standing negative stereotypes can be corrected if people of goodwill speak up and speak out against them; and that honest conversations, undertaken rather than foreclosed, can lead to advances in mutual understanding.

The next three essays reflect upon Stendahl's scholarly leadership. In "Inspecting *The School of St. Matthew*," *George Brooke* reconsiders the principal contributions made by Stendahl's doctoral thesis, which was also his first book in English: *The School of St. Matthew and Its Use of the Old Testament*. Brooke first evaluates current scholarship on the Gospel of Matthew's scriptural citations, to see how academic discourse on this subject since Stendahl's 1954 publication has changed and developed, and why. Second, Brooke sets Stendahl's contribution within the wider context of what is now known about scribes and scribalism in the late Second Temple period and beyond. Third, he juxtaposes some of Stendahl's insights with the latest scholarship on the Dead Sea Scrolls—an important comparandum in Stendahl's book—now that the full corpus of the Scrolls has been published. Fourth, Brooke attends to Stendahl's suggestions about ancient Jewish scriptural interpretation (*pesher*) and testimonia with a view toward suggesting that, in light of more recent scholarship on these issues in the Scrolls, Stendahl set an agenda for a generation of New Testament scholars. *School of St. Matthew*, Brooke concludes, remains a landmark study.

John Marshall, next, in "The Influence of 'The Introspective Conscience' on the New Paul(s)," traces the *Nachleben* of Krister Stendahl's seminal 1963 article, "The Apostle Paul and the Introspective Conscience of the West." Addressed originally to a meeting of the

American Psychological Association, "Introspective Conscience," Marshall notes, objected to easy deployments of Paul as contemporary to current modes of thought and culture. Stendahl's cautions against the facile construction of a contemporaneous Paul has been generative for the historical critical study of the apostle for the last half century. The New Perspective on Paul, drawing also on the Stendahl-influenced work of E. P. Sanders, has seen Stendahl as "effectively the father of the new perspective" (so James Dunn). Yet scholars critical of the New Perspective also claim Stendahl's work as a foundation for their opposition, either arguing against Stendahl while attempting to undermine the New Perspective (thus Käsemann, Westerholm, et al.), or, more radically, urging that the New Perspective has not internalized Stendahl's insights enough (Gaston, Gager, et al.). The essay also treats those elements of Stendahl's article that did not fully implement his own insights or that later scholars have seen as crucial loci for developing Stendahl's insights further. Guarding against false assumptions of contemporaneity, Marshall insists, is a first principle of historical criticism. Stendahl's article represented a breakthrough moment for the implementation of this principle in the study of Paul.

Bringing together the themes of anachronism, historical thinking, and the ethics of theology in "Paul, Augustine, and Krister on the Introspective Conscience of the West," *Paula Fredriksen* concentrates on the causes and the consequences of looking at Paul's change from persecutor to apostle as a moment of religious "conversion." She attends to the brilliant intuition that flashed between two pages of Stendahl's "luminous essay:" that the historical source of Luther's tormented introspective conscience was not Paul, but Augustine. Analyzing both what Stendahl got wrong (notably, his assessment of Augustine's *Confessions*) and what he got right (the effects of Augustine's views on Paul for the later tradition), she ends with another idea that Stendahl had emphasized: Paul's conviction that he lived at the edge of the end of days. Failing to heed Stendahl's points of principle when interpreting Paul—called, not converted; committed to the coming redemption of Jewish Israel; expecting the return of his Messiah within his own lifetime—will only lead to bad history, Fredriksen cautions. And bad history can never serve as the basis for good theology.

Finally, in "Krister Stendahl and the Introspective Conscience of a Friend," *James Carroll* offers a personal account of the "Krister Effect" as it was felt, especially, by Catholics of the Vatican II generation. Pointing to "Paul and the Introspective Conscience of the West," which appeared when he was a seminarian, and to its "decisive" invitation to revise assumptions about St. Paul, Carroll recounts the "astonishing" influence that the Lutheran Stendahl had on Catholics. "For us," he writes, "Stendahl focused the coming of an ecumenical mindset, which disarmed old anti-Protestant impulses and, because of the reach of his own thinking, helped prepare for the transformation of Catholic assumptions about Judaism." Becoming personal friends once Carroll was assigned to be Catholic chaplain at Boston University when, across the river, Stendahl became Harvard Divinity School dean, he describes the tumult of the Vietnam period, and Stendahl's steady commitment to theology with a social conscience. The author of *Constantine's Sword* credits Stendahl with sparking his own commitment to Jewish-Christian inquiry. This elegiac essay ends in a moving appreciation of Stendahl's gift for transforming not only the scholarship, but also the lives, of those who were privileged to know him.

I

THE LIFE

1

A TOWERING PRESENCE, BENT LIKE GRASS[1]

Jesper Svartvik

On April 7, 1991, at Maria Andersson's funeral in the Pentecostal church in Gunnamo, a small rural village in Sweden, a letter was read. It was written by Krister Stendahl. One may wonder why a former professor at and dean of Harvard Divinity School would send a letter to honor this dedicated Pentecostal woman in far-off Sweden, an unlikely event in Gunnamo. The answer is that, in the early 1920s, Ms. Andersson was a maid in the home of the chemical engineer and director of the Harbor of Stockholm, Olof Stendahl, and Sigrid (née Ljungquist). On April 21, 1921, Krister Olofson Stendahl was born, the younger of two siblings. The Stendahl children, Britt and Krister, knew that their maid was a Pentecostal, but she did not speak too much about religious matters. "The Engineer would not have approved," as Maria put it. The Stendahl family did not attend church, because, his father explained, the building was "very drafty." It would not be healthy to spend too much time there.[2]

In his letter for Maria Andersson's funeral, Stendahl remembers her as "amazingly light and spotless and a friendly presence. I can still hear her voice. They say that I have my pharyngeal 'R' thanks to her."[3] She taught the young boy how to pray.[4] Mina, one of the nurses in their home, was certain that the boy would dedicate his life to God; hence, Maria and Mina decided to pray on his behalf. And, indeed, the young Krister Stendahl chose to study theology. In interviews, he often reported that he was only twelve years old when he decided to become a minister.[5] A few years later he was confirmed by Erik Bergman, the father of the famous film director Ingmar Bergman.[6] Stendahl occasionally opined that it was easy for him to understand Ingmar Bergman's movies, presumably especially his way of depicting stern Lutheran ministers.[7]

A MASTER OF BONS MOTS

The long life and erudite learning of Stendahl cannot be accurately described in such a brief essay. This subject should be treated in a full-length biography—and, hopefully, one day it will be. However, an obstacle to such an enterprise is that Stendahl was a man of few written words. Those who knew him say that while he suffered from writer's cramp, he was a remarkable speaker. Many have witnessed how he mesmerized his listeners when he taught and preached, and in interviews one easily recognizes that journalists appreciated his way of expressing himself. In most cases, the headline of an article about him is a quotation from him. He was a master of bons mots. Journalist P. D. Lindeberg wrote that Stendahl "quickly became the media's favorite. As few others he could deliver powerful answers, not seldom with a radical content."[8]

This particular chapter focuses on Stendahl's years in Sweden in order to survey the *reception* of his person and proclamation. I draw on approximately 350 articles in major Swedish newspapers. The first was published in 1947; the last, announcing his death, in 2008. In short, this chapter primarily surveys articles and letters written in Swedish, and its particular purpose is to highlight the interplay between his Swedish and American academic and ecclesiastical milieux.

ORDINATION AND WEDDING IN STORKYRKAN

Stendahl was ordained in Storkyrkan (the Cathedral of Stockholm; henceforth called Storkyrkan) on December 17, 1944, by Bishop Manfred Björkquist for the diocese of Stockholm. Although only twenty-three years old on the day of his ordination, he was already marked for life by illness: he suffered from painful arthritis in his spine that had started when he was only sixteen years old. This disease bent his neck and made it impossible for him to move his head sideways.[9] Bishop Björkquist and Stendahl maintained a correspondence over Stendahl's years at Harvard Divinity School.[10] Stendahl often wrote to Björkquist on the anniversary of his ordination, thanking him for taking the risk of ordaining such a frail person. In a letter to Björkquist thirty-six years after the date, Stendahl recalls how difficult it was to get a doctor's certificate positive enough to allow ordination, and he writes, "I hope you think that the thirty-six years were worth the ordination—even if, on a deeper level, there is much that could have been more straight and more right [Swedish: *rakare och riktigare*] in what one has done."[11] He added that Björkquist taught him respect for both *människan* (man) and *Människosonen* (the Son of Man).[12]

Krister and Brita (née Johnsson; 1925–2016) met in Uppsala. He proposed marriage after having known her for only a few days. She did not say no; neither did she immediately say yes.[13] They were married on September 7, 1946, in Storkyrkan in Stockholm.[14] The bride's father, Johan Wiktor (Jiwe) Johnsson, who was a minister, director of *Stadsmissionen* (Stockholm City Mission), and a member of the parliament, performed the wedding.[15] The young Stendahls went on to have three children: John (in Swedish Johan; born in 1948), Anna (born in 1950), and Daniel (adopted in 1955).

Later, Brita would teach Scandinavian literature at Radcliffe College. She wrote several books, including one on Søren Kierkegaard, published in English in 1976 and in Swedish in 1980.[16] Her book *The Force of Traditions*, analyzing the discourse against ordination of women, was published in 1985 in both English and Swedish.[17] She also translated theology and poetry. Uppsala University awarded her an honorary doctorate in 1981.

STUDENT CHAPLAINCY AND DOCTORAL STUDIES

An early article about Krister Stendahl, published in December 1947 in *Stockholms-Tidningen*, reports his election as student chaplain in Uppsala.[18] This assignment had a major impact on his future scholarship: Stendahl often said that his renowned article on the introspective conscience of the West was informed by his experiences as student chaplain.[19] He felt that what he heard in confessions—presumably often guilt-filled soliloquies—were not the issues of the apostle Paul. Slowly, he began to grapple with the insight that Paul's context was quite different from Luther's—and, therefore, also quite different from that of his fallible twentieth-century Lutheran followers.

In the following years he pursued studies in Sweden and abroad. Becoming a licentiate in 1949 (an academic degree below that of a doctorate; cf. Latin *licentia docendi*, "permission to teach"), he studied in Cambridge and Paris in 1951, and from 1951 to 1954 he was first assistant in biblical studies at Uppsala University.

Stendahl sustained the *viva voce*, the public defense of his doctoral thesis in New Testament studies, on the school of Matthew the evangelist.[20] The external examiner (Swedish: *försteopponent*) was Professor T. W. Manson, who came in from Manchester. It was quite uncommon, in those days, to invite someone from that far away for a doctoral *viva*. The second "opponent" was Bertil E. Gärtner, who, after a brief period of teaching at Princeton Theological Seminary, would return to his native Sweden in 1969 to become cathedral dean in Gothenburg, and one year later also its bishop. Hence, both Stendahl and Gärtner combined scholarship and ecclesiastical service, but in different ways: whereas Stendahl always argued in favor of ordination of women (see below), Gärtner was the last bishop of the Church of Sweden to oppose it. Hence, the bishops of the dioceses of Stockholm and Gothenburg, Sweden's two largest cities, went in opposite directions in their application of scholarship and ecclesiastical praxis.

HARVARD DIVINITY SCHOOL

Even before his *viva* in Uppsala, Stendahl was invited to teach at Harvard Divinity School. In a letter of May 3, 1954, Acting Dean George H. Williams expressed his interest in contacting Stendahl because Professor Paul S. Minear of Andover Newton Theological Seminary had spoken of his work and of his forthcoming doctoral examination. In addition to looking for someone who had written a thought-provoking thesis, Harvard also wanted someone who had studied the recently discovered Dead Sea Scrolls. Although these were not the main topic of his thesis, Stendahl's work demonstrated his competence with these texts. Williams invited him to give instruction for the academic year 1954–1955,[21] and the family decided to accept this offer.[22] Initially, the Stendahls thought of their time in the United States as merely a brief intermezzo before returning to Europe. In a letter to Bishop Björkquist from the summer of

1954, Stendahl wrote that they were certainly not leaving Sweden for good, nor were they abandoning the Church of Sweden:

> My warm thanks for the kind and binding [Swedish: *förpliktande*] greetings after the commencement. No—I cannot imagine abandoning Sweden and our Church. I have grown too much into its work, needs and anguish about the future to feel that it would be nothing less than a betrayal [Swedish: *svek*]. Already the three-year period I am expected to be in America seems to be too long.[23]

As things turned out, however, these three tentative years would grow to become thirty.

In an interview published in 1958, Stendahl compared European and American universities. A doctorate in the United States, he opined, was equivalent to a Swedish licentiate. Students in the United States were good at classical languages and the classical texts, he said, and willing to work hard. He also noted that in the United States, professors first gave their courses, and then wrote their books—"It is the spoken word that becomes a book"—whereas in Germany, professors wrote primarily for their colleagues.[24] The American model, it turned out, would exemplify his own publications.

The Stendahl family enjoyed living in the States. In 1958 Harvard offered him a tenured position as the John H. Morison Professor of New Testament Studies, and in 1981 he became Andrew W. Mellon Professor of Divinity. Thus began three decades of teaching, research, and administration in Cambridge, Massachusetts. But return to Sweden remained a perpetual option, one that presented itself time and again.

THE PROFESSORSHIP AT LUND UNIVERSITY

In the spring of 1963, Stendahl applied for the New Testament chair at Lund University. As author of a highly regarded thesis and with almost a decade of teaching at Harvard, he was one of the top candidates. However, at Swedish state universities, unsuccessful candidates may file appeals both to the university and, eventually, also to the state—a procedure that can prolong the process of appointment for months and even years. This is exactly what happened. After a year, not even the external advisors of the search committee had been elected, and it would take another year before an appointment would be made. Stendahl withdrew his application and, deciding to settle in Harvard for good, the Stendahl family bought a house at 29 Woodland Road in Lexington.[25] However, his Swedish ordination always lingered in Stendahl's mind, tugging him to journey back across the Atlantic. In a letter of December 1964 to Björkquist, he expressed his ambivalence:

> I hope…that my decision not to fight for the chair in Lund was not a betrayal [Swedish: *svek*]. Partly it feels that way, because I so wanted to do something for our miserable Church of Sweden. Even if she is God's problem child, she is still my mother, and the longer I am here, the more I understand this. But when the appointment [at Lund] dragged on absurdly, I could not leave Harvard and my doctoral students waiting in suspense.[26]

Birger Gerhardsson eventually won the appointment as professor of New Testament studies at Lund University. He, too, had written his doctoral thesis at Uppsala University, and under the same *Doktorvater* as Stendahl and Gärtner. Like Stendahl, Gerhardsson also emphasized the Jewishness of the early Christian movement. However, Gerhardsson's scholarship had a more conservative and certainly more apologetic aspect. In his books, such as *Memory and Manuscript* and *Tradition and Transmission in Early Christianity*, he challenged form criticism for not being historical enough in its method. Hence, his reason for exploring early Jewish oral tradition and written transmission was to prove the historical reliability of the Gospel tradition.[27]

In a letter to Manfred Björkquist, written in December 1966, probably replying to Björkquist's request that Stendahl become the director of Sigtunastiftelsen, a retreat and cultural center situated outside of Stockholm, Stendahl writes,

> And as far as I can see, it is highly unlikely that we will return to Sweden definitely.…And now we have applied for American citizenship and it will be finalized in the coming days. We cannot cope with living in two worlds, and the children are now entirely American.…We have drifted apart from the

> Swedish context, and it is difficult to believe that we can fit back in there.[28]

However, within a matter of weeks this situation would alter dramatically.

ARCHBISHOP IN UPPSALA?

It had taken twelve years for the Stendahl family to decide to apply for US citizenship.[29] This was a major step for them, especially since it required renouncing their Swedish citizenship. However, in early 1967, they filed their applications, which were approved on January 23.[30] Stendahl informed the cathedral chapter in Stockholm the following day and asked for instructions about the consequences for him as a minister in Church of Sweden, now that he was no longer a Swedish citizen.

Events moved quickly. Only ten days after they were granted citizenship in the United States, which expressed their will and determination to remain at Harvard, Stendahl was nominated for the highest office in Church of Sweden: the archbishopric. What happened is this: On February 2, the ministers in the archdiocese met in the city of Gävle to discuss and nominate candidates for the upcoming elections. One of these ministers, Per-Olof Lundberg, nominated Stendahl, and this was received favorably by the other ministers. The next day Lundberg wrote to Stendahl, who responded five days later, on Ash Wednesday:

> Dear Per-Olof: Your letter of February 3 was like a bolt from the blue. What can I say?...My personal answer is a yes. If there is a feeling in Church of Sweden that I could be useful at this position, I would not like to say no....
>
> With thanks and fear
>
> Krister[31]

A statement records that "Professor Stendahl has informed the Swedish authorities that he would accept the appointment were he to be chosen. Says he: 'I did not find my decision to be a difficult one. If I am asked to take such an impossible assignment, it is obvious to me that I should try.'"[32]

However, there was now a major obstacle. He was no longer a Swedish citizen. The Church of Sweden was a state church. To take up the post, Stendahl would have to reclaim his native legal standing. In a statement, he said that he was willing to return to Sweden if he were elected as archbishop; but he hesitated to apply for Swedish citizenship just for the elections. After twelve years in the United States, he and his family had finally decided that they did not want to live there as strangers.

> We cannot look upon our citizenship as a sheer technicality. It is a serious matter, and I am sure that people in Sweden will understand how inappropriate it would feel for me to reclaim my Swedish citizenship only three weeks after January 23 in order to offer myself as a candidate in Sweden.[33]

Following correspondence with Swedish authorities and leaders of Church of Sweden, he finally decided to apply for Swedish citizenship, which was granted on March 3. Thus Stendahl had been a US citizen for forty days less one before becoming a Swedish citizen again, all because of the archepiscopal election. In mid-February, Minister of Justice Herman Kling announced that it would take approximately one week to attend to repatriation. "He is well known, so there should be no problems."[34]

An interview from 1967 described Stendahl as a bridge builder between different theological communities in the Church of Sweden, as someone who could reach out from the church to the "living room" (i.e., people's ordinary life), as well as to the wider church world outside of Sweden. There is, the article says, only one bridge that Stendahl did not appreciate: the strong bonds between the state and the church.[35] Until the year 2000, the Church of Sweden was a state church, over which the state exerted considerable influence, and from which the church benefitted economically: people born in Sweden automatically became members of Church of Sweden, and the state collected the members' fees via the fiscal administration. Stendahl maintained that he wanted all this to change. The Church of Sweden should not have these privileges, he felt, but should become one Christian denomination among other denominations.

Theologically he was depicted—and depicted himself—as "high church," and politically as "liberal."[36] One Swedish article opined that Sweden would get an archbishop who was "left-leaning [Swedish: *åt vänster*]."[37]

Precisely when the government was meeting to decide between the three candidates for this position, Stendahl was on his way to Sweden in order to give a lecture on April 23 in Malmö at *Allmänna Kyrkliga Mötet* (the general church meeting) to an audience of four thousand. The topic he had chosen was "Security or Vitality: A New Stream within the Church." When boarding in the United States, Stendahl did not know if he would deplane as the archepiscopal appointee.[38]

In the elections, Bishop Ruben Josefson received the most votes, Bishop Gert Borgenstierna came in second, and Krister Stendahl third.[39] One might assume that this settled the matter, but the government was free to choose any of these three—and there was a precedent in Swedish church history. This precedent-setting event had occurred fifty-three years earlier. An academic "dark horse" had been elected before. Nathan Söderblom, who at the time was a professor in Leipzig, had been nominated for the archbishopric in 1914. In those elections, Bishop Hjalmar Danell got 373 votes, Bishop J. E. [Johan Alfred] Eklund got 271 votes, and Professor Söderblom, only 106 votes.

The story of how Söderblom reached the third place is worth recounting. He was one of the three top candidates in the diocese of Västerås, all of whom had received an equal number of votes. The decision was made by a draw. A young teacher drew the lot, which fell on Söderblom—and thereby Söderblom was their candidate, and thus also one of three with the most votes in the entire election.

Foreign Minister Knut A. Wallander was one of those who argued in favor of Söderblom. He managed to convince the prime minister, and King Gustav V approved the appointment.[40] The decision was made on May 20, 1914, and Söderblom went on to become not only an archbishop, but also the most famous Swedish archbishop of all time. A decade after his consecration, he invited Christians of all denominations from all over the world to the Universal Christian Conference on Life and Work, held in Stockholm, August 19–30, 1925.[41] In 1930, he received the Nobel Prize for Peace. All this had been made possible by the chance of a single lot! In short, the government had chosen the third-place candidate once before and, therefore, could well do so again.

In interviews and to an even greater degree in correspondence, one sees how torn Stendahl was. On the one hand, he seems to have enjoyed teaching at Harvard Divinity School; on the other hand, he thought of himself as a man of the church. And what does one do when one is asked to become the archbishop in one's native country? Eventually Josefson was chosen, freeing the Stendahl family to stay in the United States. In 1967, Stendahl was still quite young, only forty-six years old, and the candidates are often, if not always, already bishops before becoming archbishops.

Stendahl was encouraged to be nominated for another bishopric in the northern part of Sweden, but this time he abstained: "It might seem snobbish to say yes to the archbishopric but no to Härnösand [the northern city]. But that is how I felt."[42]

In that year's Christmas letter, he described the ambivalence that he and his family felt, not knowing whether they were to stay in the States or to move back to their native Sweden. He called it a "schizophrenic spring": "A whole world that had faded much in our minds took on new intensity."[43]

After the elections and the appointment of Josefson, Stendahl said that, as all Swedes living abroad, he was torn between two worlds, and thus between two lives:

> To be summoned suddenly and unexpectedly to Sweden is one thing. To plan on returning is something completely different. I thrive in America. It is here I live and build. In Sweden one probably has to tear down so much before one can build anew.[44]

But on March 19, 1972, Archbishop Ruben Josefsson passed away, and his successor was to be elected. Stendahl was asked, once more, to accept a nomination:

> Professor Krister Stendahl has in a statement for TT [the news agency *Tidningarnas Telegrambyrå*] declared that he would seriously consider the offer were he to be nominated to become archbishop. [Stendahl adds:] "However, the question is whether I am tied to Harvard in such a way that I should continue there for some more time."[45]

Olof Sundby, then bishop in the diocese of Växjö, was elected. A few years later, in 1979, when a bishop in the diocese of Stockholm was to be elected, Stendahl declined nomination. In February 1977 he had said that he was interested in being nominated, and in September 1978 he stated that he had promised to be available.[46] However, in a letter intended for all the ministers in the diocese and delivered *aux mains* by his son John Stendahl to Bishop Ingmar Ström, Stendahl explained that because his illness was growing more severe, it would be somewhat easier to perform duties as a university professor than as a bishop.[47] By then, his health had deteriorated so much that he had to use a wheelchair. However, in 1982 he underwent hip surgery, and that made all the difference.

THE ARCHBISHOPRIC FOR A THIRD TIME

In 1983 it was time to elect a new archbishop and, once again, Stendahl was nominated. Ragnar Holte, a professor of ethics at Uppsala University, wrote an article in *Dagens Nyheter*, the major daily newspaper, in favor of Stendahl: "He stands a head taller than his fellow candidates in terms of ability for spiritual leadership, for clear and fresh profiling of the Christian message, and for presenting and convening visions for the future."[48] A text from *Tidningarnas Telegrambyrå*, published more or less verbatim in at least four newspapers, presented him as "Gossen Ruda," a fictive character, known for being unconventional, even irreverent. In an interview published in the major Swedish newspaper on the very day of elections for the archbishopric, Stendahl said,

> I enjoy testing a line of thought, throwing myself into a line of argument, even if I am not sure whether it holds in the end. In Sweden one is supposed to keep to the book and the instructions. Things are supposed to stay straight [Swedish: *rakt*].[49]

However, in other interviews he expressed himself in other ways. What is "most important is that the church is genuine....If the church has something substantial [Swedish: *väsentligt*] to say, the future will take care of itself."[50]

A somewhat condescending article about him was published in *Sydsvenska Dagbladet*, asserting that, other than his 1954 dissertation, Stendahl had few publications. "It is, however, difficult to point at any particular idea that he has brought forth"—quite a statement about someone who authored one of the most influential scholarly texts ever written about the apostle Paul.[51]

Representatives of all the thirteen dioceses in Sweden voted in the elections. Bishop Bertil Werkström got 9 2/3 votes; Cathedral Dean Clarence Nilsson got 9 1/6 votes; Bishop Arne Palmqvist got 5 1/3 votes; and Stendahl got 5 votes.[52] Hence, the difference between the third and the fourth candidates was only one-third of a vote. Had Stendahl been one of the first three candidates, it would not have been remarkable for the government to choose him, given his recognition and esteem among high-ranking leaders of the Social Democrats. Based on precedent, the government had its choice of the first three. But in this instance, that did not happen. Once again, one is reminded of the circumstances surrounding Nathan Söderblom's election in 1914. What tipped the scales that time was the ballot, and this time one-third of one vote.

When reading and rereading these articles and interviews, a particular issue figures prominently, one very much discussed in all these archepiscopal elections: the fact that at that time the Church of Sweden was a state church. The choice of archbishop rested with the government. The state-church system also meant that people went to the local Lutheran minister for all sorts of personal matters, such as when they needed a license to marry, when they applied for passports, and when they sought a divorce. The economy of the state church was solid: as noted, everyone born in Sweden *ipso facto* became a member of the church, and the state collected church taxes and transferred the amount to the church. But Stendahl was very much in favor of ending the state-church system. He considered it unfair to other Christian groups that one particular denomination prospered in most-favored status from a better economic situation. He often said that it was arrogant to treat other Christians that way.

A sufficient number of delegates voting in the archbishopric elections decided that they needed a candidate who was less outspoken on this state-church issue. In fact, the system did not change until 2000. With more than six million members, Church of Sweden remains by far the largest denomination; nevertheless, it is now simply one among many other Christian denominations, though perhaps *prima inter pares* (the first among equals).[53] The future proved Stendahl right: time was running out for the Swedish state-church system.

Yet another opportunity to return to Sweden emerged: Sigtunastiftelsen. The retreat center outside of Stockholm, founded in the 1910s by Bishop Manfred Björkquist (who had ordained Stendahl in 1944), had grown to be a spiritual and intellectual center. When a new director was to be chosen in 1983, a letter was sent to Cambridge, encouraging Stendahl to take this position. Björkquist was still alive (ninety-nine years old).[54] It seems that Stendahl, eventually, turned down this offer also, choosing instead to remain in the United States—but not for long.

BISHOP NOT *OF* STOCKHOLM, BUT *IN* STOCKHOLM

Once again in 1984 it was time to choose a bishop for Stockholm. By then, Stendahl was sixty-three years old, and that also was the strongest argument in the diocese of Stockholm against his nomination: Was it wise to elect someone who would retire in a few years? Stendahl accepted the nomination, committing to stay in Stockholm for four years: "I will do everything to become worthy of this task, and I am willing to stay as long as I can and as long as they want me."[55]

In the election held on April 25, Stendahl won 237 votes, Cathedral Dean Henrik Svenungsson (he was to succeed Stendahl as bishop in 1988) 197.5 votes, and Rev. Dr. Gösta Wrede 157 votes.[56]

The Stendahls arrived in Stockholm on September 21, and Krister took office on October 1.[57] From the start, he was eager to emphasize that he was not about to become *the* bishop of Stockholm, but *one of* its bishops. "I emphasize that I will be one of the bishops in Stockholm.…More and more Sweden must learn to live with a multitude of churches and denominations."[58]

Stendahl's consecration took place on October 7 in the Cathedral of Uppsala. Among the many guests was the US ambassador to Sweden, because of the many years that the Stendahls had lived and worked in Cambridge. One invited guest who was absent was the Polish bishop Janusz Narzynski. He was unable to attend because he was refused to leave Poland at that point, and "in order to show solidarity with the Polish people in their struggle, his seat was left empty."[59] Another guest at the consecration was Maria Andersson, the Pentecostal maid in his childhood home—"Mary, the mother of my faith," as Stendahl called her.[60]

In his speech to Stendahl, the Archbishop Werkström cited 2 Corinthians 4:7: "But 'we have this treasure in clay jars,' so that it may be clear that this extraordinary power belongs to God and does not come from us."[61] He may have chosen this particular verse because Stendahl was a renowned Pauline scholar. Perhaps it was also an oblique reference to Stendahl's arthritis, which had plagued him since he was a teenager.

The chief rabbi of Sweden, Morton H. Narrowe, was not only invited to the consecration, but also actively participated in the liturgy. He chanted a text from Isaiah 51 in Hebrew, and then read it in Swedish. Later, Stendahl recounted the background to this part of the service:

> I had given many suggestions how my consecration in the Cathedral of Uppsala in the fall of 1984 could become more ecumenically trustworthy. Most of the suggestions were rejected, but it was accepted that the chief rabbi read that Sunday's "Old Testament" text. Morton did more than so. When the moment came he intoned the Hebrew text with cantorial power. Brita Stendahl, who was sitting opposite the king and queen, recounts how the king was startled in unkingly surprise. And no wonder. It was probably the first time that the holy tongue of Jesus was heard in the Cathedral of Uppsala during its 700-year-old history.[62]

Today, some three decades later, improved interfaith relations are an important issue for politicians and theologians alike; in the eighties, however, this was far from a matter of course. Stendahl blazed the trail.

PAUL AND BIBLICAL INTERPRETATION

In what way did Stendahl influence both Church of Sweden and public discourse in Sweden? Most articles in the Swedish press cluster around his four years as Lutheran bishop in Stockholm. But his influence well predates that period, beginning already when he was first a candidate for the archbishopric, in 1967. What follows is a presentation of eight of the most important issues identified in articles and interviews in Swedish newspapers.

A good starting point for this summary and assessment of his impact is his scholarship on Paul. Its main thesis is that Paul never converted from Judaism, but was called by the God of Israel to reach out to the Gentiles. In general, his book *Paul among Jews and Gentiles* was favorably reviewed in Swedish media.[63] To trace exactly when Stendahl (not Paul) converted from the "conversion" paradigm to one of "calling" is a topic for an article of its own. Here, however, we note that in a 1960 article Stendahl cites the scholarship of Johannes Munck, which is quite interesting, as his conclusions were quite similar to Stendahl's. (For further comments on the interplay of the scholarship of Munck and Stendahl, see the articles of John Marshall and Paula Fredriksen in the present volume.) In this article Stendahl discussed the issue of "the not yet converted Jews" (Swedish: *de ännu oomvända judarna*) when referring to the narrative context in the Acts of the Apostles. He also refers to the ecumenical week of prayer, from St. Peter's Day (January 18) to the day of St. Paul's conversion (January 25), without any comment about the anachronism of the term *conversion* in reference to Paul.[64]

In the coming few years, however, he began to address this issue very differently. What would become known as the Stendahlean approach to Paul first appeared in an article published in Swedish in 1960 and in a 1961 lecture to a meeting of the American Psychological Association.[65] All this suggests that these were formative years for Stendahl's Pauline interpretation.

A service he led in 1985 for the staff at the courts—the court of appeal, the administrative court of appeal, the district courts, and the county administrative court—illustrates his desire to offer an alternative to the law/grace dichotomy that has governed so much of Lutheran theology. The service included readings from the Nineteenth Psalm, which praised the Torah, and the starting point of his sermons was the psalm's seventh verse: "The law of the LORD is perfect, reviving the soul."[66]

By way of summary, the impression one gets from the Swedish sources is that journalists and intellectuals generally accepted his approach to Paul. In this new view, Paul did not have to pass through the valley of despair, as Luther had.[67] A possible explanation for this embrace of Stendahl's interpretation of Paul might be that Swedes, in general, have a rather negative image of Luther, who is associated with sin and guilt and, therefore, they welcomed Paul's liberation from the Lutheran straightjacket. Sadly, however, even to this day numerous sermons in Sweden continue to counterpose law and grace when speaking of Paul.

IMMORTALITY, RESURRECTION, AND WATERLOO

A second topic discussed intensely during Stendahl's tenure as bishop was his views on immortality. Approximately thirty articles, some of them quite extensive, addressing this issue were published in major Swedish newspapers, most of them in 1987. In addition, he received hecatombs of letters from laity and clergy both. My recollection (at the time I was twentyish) is that everyone everywhere in Swedish Christian circles was discussing Stendahl's statements on this topic.

As early as 1972, the topic arose in a lecture that Stendahl delivered at Gustavus Adolphus College in St. Peter, Minnesota. Cultivating its historical ties with Sweden, this college sponsors an annual Nobel conference, with participation from recent Nobel laureates. In 1972 the chosen theme was "The End of Life" and, as Stendahl notes in the preamble to the article, "Since there are no Nobel Prizes in Theology, that field must be represented by lesser lights." His presentation was eventually published in *Meanings: The Bible as Document and as Guide*, a collection of sixteen essays with an introduction.[68] This book was translated into Swedish and published in 1986, though without the subtitle (*The Bible as Document and as Guide*), a fact that partly may explain the riptides of subsequent debate. Whereas Stendahl sought to present essays on the Bible as thoughtful reflections, some of his readers perceived him as wanting to undermine what they understood to be one of the fundamental pillars of Christian faith and doctrine.

Although Stendahl wrote the essay in *Meanings* when he was a university professor, it became accessible to a wide Swedish-speaking audience only once he was bishop. In this piece he pointed out that, according to the biblical texts, immortality is not an inherent quality of human beings. The New Testament deploys the Greek word *athanasia* to state that "God alone is immortal" (1 Tim 6:16; *ho monos echôn athanasian*). Stendahl wanted to emphasize that, in biblical perspective, human beings are mortal, and that resurrection is—and always should be—a theocentric notion. It is not a matter of human beings being immortal per se, but of a powerful God who chooses to give life back to humans. A belief in an inherent immortal soul, opined Stendahl, might put too much emphasis on life after death, and thus risked being too selfish. To paraphrase the message of the article, stern statements about immortality may lead, to use a neologism, to the "importality" of the ego. A belief in resurrection as a gift is far less likely to be self-centered and more likely to be God-centered.

Reaction was intense. Stendahl received numerous letters (some of which the mailman chose to put in large brown envelopes, to conceal what was written on the envelopes' outside). Several fellow bishops publicly said that they disagreed. The editor in chief of the major Christian weekly journal *Kyrkans Tidning*, Ingvar Laxvik, even penned a thirty-two-page pamphlet called "Against Stendahl" (*Mot Stendahl*), the title of which recalls patristic intra-Christian polemics, for example, Tertullian's *Adversus Marcionem* and Augustine's *Contra Faustum*. The minister Hans Fredriksson (and subsequently two other ministers, Jan-Åke Karlsson and Börje Rundgren) reported Stendahl to the disciplinary committee of the bishops (Swedish: *Ansvarsnämnden för biskopar*), which was to decide whether he, as a bishop, was guilty of misconduct beyond reasonable doubt. If the committee agreed, Stendahl would have to resign. The committee's four members—President of the High Court Birgitta Blom, Chief Judge emeritus Carl Hamilton, Professor Per-Erik Persson, and Dr. Anne-Marie Thunberg—ruled to acquit him; however, two of its members, Persson and Thunberg, wrote an addendum in which Stendahl was criticized for not expressing himself clearly enough to avoid misunderstandings.[69] The debate went on and on, month after month, year after year and, ultimately, Stendahl chose not to respond. He held his peace.

An interview published years later, in 2002, bore a headline with a punch, because the Swedish word *uppståndelse* means both "resurrection" and "turmoil," thus, "What Resurrection and Turmoil!" In this interview, Stendahl spoke quite openly about this skirmish. He said that until that moment in time, he had always thought that he had a gift for explaining complicated issues to a wide audience. Yet this time he failed utterly. "But this, it was my Waterloo." In addition, there were consequences for his family: "It was one of the few things I have written that made my mother sad."[70] Ironically, the most undying controversy of his bishopric concerned resurrection and immortality—the very concepts that he wanted to call into question.

In an article about Stendahl's theology, Professor Per Beskow describes the problem of communication between Stendahl and some of his fellow Swedes. The headline was "Too Biblical, Too Liberal." Beskow writes, "To a large extent his [Stendahl's] notorious liberalism springs from his respect for the biblical text....Stendahl is too biblical for the secularized, too liberal for the Bible believers—that is the dilemma in which Krister Stendahl, with all his exegetical and rhetorical talents, seems to end up."[71]

NOT KNOWING WHAT THE JAM TASTES LIKE

A third area where Stendahl weighed in was the interplay between theology and politics. Stendahl often criticized dichotomizing the two. In an interview given in 1985 he proclaimed,

> It is one's duty to acquaint oneself with important questions and to ask oneself what is right and what is wrong. Furthermore, there is no important moral question that does not have a political, and probably also a party-political, side to it. In the history of the church one can see that all martyrs were martyrs for political reasons, from the point of view of the state.[72]

In an interview given in 1972, during his Harvard years, he criticized indirect theological discourse—a phenomenon more common in Sweden than in the United States. He maintained that theologians are good at stating what the Bible and Luther say, but if asked what the theologians themselves think, a condition of embarrassment [Swedish: *förlägenhet*] arises.[73]

Since Laura Nasrallah's chapter in the present volume focuses on his thirty years at Harvard Divinity School, the present chapter will simply note that Stendahl was dean at Harvard Divinity School from 1968 to 1979—the stormy years of countercultural growth and of the escalation of the Vietnam War.[74] In a 1971 interview, Stendahl confessed that "it is a difficult time to be an American." Hopeful signs were the many and massive protests against the war: he refers to a recent protest in Boston with some one hundred thousand participants.[75] In December 1972, he preached in Storkyrkan on the topic "Blessed are those who make peace" (Matt 5:9). The sermon was taped and published in one of Sweden's daily tabloid newspapers.[76]

Having renewed his US citizenship, in 1968 Stendahl voted for the Democratic presidential candidate, Hubert H. Humphrey, adding "but there was not much of a choice."[77] The Republican candidate was Richard M. Nixon.

In a discussion in Sweden in 1987 on taxes, to which we will return below, he mentions that he, born in 1921, vividly remembered the military shootings of five workers during a protest march in Ådalen in 1931. (At that time there was no national police force in Sweden.) An article from 1987 reports that "the bishop has also declared that his heart is to the left."[78]

In 1985, Stendahl commented favorably on President Jimmy Carter's success in peace negotiations between Egypt and Israel and also on his dedicated awareness of and attention to civil rights throughout the world.[79] And in 1984, before returning to Sweden, Stendahl admitted that "it is also good to get away from [Ronald] Reagan and [his involvement in] Central America."[80]

While in Sweden during his bishopric, Stendahl accepted an invitation to give a speech on May 1 in Bergsjön in northern Sweden. This is not something that Swedish bishops normally do. Traditionally, May 1 in Sweden is a day when only socialist and communist parties and trade unions demonstrate. In interviews, he said that he was not a member of a political party, but that it was his custom to accept invitations when asked to speak. In his speech, he referred to the words in the Swedish socialist songs "The Sons of Work" (Swedish: *Arbetets söner*), "Human dignity we demand back." Stendahl characterized human dignity as a most precious asset, one to be preserved and guarded by taking a stand, daring to say yes and no between elections rather than delegating everything to politicians.[81] He spoke out against nuclear power and in favor of a nuclear-free world.[82]

Stendahl never shied away from voicing political opinions. He maintained that the United States and the Soviet Union, 10 percent of the world, had decided to rule over the remaining 90 percent.[83] He also spoke at a demonstration against the Soviet Union's invasion of Afghanistan.[84] During the period of apartheid, he favored boycotting South

Africa.[85] On September 7, 1986, he attended the consecration of Desmond Tutu as archbishop in South Africa and later invited him to speak in Stockholm when he was in Scandinavia to receive the Nobel Peace Prize in December 1984.[86] Stendahl also praised the Quakers for setting a good example: "They speak about peace with tenderness, so that it sounds like peace."[87]

This extensive list of examples and quotations communicates the contours of Stendahl's political priorities and his emphasis on political responsibility. The heading of this section—"not knowing what the jam tastes like"—refers to something Stendahl said in a 1984 interview, before returning to Sweden for four years, following thirty years of life in the States. "The advantage of having been away is that I am not 'in the jam' [Swedish: *insyltad*, meaning 'mixed up with anything'] but, on the other hand, that means that I do not know what the jam tastes like."[88]

The reason for mentioning this now is that there was one particular instance when something he said was debated and criticized quite harshly for an extended period of time. The starting point was a sermon Stendahl preached on New Year's Day in 1985 that gave rise to at least forty articles in major newspapers.

In one single sentence of the sermon he expressed the view that leaving Sweden in order to evade taxes was a sin.[89] Some people reacted strongly to this statement, especially the right-wing politician Gösta Bohman. Bohman's main argument was that he did not want someone preaching politics from the pulpit. However, others did not object to political implications in the sermon; they could not understand how someone who had lived in the United States for three decades, thereby avoiding the high taxes of socialist Sweden, could say something like this from the pulpit. (Sweden at that point had been governed by socialists for decades, apart from a six-year interregnum, 1976–1981; taxes had been high.) "I am very surprised," Stendahl said. "I must have addressed an issue that one prefers not to talk about in Sweden."[90]

One way to interpret what happened in the aftermath of this sermon was that he, as a teacher of divinity in the United States, was used to drawing connections between Christian principles and daily life. He fought both for freedom of speech and for freedom of religion. However, high taxes were very much discussed in Sweden at that time. Relevant to the picture is that in one year, the famous author of children's books Astrid Lindgren—who, incidentally, was a dedicated Social Democrat her entire life—was taxed 102 percent (!) on her income. In response, Lindgren wrote *Pomperipossa in Monismania,* a satirical attack on the Social Democratic taxation policies.[91] Minister for Finance Gunnar Sträng shot back that she must be deeply ignorant about the tax system, but that one should not expect a storyteller to understand complicated issues about taxes and economy. Lindgren then responded that Sträng was far better at telling fairy tales than she and suggested that they change jobs.

There are good reasons to believe that Lindgren's satire tipped the scales in the elections of 1976, such that after four decades in power, the Socialists were replaced by a right-centrist government. This public debate forms the context for the discussion on taxes. Whereas Stendahl pushed for the freedom to speak freely from the pulpit, many interpreted his statement as inappropriate, coming from someone who had lived overseas for three decades, unaffected by the drawbacks of the Swedish tax system. The Stendahls were favorably impressed with the Swedish welfare state, and well aware of the problems with the patchy system of Social Security in the United States. This also formed part of the picture.

In many ways the metaquestion, the interplay between theology and politics, is far more interesting than is determining exactly what Stendahl said in the sermon on emigration to avoid heavy taxation. In an interview as early as in mid-February that year, he admitted that he had expressed himself less than carefully. "The issue of taxes...was [handled] unskillfully. I am as aware as many others that tax systems constantly need to be evaluated. But I actually had no intention to emphasize tax evasion. It was only a minor part of a long sermon."[92]

WOMEN AND EQUALITY

A fourth issue identified with Stendahl is feminist theology and the ordination of women. In the preface to the book *Meanings*, he described how he gradually became aware of gender issues: "Now I see that inclusive language did not enter my consciousness until I was awakened by the women of the Harvard Divinity School in the 1970s."[93]

At Harvard Divinity School, Stendahl earned the sobriquet "Sister Krister" for his dedicated work toward the ordination of women, the establishment of women's studies programs, and the hiring of female faculty. An interview published in 1977 in a major Swedish newspaper observed that "Krister Stendahl joyfully welcomes a theology that is aware of gender issues [Swedish: *kvinnomedveten*]....Priests and ministers should learn how to talk about the spiritual world in a way that eliminates the impression that it is an exclusively male pantheon."[94]

However, Stendahl's involvement and influence on these issues well predates the seventies. Knowing the Swedish context makes the point more clearly. In 1951, with the single exception of Dr. Gosta Lindeskog, all Swedish professors and *docenter* (approximately, associate professors) in biblical studies at the universities of Lund and of Uppsala signed what became known as *Exegetdeklarationen* (the declaration of biblical scholars). In this declaration, all but one of the biblical scholars at the two universities in Sweden where one could study theology stated that the ordination of women was irreconcilable with the New Testament's teachings on ministry. Few texts in the Swedish debate about female ordination have had such an impact as this statement. It turned the debate into one of loyalty to the plain meaning of the Bible. To ordain women would be to contravene the teaching of the word of God.

What did Stendahl say? On the one hand, in 1946, Stendahl's father-in-law, who was a member of the parliament, had suggested that a committee be appointed to investigate this question of female ordination. Out of the committee's fourteen members (six of whom were women), ten voted in favor of ordination and four against. Gender issues also frequently were discussed in the Stendahl family, and Brita, as noted, would later write a book on this topic.

On the other hand, in an interview, John Stendahl, the son of Krister and Brita, says that his father "grew up in a very patriarchal context" in Stockholm and that "it did not change overnight."[95] Krister Stendahl's theological moorings were high church, with an emphasis on a rich traditional liturgy and the Eucharist. Some were surprised that he traveled directly from the World Council of Churches in Uppsala in 1968, a liberal conclave, to the annual meeting of the more conservative Societas Sanctae Birgittae in Vadstena, Sweden.[96] As Societas Sanctae Birgittae arguably is the most high church society in Sweden, he was asked about this, and he responded in a comparatively extensive text on the new radicalism in Uppsala and the high church traditionalism in Vadstena.

Describing appreciatively his own high church feelings, he compared it favorably to "the withered and petrified services" of the mainstream Church of Sweden, and he denounced what he called "liberal theology."

> I think that it is wonderful that we have this remarkable starting position [i.e., high church spirituality] instead of...a worn-out liberal theology....It was in *Societas Sanctae Birgittae* that I myself could get hold of what devotion and services are all about.[97]

On February 17, 1958, Ruben Josefson wrote to Stendahl, asking for an article on the ordination of women:

> We are in an emergency situation here because we cannot find a single biblical scholar in this country who is not already burdened with his standpoint....Hence, in this essay you need not take a stand for or against, but it would of course give me and the others who are working on this issue great pleasure if your text were such that it allowed conclusions in the direction towards a positive settlement of this issue.[98]

Stendahl accepted this assignment in a letter of February 24 and wrote his text for this collection of essays, which was instrumental when the Church of Sweden in that very year decided to permit the ordination of women.[99] On Palm Sunday two years later, the church ordained its first three women pastors: Elisabeth Djurle, Ingrid Persson, and Margit Sahlin.

Some of Stendahl's high church colleagues and friends did not see this coming. After the publication of his article, however, there was no longer any doubt about his views on the matter. He had argued for justice and for equality. "I do not believe in pseudo-psychological arguments that if we have more women ministers, the church will be enriched. I do not believe in the women's mysticism. But I do believe in justice."[100]

Thus, from 1958 on, everyone knew that Stendahl favored the ordination of women. Before the elections for the bishopric in Stockholm in 1984, however, a related but different question was put to him: What did he think about ordination of those who did *not* concur with the ordination of women? Stendahl would ordain them, he said; but he would want to talk with them about their position. This interview was not received favorably.[101] Eventually he went in the direction of ordaining only those who accepted both men and women as ministers. When pressed further about the possibility of cooperation—how those in favor and those against female ordination could live and work together in the church—he often stated that the way forward was to emphasize the role of laity. The church does not consist solely of the ordained.[102]

TRADITIONALISM AND THE STATE CHURCH

Stendahl, as we have seen, had early on expressed his opposition to the state-church system.[103] His position was part of a wider opposition to traditionalism in the sense of upholding a status quo for its own sake. When in 1967 (at the time of elections for the archbishopric) he gave a speech in Malmö, on "Security or Vitality: A New Stream within the Church," he spoke by appeal to a parable. A security-oriented church treats tradition like an elderly relative, who is invited for major holidays but never in daily life. And on the major events, this elderly person perhaps sits in a rocking chair, the very symbol for someone moving without moving ahead. He used the Swedish military term *på stället marsch* (for soldiers who walk without actually advancing forward).[104] Another parable that he repeatedly used was of a snake and its relation to its skin: "The Christian tradition is like the snakeskin. It sometimes drops, and scholars study it, but the happy snake slithers away."[105]

A third parable, in addition to the rocking chair and the snake, referred to the Church of Sweden as the Vasa ship, which capsized and sank outside Stockholm in 1628. It was salvaged after 333 years on the seabed, but then had to be sprayed frequently with water to prevent decomposition.[106] By comparing the church to this recently discovered old ship, he wanted to convey the idea that some treat the church as a fragile museum exhibit that demands constant tending lest it fall to pieces.

Stendahl once spoke about Christmas, describing the Magi from the East as foreigners who brought renewal, whereas Herod sought only to defend the established order and the existing power structure.[107]

Thus, Stendahl argued that the Church of Sweden should be one religious community among other such communities, with equal rights and duties. He envisaged the church as a community of the willing, composed of those who chose to be a part of it. However, he gradually began to define Christian identity and church affiliation more broadly: "I now think that I have become more sensitive to these shy and gawky [Swedish: *tafatta*] people and their need for a church that provides them with service."[108] Ultimately, he said, "the real mission of the church is to create an environment wherein God's will be done."[109]

SAME-SEX RELATIONS: CELIBACY OR BLESSINGS?

What is the theological status of same-sex relations? In 1984 the Swedish government published the report *Homosexuals and Society*.[110] In his response, Archbishop Werkström argued that the church could accept the homosexual orientation, but not homosexual acts. Hence, said the archbishop, celibacy was the only theologically valid behavioral option for homosexuals. In response, Stendahl led a service on "Sexuality and Responsibility" in solidarity with homosexuals, which took place in Storkyrkan, with a congregation of some eight hundred people. When some protesters shouted, "This is the synagogue of Satan" (Rev 2:9 and 3:9), Stendahl started singing "We Shall Overcome," and the congregation joined him.[111] He also led a eucharistic service, again in Storkyrkan, which took place during "Homosexuals' Liberation Week," marked by a demonstration of approximately five thousand supporters.[112]

The mid-1980s were marked as well by a terrible surge in HIV/AIDS-related deaths within this community. Bishop Stendahl spoke out in favor of anonymous HIV tests, and he was sought out by those who suffered from AIDS.[113] Sighsten Herrgård, a fashion designer and the first in Sweden to go public about his disease, reached out to Stendahl as the only person he felt that he could turn to in the entire church.[114]

After Stendahl returned to the United States, he participated in the ordination of Anita C. Hill in 2001.[115] This attracted some attention in Sweden because a minister wrote an article in the conservative journal *Göteborgs Stifts-Tidning* about the fact that Stendahl had participated in ordaining a woman who lived in a same-sex relationship, at a time when the Evangelical Lutheran Church of America demanded that homosexuals be celibate. Unrepentant, on November 2, All Saints' Day 2003, Stendahl took part in the consecration of V. Gene Robinson as bishop of the Episcopal Diocese of New Hampshire. Robinson had lived in a same-sex relation since 1989.[116]

In an article from 2000, Stendahl recounted the discussions held in the Council of Bishops (Swedish: *Biskopsmötet*) during his time as bishop in Sweden: "A majority of us were unwilling to consider celibacy the only lifestyle for gays and lesbians."[117] In this situation, when his archbishop argued in favor of compulsory celibacy, Stendahl pointed to the miseries and moral distortions of an obligatory celibacy, and he publicly stated, "I am willing to bless homosexual couples in the church."[118] In 2005, the General Assembly of the Church of Sweden voted on and passed the petition that there be a liturgical order for blessings of same-sex couples.[119] Stendahl anticipated this decision by two decades.[120]

INTERRELIGIOUS RELATIONS: A GRADUAL AWAKENING

Stendahl was also in the forefront of interreligious relations. Questioned on this issue immediately upon arrival at Arlanda Airport outside of Stockholm to assume the bishopric, he responded,

> We Christians must be able to have a dialogue with other religious movements without fear. Christ is so strong that he shines through everything.…One should keep one's own distinct character, but not at the expense of others.[121]

Comparative theology of religion was not Stendahl's initial area of specialization. He had written his thesis in New Testament studies. His *Doktorvater*, the legendary Norwegian scholar Anton Fridrichsen, directed doctoral candidates who became professors all over the world: at Åbo Akademi University (Gösta Lindeskog); at the University of Basel (Bo Reicke); at the University of Copenhagen (Olof Linton); at Harvard Divinity School (Stendahl); at Lund University (Birger Gerhardsson); at Princeton Theological Seminary (Bertil E. Gärtner); and at Uppsala University (Carl-Martin Edsman and Harald Riesenfeld).[122] Fridrichsen was sternly anti-Nazi. However, it can hardly escape notice that some of his texts exhibit a negative stereotyping of Jews and Judaism. This is particularly manifest in the book *Fyrahanda sädesåker* (a Fourfold Field, a reference to the parable of the sower; Matt 13:1–9, Mark 4:1–9, and Luke 8:4–15), a collection of extraordinarily influential essays intended for ministers preparing their sermons.[123] Ministers in the Church of Sweden have read and referred to this book for decades, thereby reinforcing the Christian negative stereotyping of the people that Jesus knew as his own.

Thus, it was not Stendahl's *Doktorvater* who encouraged him to become acquainted with vibrant Jewish spirituality. It was only upon arrival in the United States that Stendahl encountered living Judaism. Brita Stendahl writes that "Jewish customs and Jewish prayer were totally foreign to us when we came to Cambridge."[124] In a lecture in Jerusalem, Krister Stendahl even names those who helped him understand Jewish spirituality:

> It was only when I came to the US that I started to experience Jews as a people, as human beings, as a reality. I had the great privilege to meet with and to be inspired by people like Abraham [Joshua] Heschel, Alexander Altman, Emil Fackenheim, Nathan Glazer, and many others.[125]

An early example of how he started to recontextualize the New Testament within Judaism occurs in a text from 1960:

> The distinctive character of Christianity is not to be found in its doctrine, but in the course of events [Swedish: *skeendet*]. In the Sermon on the Mount there is hardly one word that does not have parallels elsewhere. The distinctiveness is to be found somewhere else, in the course of events. Jesus did not bring a new teaching.[126]

However, even in a few later texts, Stendahl used the label *Pharisaism* in a derogatory way. In an article from 1966, which discusses the US attempts to block China's membership in the United Nations, he calls this endeavor "a top political version of the individual American's naïve moral idealism with its accompanying Pharisaism—China is too naughty to be allowed to join [the UN]."[127] In 1972, he used a similar expression:

"The shyness here has been impressed through 400 years of Lutheran teaching that has created a spiritual Pharisaism [Swedish: *andefariseism*]."[128] (For contemporary usage of *Pharisaism* as a derogatory term, see Amy-Jill Levine's chapter in the present volume.)

Nonetheless, Stendahl grew to become a great force in the field of interreligious relations. He used to say that for thirty years he taught students at Harvard Divinity School from thirty different denominations and religious traditions.[129] His colleague Helmut Koester described Stendahl's endeavor as "the exploration of Christian integrity as a basis for, rather than contradiction of, pluralism."[130]

Stendahl often returned to the thought that there is something odd with the expression that people of different faiths "believe in the same God." What else would a monotheist say? It is more correct to say that "there is only one God, but that there are different experiences of God and various interpretations of God."[131]

When Essinge, a relatively new congregation in Stockholm, celebrated its thirtieth anniversary, Stendahl was invited to speak. He wanted to talk about the importance of young people in the churches, and referring to Simeon's song *Nunc dimittis* ("Now you are dismissing your servant in peace," Luke 2:29), he said that both the young and the elderly are needed in the church. But he turned this observation into a moment of nonsupersessionist theology. So also, he said, does the church need Israel: it is not a matter of "either-or, but both-and."[132]

Stendahl's language was often drastic, perhaps no more than in the following similitude: Two images run through history. What happens when God comes to the office in the morning? What does God say? There are two options, speculates Stendahl. In one scenario God asks for statistics; in the other, God is interested in the kingdom. Does God ask, "How are the statistics on saved souls? Give me the figures for saved souls [...or does he ask] has there been any progress for the Kingdom of Heaven today? For justice in the world?"[133]

In lectures and table talks Stendahl often spoke about apologetics as a problematic approach to religion and religious studies: "Nothing destroys spiritual life more than a theology that is dominated by a defense for God and Christianity."[134]

Probably his most well-known bon mot on apologetic faith is "it is pathetic to hear mosquitos cough." His friends and admirers quote this saying of his, but no one seems to understand what it means. In his own words: "I don't know why that is funny, but in Swedish it is funny. And apologetics is [like] mosquitos coughing. It kills so much of the joy in reading and practicing the love of the scriptures."[135]

"NOT EVEN A SWEDE CAN BE OBJECTIVE"

Interreligious dialogue is one thing; the Israeli-Palestinian conflict is another. Well known for his pioneering texts and mesmerizing lectures on Jewish-Christian relations, Stendahl dealt with this issue as well. As few others could, he managed not only to present sympathetically the fundamental beliefs and concerns of Jews so that Christians were able to understand better the Jewish tradition; he also presented central Christian beliefs so that Jews could better apprehend and even appreciate them. The study of the *Wirkungsgeschichte* of the biblical texts made him aware of the fact that some groups have suffered more than others because of how these texts have been interpreted. "The Christian Bible includes sayings that have caused much pain, both to Jews and to women. Thus I have felt called to seek forms of interpretation which can counteract such undesirable side effects of the Holy Scriptures."[136]

From 1975 to 1985, Stendahl chaired the World Council of Churches' Consultation on the Church and the Jewish People, and throughout his time as a bishop in Stockholm he was the chairperson of the Council of Christians and Jews.[137] This dedicated involvement in Jewish-Christian dialogue did not, however, mean that he was ignorant of or indifferent to the plight of suffering people and peoples in the Middle East.[138]

In 1984—that is, fully a decade before the Oslo Agreement of 1993 with its mutual recognition of Israel and PLO—Stendahl said the following in public debate:

> Occupations have satanic effects....As a theologian I can say that occupations always are devilish....Among the most important [things] in order to solve the problems is for Israelis to learn to say "Palestinians," not only "PLO." They cannot define away an entire people....Israel need not be ashamed of being ashamed.[139]

One has to keep in mind that this was uttered at a time when Israeli politicians and civil servants were forbidden to have contact with representatives of the PLO. He also strongly encouraged Christian pilgrims visiting the holy sites in the Holy Land to demand that the tour guides take them to the West Bank.[140]

At times, he could be quite explicit about his opinions about Israeli politicians: "In Israel I meet with people who dislike [Swedish: *avskyr*] [Menachem] Begin and [Ariel] Sharon as much as I do."[141]

Stendahl recognized the apologetic *Tendenz* that at times governs some descriptions of and discussions about the Israeli-Palestinian conflict: The situation is so difficult, he said, "that not even a Swede can be objective.…It is meaningless, I think, to try to figure out who has the most claims on the land. It is a long history of thousands of years. Both Palestinians and Israelis have deep roots in the Land."[142]

THE PRIME MINISTER ASSASSINATED AND STENDAHL'S STROKE

During Stendahl's time as bishop in Stockholm, Prime Minister Olof Palme was assassinated on February 28, 1986. Many Swedes still recall how Stendahl, a few days after the murder, looked into the TV camera in order to reach out to the murderer.[143]

In December 1987, Stendahl wrote to the government requesting leave to retire on October 1, 1988.[144] Only two days before an ordination service in Storkyrkan on June 5, 1988, he experienced a stroke and had to be taken to Danderyd Hospital. He was paralyzed on the left part of his body. The ordination was carried out by his predecessor, Lars Carlzon. Two days later, the media reported that he was feeling somewhat better.[145] He was, however, on sick leave, and it was uncertain whether he would be able to resume working before his retirement in October. Senior physician Nina Rehnqvist said that he was weak but that he could move and that he had been up briefly. Her prognosis was that he would recover but that it could take several months. Cathedral Dean Gösta Wrede assumed his duties. In an interview in September, Stendahl said that during his illness he kept thinking of a Swedish hymn: "Release into the hands of the Lord your hardship and your way."[146]

THE STENDAHLS RETURN TO THE UNITED STATES

Stendahl often referred to the four years in Stockholm in enthusiastic terms. "It is the only time I have had the opportunity to be firing on all cylinders: theology, sermons, administration, yes, everything. I had a tremendously good time and loved almost every day."[147] He called this period the culmination of his life. "The four years were one long celebration. It feels like everything else that I have done for almost sixty years was meant for those years."[148]

Journalist P. D. Lindeberg wrote, "Maybe a church can only cope with one Stendahl at a time. But it feels a little empty now when he is gone, this colorful and unafraid theologian."[149] (During his years in Stockholm, Stendahl's answering hour for media was 7–7:30 in the morning. When asked whether this was such a good idea, he replied that it certainly was: he arose at 5:30 a.m., offered Brita a glass of juice in bed, then read the newspapers and had time to think about what the journalists might want to ask him, so that he was prepared when they started calling at seven o'clock.[150])

Upon Krister's retirement in 1988, the Stendahls returned to Cambridge. For one semester he taught at Harvard Divinity School. In an interview he complained that there were too many student papers to read. The university then appointed him the first chaplain of Harvard Divinity School, perhaps the first bishop ever to assume such a position. One is reminded of the fact that he was a student chaplain in his youth.[151]

After retirement, he became even more involved in interreligious relations. In 1991 he was appointed the first Myra and Robert Kraft and Jacob Hiatt Distinguished Professor of Christian Studies at Brandeis University. (At the same time a comparable position in Jewish studies was endowed at the College of Holy Cross.)[152] Stendahl retired from Brandeis in 1993.

As a tribute to him from Sigtunastiftelsen, a series of seminars on religious pluralism were hosted in 1999–2000, at which he gave the keynote address (which is a reference to 1 Cor 13:12): "For Now We See in a Mirror, Dimly: Theology That Knows Its Limits."[153]

THREE INSTITUTES CLOSE TO HIS HEART

Uppsala University was Stendahl's alma mater. He taught for thirty years at Harvard Divinity School. Sigtunastiftelsen has already been mentioned several times. However briefly, three more of Stendahl's institutional affiliations deserve mention. Each one connected him to Sweden in a different and special way.

The first was his association with the Swedish Theological Institute in Jerusalem. Founded in 1951—only a few years after the Shoah—this institute strives to teach theology students about vibrant Jewish, Christian, and (more recently) Muslim spirituality, in order to promote improved interreligious relations. Generations of theology students have studied in this beautiful building, designed by one of Jerusalem's most famous nineteenth-century architects, Conrad Schick. Known as Beit Tavor (the house of Tabor; cf. Ps 89:12), it reposes like an island of calm on the Street of the Prophets in busy central Jerusalem.

Lund University, in cooperation with Church of Sweden, has established the Krister Stendahl Chair in Theology of Religions, the holder of which is the present writer. This chair is located at the STI. For decades, Stendahl served as the unofficial *episkopos* of this educational enterprise, always visiting when he was in town; lecturing, preaching, and counseling students and staff alike.

A second important affiliation was with Jerusalem's Shalom Hartman Institute. Named after the father of founder David Hartman, it was established in 1971. One day, the then-mayor of Jerusalem, Teddy Kollek, phoned Hartman, saying that there was a person he wanted him to meet. That person was Stendahl. Over the years, Hartman and Stendahl came to influence each other intensely, learning together how to articulate one's theology in the presence of the Other. The exercise mattered profoundly, they both felt, because it creates in oneself a salubrious humility and deeper ability to be meaningfully self-critical.[154]

From the 1980s, the Hartman Institute has sponsored interfaith theology seminars. Jews, Christians, and subsequently also Muslims have met there annually to engage in soul-searching discussions of topics such as sacred space, sacred time, holiness, death, hope, fundamentalism, and ways to confront religious dogmatism and intolerance. Characterized by *hevruta*, the close group study of texts, these seminars have tutored scholars from the three different faith traditions in the sacred literatures of the Other, while offering the opportunity to reflect both critically and appreciatively on one's own.

Swedish Consul General in San Francisco Barbro Sachs Osher had met with the Stendahls already in the 1980s in Stockholm. She and her husband Bernard Osher, both dedicated philanthropists, decided to support the Shalom Hartman Institute substantially. Thanks to their generosity and vision, the Hartman Institute now houses the Osher Center for Religious Pluralism and Tolerance. In 1994, Stendahl was appointed its codirector along with Hartman.

Mayor Kollek, whom Stendahl had also known for decades (Stendahl became a member of the Jerusalem Committee in 1978, and Kollek received an honorary doctorate from Harvard in 1984), offered the Shalom Hartman Institute three acres of land on Gedalyahu Alon Street in Jerusalem, where the $10 million premises were built. The locale was singularly appropriate. The site sits opposite the Hansen House (earlier known as Jesus Hilfe Asyl, a hospital and home for lepers designed and built by Conrad Schick in 1887), and not far from the Jerusalem Theater and the L.A. Mayer Institute of Islamic Art—a nice confluence of Christian, Jewish, and Muslim cultural centers. In its new location, the Shalom Hartman Institute continues to develop new and diverse voices within the Jewish tradition, *panim el panim* (Hebrew: face to face) with people who identify with other faith traditions. Stendahl's contribution both to the development of the Shalom Hartman Institute and to the role that it plays in Israeli society and worldwide was decisive.

In 2000, Paideia—the full name of this nondenominational institute being "Paideia: The European Institute for Jewish Studies in Sweden"—was established with funding from the Swedish government and also the Jewish communities of Stockholm, Gothenburg, Malmö, and Borås. Its website describes its mission:

> Dedicated to the revival of Jewish culture in Europe, Paideia educates leaders for Europe—academicians, artists and community activists—towards fluency in the Jewish textual sources that have served as the wellsprings of Jewish civilization. In renewing interpretation of Jewish text, Paideia is reviving a European Jewish voice long silenced by Communism and post-Holocaust trauma—a voice that can contribute to a culturally rich and pluralistic Europe.[155]

Paideia provides scholarships for students from all over the world to come to Stockholm for a year in order to study Jewish culture, the Hebrew language, Jewish classical texts, and Jewish hermeneutics. Paideia was founded by Barbara Lerner Spectre, and Stendahl was a trustee of this institute. The diocese of Stockholm in the Church of Sweden, in cooperation with Paideia, hosts the annual Krister Stendahl Memorial Lecture. When Paideia in May 2004 sponsored a conference at Hässelby Castle outside of Stockholm, Stendahl gave a lecture on religious pluralism and the reading of Holy Scriptures. It is his very last text (except for one published article and personal letters) that I have had access to when doing research for and writing this article. He writes,

> I think that what happens to my Holy Scripture, my holy canon, my revelation, is that it becomes potential wisdom for the others, and their truths become potential insight for me....The great watershed in intercultural and inter-religious relations was the opening of the Second Vatican Council, when Pope John XXIII declared contrary to centuries of tradition, that this council would not utter condemnations. Formerly all council decisions had each paragraph stating the faith followed by what was called the *anathema* [i.e., a person or thing to be detested and renounced], the condemnation of those who thought otherwise. But Vatican II did not utter condemnations. That implies a new attitude toward truth....The Enlightenment was very good in stressing the individual and very good in stressing the universal, but it had no patience with the particular....So, the time has come to understand the community of communities each with their distinct cultures....How much diversity do we need in order not to oppress or suppress?[156]

A TOWERING PRESENCE, BENT LIKE GRASS

For his last three years of life, Stendahl was on dialysis. He passed away of renal failure at Massachusetts General Hospital on April 15, 2008, only a few days before what would have been his eighty-seventh birthday. Memorial services were held on May 8 in Storkyrkan, Stockholm, and on May 16 in Memorial Church in Harvard Yard, Cambridge.[157]

In his essay "Why I Love the Bible," published in 2007, Stendahl wrote about the biblical passage that he wanted to have in mind when the end came: "And all of us, with unveiled faces, seeing the glory of the Lord as though reflected in a mirror, are being transformed into the same image from one degree of glory to another; for this comes from the Lord, the Spirit" (2 Cor 3:18).

In lectures, articles, books, letters, and conversations, Stendahl taught how necessary it is for religious studies scholars to be members of what he called "the Public Health Department." You have to know, so to speak, "the rough neighborhoods" of your own religious tradition. Christians need to know more about how their religion has been used *against* people, for example, against women, against people of color, against homosexuals, and against the Jewish people: "The Bible is a medicine cabinet with many medicines. The right way to live with this cabinet is to see what medicines are God's word for us right now."[158] He said that his own biblical interpretation and preaching could be described with the help of three words: "light, quick and tender" (Swedish: *lätt, snabb och öm*).[159]

Stendahl was a person who not only talked about the concept of "holy envy"—the willingness to recognize and celebrate elements in the other religious traditions without making them your own—but also someone who created holy envy within us who met him, who listened to him, and who worked with him. He was a person who generated trust. In the words of Diana L. Eck, professor of comparative religion and Indian studies at Harvard: "He was just a wonderful, towering presence in the Christian ecumenical community, both in interfaith and in Jewish-Christian relations."[160] And at Stendahl's memorial service in Cambridge, Susannah Heschel, describing the mayhem, the agony, and the suffering of the Jewish people during the Shoah, said simply, "And, then, after the war, God sent us Krister Stendahl."[161]

In the beginning, Stendahl was a New Testament scholar, but more and more he moved in the direction of theology of religions. One is reminded of what Job says: *ba-chuts lo-yalin ger, dlatai la-orach eftach*: "The stranger has not lodged in the street; I have opened my doors to the traveler" (Job 31:32). More and more, Stendahl addressed the issue of such hospitality to those who are "outside" of one's own theological tradition. His favorite question was, "How can I [i.e., as a Christian] sing my song to Jesus without telling negative stories about others?" This illumines how, for Stendahl, religious conviction was not a zero-sum game, in which one's gain has to be the other's loss. He always emphasized that one's religion must not be at other people's expense. Christians should not seek to find a dichotomy between a Christian type of alleged "unique" love that is better than other people's love. And his expression "sing my song" highlights his idea of what kind of activity religion actually should be: not doctrinal fencing, but devotion. Is it not a Eurovision Song Contest, with a complicated procedure of voting, but it is a song, a song of praise.

Beginning as a biblical scholar, Stendahl indeed remained a biblical interpreter throughout his life. The full title of his last article, "Why I Love the Bible: Beyond Distinctions of Intellect and Spirit, an Ever-Transforming Affair of the Heart," captures this well. But by and by, he was exploring new angles of religious pluralism. He often returned to the thirteenth chapter in Paul's first epistle to the Corinthians: *hê agapê... ou zêtei ta heautês*, which is sometimes translated as "love is not selfish" (1 Cor 13:5). But he wanted to understand it more literally: "love does not seek its own"; in other words, love yearns for what is different, it longs for pluralism. He called this understanding "the Corinthian Model": a Christian theology of religion that recognizes and integrates pluralism and difference. That is another way to express what he meant by "holy envy." Love—which Paul, by the way, says is greater than knowledge, hope, and faith—yearns for what is different. Holiness envies the beauty of the other—but still lets the other remain what he is, remain what she is. Religious curiosity must not become the servant of religious arrogance.

Furthermore, "holy envy" is what you experience when you meet "the Other." But you have to transform this experience into theological discourse. In other words, how do we provide theological space for the Other? How is my own faith influenced by this encounter?

HIS IMMORTAL TEXT ON IMMORTALITY

Of all the texts that Stendahl wrote, there is one that has meant more to me than the other books and articles. This text is even more important than his tour de force on Paul and the introspective conscience, profoundly influential though that has been in rooting out individualistic and problematic readings of Paul's epistles in the West.

The text that I am thinking of is more important than his article on women and ministry, published in 1958, when the decision was made in the Church of Sweden to allow ordination of women. That writing of his was one of the most significant contributions to the debate; one could perhaps even state that it was what tipped the scales in favor of a positive decision. But I am thinking of something else.

The text I am thinking of is more important than his often-quoted article on contemporary biblical theology in the *Interpreter's Dictionary of the Bible*, published in 1962, in which he underlined that we have to separate what biblical texts "meant" (in a way, his emphasis when he was a doctoral student at Uppsala University in Sweden) from what they "mean" (which gradually became his focus at Harvard Divinity School).[162]

The text I am thinking of is more important than his thought-provoking book *Energy for Life: Reflections on the Theme "Come, Holy Spirit—Renew the Whole Creation."*[163] Written for the Seventh General Assembly of the World Council of Churches in Canberra in 1991, this book seeks to articulate an alternative to androcentric theological discourse.[164]

All these texts are, no doubt, paradigmatic, illuminating, and important. But now I am thinking of another text. It is Stendahl's short article on immortality and resurrection, the text that was debated so fiercely in Sweden during his bishopric.[165]

A cantata sung at Krister Stendahl's memorial service reminded those present that people are like grass. Anna Langenfeld, Krister and Brita Stendahl's daughter, said in her remarks to those assembled that day,

> And, yes, father was like grass—very tall grass. He was tall and graceful, even though his body tried to bend him to be otherwise.[166]

We are all like grass; perhaps not as tall and not as graceful, but we are all like grass. We live for a short time on this earth, and when our days are over, we are no more, as the Psalmist reminds us.[167]

And when quoting the concluding paragraph in Stendahl's immortal text on immortality and resurrection, it seems that the descriptions of him—a person bent like grass, but nonetheless and in so many ways, a towering presence—all converge. Here we hear his message, his *viva vox*, always emphasizing God's greatness, human humility, and also the limits of our knowledge:

> So, sisters and brothers, we are very small but we are small in the hands of God. . . . To me it seems that if God is God, I neither care for nor worry about the hereafter; I celebrate the coming of the kingdom by singing hymns and by caressing with words the heaven with angels and saints and the messianic banquet with light and joy and glory. And I know that I paint, but I like to paint and I paint out of love and hope and faith. But when all is said and done I pray that the evil I have put into the world will not cause others to suffer too much, and that my little life will fit somehow into God's plan for the kingdom. The rest I leave. May his kingdom come.[168]

NOTES

1. Profound thanks are primarily due to Annika Wenemark, and also to Jan-Olof Aggedal, Gunnel Borgegård, Tamara Cohn Eskenazi, Göran Larsson, Laura Nasrallah, Kristina Selén, Barbara Spectre, John Stendahl, and, of course, to my coeditor Paula Fredriksen, for stimulating conversations and helpful observations. Sincere thanks go to Jessica Suarez, curator of manuscripts and archives at Andover-Harvard Theological Library for kind assistance during one full week of archive research in July 2017, and to Maureen Jennings for additional research in November 2017. Many thanks also to the library staff at Sigtunastiftelsen for providing me with numerous articles about and texts by Krister and Brita Stendahl. The concluding paragraphs of this essay build upon and expand my presentation in memory of Krister Stendahl, which took place at the Shalom Hartman Institute in Jerusalem on March 24, 2009.

2. See, e.g., the interview with John Stendahl by Laura Nasrallah, "A Conversation with John Stendahl," YouTube video, 48:16, part of HarvardX course, "Early Christianity: The Letters of Paul," posted by Harvard Divinity School, January 14, 2014, https://www.youtube.com/watch?v=8qYPcZ8WvSU.

3. Krister Stendahl, "Om Maria: Min tros moder," *Växjö stifts hembygdskalender* 82 (1991): 30.

4. *Dagen*, August 24, 1985.

5. See, e.g., *Dagens Nyheter*, June 10, 1984; *Svenska Dagbladet*, September 25, 1988; and *Expressen*, January 14, 1983.

6. *Svenska Dagbladet*, September 21, 1986, and *Expressen*, October 20, 1984.

7. *Sydsvenska Dagbladet*, April 20, 2001. The name of this newspaper has shifted over the years from *Sydsvenska Dagbladet Snällposten* to *Sydsvenskan*. For the sake of congruity, in this article it is always referred to as *Sydsvenska Dagbladet*.

8. P. D. Lindeberg, "Paulus är idealgubben," *Sydsvenska Dagbladet*, April 20, 1996.

9. Douglas Martin, *New York Times*, April 16, 2008.

10. The earliest letter I have found is a recommendation written by Stendahl on March 29, 1949, for a man who would like to become a minister in Church of Sweden. One letter was written on a flight to San Francisco in 1968. It is very much marked by Stendahl's outrage over the Vietnam War, which he calls "lunacy" (Swedish: *vanvett*), and over the racism in the United States. "The future," he says, "belongs to God; it is not mine, not ours, not even 'Christianity's,' but God's." Stendahl, Papers, Sigtunastiftelsen.

11. Stendahl to Björkquist, January 12, 1981. Stendahl, Papers, Sigtunastiftelsen.

12. The word *människan* in Swedish is feminine.

13. Nasrallah, "A Conversation with John Stendahl."

14. *Sydsvenskan*, April 20, 2001.

15. Stockholm City Mission is a nonprofit organization that provides help to people who are homeless or living with substance abuse, and to children, young adults, and the elderly.

16. Brita K. Stendahl, *Søren Kierkegaard* (Boston: Twayne, 1976) and *Søren Kierkegaard*, trans. Hans-Erik Johannesson (Stockholm: Atlantis, 1980).

17. Brita K. Stendahl, *The Force of Tradition: A Case Study of Women Priests in Sweden* (Philadelphia: Fortress, 1985) and *Traditionens makt: Kvinnan och prästämbetet i Svenska kyrkan*, trans. Ingela Åstrand (Stockholm: Petra, 1985).

18. *Stockholms-Tidningen*, December 11, 1947. He had previously been a minister in the parishes of Västerhaninge and Hedvig Eleonora. See also *Svenska Dagbladet*, September 21, 1986.

19. E.g., Krister Stendahl, "Vad jag har lärt mig om judendomen mellan 1951 och 1991," *Tro möter tro: Med KJ-information* 1, no. 2 (1991): 16.

20. *Stockholms-Tidningen*, May 20, 1954, and *Stockholms-Tidningen*, April 4, 1954.

21. Williams to Stendahl, May 3, 1954, Stendahl Papers, bMS 760, Andover-Harvard Theological Library, Harvard Divinity School, Cambridge, MA.

22. *Hudiksvalls Tidning*, June 3, 1954, and Brita K. Stendahl, *Sabbatsår: Tio Guds bud i vår tid*, trans. Astrid Lundgren (Stockholm: Legenda, 1986), 13; originally published as *Sabbatical Reflections: The Ten Commandments in a New Day* (Philadelphia: Fortress, 1980).

23. Stendahl to Björkquist, July 23, 1954. Stendahl, Papers, Sigtunastiftelsen.

24. *Svenska Dagbladet*, September 7, 1958.

25. The Stendahl family's Christmas letter, Advent 1965. Stendahl, Papers, Sigtunastiftelsen, and *Sydsvenska Dagbladet*, April 20, 2001.

26. Stendahl to Björkquist, December 12, 1964. Stendahl, Papers, Sigtunastiftelsen.

27. Birger Gerhardsson, *Memory and Manuscript: Oral Tradition and Written Transmission in Rabbinic Judaism and Early Christianity*; with *Tradition and Transmission in Early Christianity* (Grand Rapids, MI: Eerdmans, 1998, originally published in 1961 and 1964). The reception history of his scholarship has been formed and forged to a high extent by Morton Smith's review article, "A Comparison of Early Christian and Early Rabbinic Tradition," *Journal of Biblical Literature* 82 (1963): 169–76. Gerhardsson himself describes these two books as "youthful works" (Swedish: *ungdomsarbeten*); see *Evangeliernas förhistoria: Nyutgåva med tillägg* (Lund: Novapress, 1991), 7. See also his preface in *The Reliability of the Gospel Tradition*, foreword by Donald A. Hagner (Peabody, MA: Hendrickson, 2001), xvii–xxiv, especially xxiv: "For my part, I have become convinced that we can hear the voice of Jesus himself in the Gospels. His pronouncements and the narratives about his actions have been interpreted and clarified by his disciples, but they reach us nevertheless in a *reliable* form" (emphasis added).

28. Stendahl to Björkquist, December 10, 1966. Stendahl, Papers, Sigtunastiftelsen.

29. Brita K. Stendahl, *Sabbatsår*, 142.

30. *Dagens Nyheter*, February 21, 1967. Their son Johan, now called John, experienced some problems, because he had taken part in anti-Vietnam activities.

31. Stendahl to Lundberg, February 8, 1967. Stendahl, Papers, bMS 760.

32. Stendahl, Papers, bMS 760.

33. Stendahl, Papers, bMS 760.

34. *Svenska Dagbladet*, February 17, 1967.

35. *Expressen*, February 19, 1967.

36. *Expressen*, August 13, 1967, and *Svenska Dagbladet*, August 15, 1967.

37. *Kvällsposten*, March 27, 1967.

38. *Aftonbladet*, April 21, 1967.

39. In an article in *Aftonbladet*, August 15, 1967, another newspaper, *Dagens Nyheter*, was blamed for the results because of how Stendahl had been presented.

40. Jonas Jonson, *Jag är bara Nathan Söderblom satt till tjänst: En biografi* (Stockholm: Verbum, 2014), 198–201.

41. Olof B. Malm, *Bilder och blad från Ekumeniska mötet i Stockholm 1925* (Stockholm: Svenska kyrkans diakonistyrelses bokförlag, 1925).

42. *Kvällsposten*, January 20, 1968.

43. The Stendahl family's Christmas letter, Advent 1967. Stendahl, Papers, Sigtunastiftelsen.

44. *Expressen*, August 13, 1967.

45. *Svenska Dagbladet*, May 17, 1972.

46. *Svenska Dagbladet*, February 15, 1977 and September 3, 1978.

47. *Svenska Dagbladet*, November 11, 1978, and *Dagens Nyheter*, November 14, 1978.

48. Ragnar Holte, "Välj Stendahl till ärkebiskop!" *Dagens Nyheter*, January 20, 1983.

49. *Dagens Nyheter*, January 20, 1983.

50. *Tidningarnas Telegrambyrå*, January 16, 1983 and *Vestmanlands Läns Tidning*, January 17, 1983; *Sydsvenska Dagbladet*, January 17, 1983; *Dagens Nyheter*, January 17, 1983; and *Östersunds-Posten*, January 17, 1983.

51. A response from Sven Hernqvist was published on the 27th, criticizing the author of the text, who defended himself saying that he had consulted several outstanding biblical scholars. "They gave a rather homogeneous judgment [Swedish: *ett tämligen enhetligt omdöme*] about Stendahl's theology."

52. *Dagens Nyheter*, January 29, 1983 and *Vi* #16 (1984). In the elections the votes of the archdiocese count six times more than votes of the other dioceses.

53. The Latin expression *primus inter pares* is often used to describe the relation between the archbishop and the other bishops in Church of Sweden. Although the archbishop often is the spokesperson for the bishops, she (since

2014 Antje Jackelén is the archbishop) is among equals. In that sense, the Church of Sweden is a distinctly episcopal church.

54. *Sydsvenska Dagbladet*, February 12, 1983.

55. *Svenska Dagbladet*, February 9, 1984.

56. Stendahl was appointed on June 7, but did not have much time to celebrate, because on that very same day it was commencement at Harvard Divinity School: both King Juan Carlos of Spain and Teddy Kollek, mayor of Jerusalem, were there to receive honorary doctorates, see *Dagens Nyheter*, June 8, 1984.

57. *Tidningarnas Telegrambyrå*, September 13, 1984.

58. *Sydsvenska Dagbladet*, September 25, 1984, and *Göteborgs-Posten*, September 25, 1984.

59. *Arbetet*, October 8, 1984, and *Sydsvenska Dagbladet*, October 8, 1984.

60. Stendahl, "Om Maria: Min tros moder."

61. *Dagens Nyheter*, October 8, 1984.

62. Undated correspondence from Margareta Nudel to Stendahl. See Stendahl, Papers, bMS 760.

63. See, e.g., Gunnar Dahmén in *Svenska Dagbladet*, August, 29, 1977; Bernt Eklundh in *Göteborgs-Posten*, April 16, 1978; Allan Sandström in *Västerbottens-Kuriren*, July 8, 1978; and Leif Carlsson in *Svenska Dagbladet*, June 2, 1985. However, Olov Hartman's impression in *Aftonbladet*, February 12, 1978, is that Stendahl portrayed Paul as someone involved in "church politics" (i.e., merely seeking to reconcile Jews and Gentiles in the early church).

64. *Svenska Dagbladet*, January 28, 1960.

65. Krister Stendahl, "Paulus och samvetet," *Svensk exegetisk årsbok* 25 (1960): 62–77; address delivered at the Annual Meeting of the American Psychological Association, New York, September 3, 1961.

66. Ps 19:7 and *Svenska Dagbladet*, January 8, 1985. The article's headline is "Biskopen 'läste lagen' för lagfolk," which means both that he read the law and that he gave them a lecture.

67. *Västerbottens-Kuriren*, July 8, 1978.

68. Stendahl, "Immortality Is Too Much and Too Little," *Meanings: The Bible as Document and as Guide*, 2nd ed. (Minneapolis: Fortress, 2008), 193–202. As a young scholar, Stendahl actually published a book in Swedish called "The Meaning of the Bible": *Bibelns mening* (Stockholm: Sveriges kristliga studentrörelses bokförlag, 1952). In a way, his book from 1984, celebrating plurals and pluralism, is an oblique reference to his previous

book, published thirty-two years earlier. His book *Meanings* opens with the following words (p. 1): "The longer I have lived, the more I have come to like plurals. I have grown increasingly suspicious of singulars. I have come to question the incessant theological urge toward oneness."

69. *Tidningarnas Telegrambyrå*, June 18, 1987.

70. *Kyrkans Tidning* #7 (2002): "Vilken uppståndelse det blev!"

71. *Sydsvenska Dagbladet*, February 6, 1987. Cf. *Nya Wermlands-Tidningen*, April 4, 1995, in which Stendahl complains that Swedish ministers do not know the Bible well enough; they think that they can get away with just reading the lectionaries.

72. *Göteborgs-Posten*, January 20, 1985.

73. *Sydsvenska Dagbladet*, January 16, 1972.

74. Brita Stendahl, presumably and hopefully to some degree a tongue-in-cheek commentary, writes that the student revolt in 1969 destroyed their sex life, see *Sabbatsår*, 101. For her definition and critique of capitalism, see p. 117.

75. *Kvällsposten*, April 28, 1971. In addition to talking about himself as an American, he also thinks of himself as a Swede; see, e.g., *Expressen*, January 14, 1983, where he says that "he feels a wave of warmth [Swedish: *värmeström*] every time someone says 'Sweden.'"

76. *Expressen*, December 3, 1972.

77. *Expressen*, July 26, 1970.

78. *Svenska Dagbladet*, November 6, 1987.

79. *Vestmanlands Läns Tidning*, March 29, 1985.

80. *Expressen*, May 5, 1984.

81. *Dagen*, March 7, 1987 and *Tidningarnas Telegrambyrå*, May 1, 1987.

82. *Dagen*, May 15, 1986. In Sweden a national referendum on nuclear power was held on March 23, 1980. On Stendahl's comparison of theology to nuclear power (maximum energy, minimum waste), see *Sydsvenska Dagbladet*, January 16, 1972.

83. *Dagens Nyheter*, October 28, 1984.

84. *Tidningarnas Telegrambyrå*, December 27, 1985.

85. *Tidningarnas Telegrambyrå*, September 3, 1986.

86. *Tidningarnas Telegrambyrå*, August 28, 1986.

87. *Dagen*, February 6, 1985.

88. *Göteborgs-Posten*, June 8, 1984.

89. The sermon "In the Name of Jesus" is in Stendahl, Papers, bMS 760.

90. *Göteborgs-Posten*, January 20, 1985.

91. *Expressen*, March 10, 1976. The name of the protagonist is a reference to Falstaff Fakir's book from 1895: *The Fairytale about Pomperipossa with the Long Nose*.

92. *Svenska Dagbladet*, February 17, 1985.

93. Stendahl, "Preface," in *Meanings*, vii. The preface is dated December 13, 1983.

94. *Svenska Dagbladet*, October 10, 1977.

95. Nasrallah, "A Conversation with John Stendahl."

96. See, e.g., *Vestmanlands Läns Tidning*, June 30, 1984, where he is described as a combination of high church theology and broadness of views.

97. *Svenska Dagbladet*, August 6, 1968: "Jag tycker det är underbart att vi har detta rika utgångsläge i stället för att starta från en nersliten liberal teologi....Det var i *Societas Sanctae Birgittae* som jag själv fick grepp om vad andakt och gudstjänstliv handlar om." It is stated that the text had been checked (Swedish: *granskad*) by Stendahl, which probably means that he gave an interview, perhaps over the phone, and that he then read and approved the text before it was printed.

98. Stendahl, Papers, bMS 760.

99. Krister Stendahl, "Bibelsynen och kvinnan," in *Kvinnan—Samhället—Kyrkan* (Stockholm: Svenska kyrkans diakonistyrelses bokförlag, 1958), 138–66. See also his article "Kvinnan i Bibeln och kyrkan," *Handlingar rörande prästmötet i Stockholm den 2, 3 och 4 juni 1975* (Stockholm: Diocese of Stockholm, 1975), 56–73.

100. *Expressen*, July 26, 1970.

101. See, e.g., *Dagen*, February 28, 1984; *Expressen*, February 29, 1984; *Aftonbladet*, March 28, 1984; and *Dagen*, June 8, 1984. See also *Vestmanlands Läns Tidning*, September 25, 1984.

102. See, e.g., *Svenska Dagbladet*, April 7, 1984. A related topic to active participation of laity in the services is his views on the charismatic movement. During the years of the Jesus movement, he spoke in favor of more charismatic services. He said that the Jesus movement had a contribution to offer to mainstream Christianity, which often had services that were too boring; see, e.g., *Upsala Nya Tidning*, January 29, 1975.

103. See, e.g., *Svenska Dagbladet*, September 25, 1988.

104. *Svenska Dagbladet*, April 24, 1967.

105. *Upsala Nya Tidningar*, December 6, 1984. He refers to the snakeskin parable also in a conversation about "theology about important things"; see "Angelägen teologi: Teologi om viktiga ting. Samtal mellan Krister Stendahl och Lars Gyllensten," *Vår Lösen* 67, no. 7 (1976): 350.

106. *Upsala Nya Tidning*, June 5, 1972.

107. *Svenska Dagbladet*, January 7, 1987.

108. *Expressen*, July 26, 1970: "Nu tror jag att jag har blivit lite känsligare för dessa blyga och tafatta människor och deras behov av en servicekyrka."

109. *Svenska Dagbladet*, August 13, 1975: "Kyrkans verkliga uppgift är att skapa ett klimat där Guds vilja kan ske."

110. *Homosexuella och samhället: Betänkande av utredningen om homosexuellas situation i samhället*, Statens offentliga utredningar 1984:63 (Stockholm: Liber, 1984).

111. *Svenska Dagbladet*, April 22, 1985, and *Dagens Nyheter*, April 22, 1985.

112. *Tidningarnas Telegrambyrå*, August 17, 1985.

113. *Göteborgs-Posten*, October 24, 1986.

114. *Tidningarnas Telegrambyrå*, August 13, 1987.

115. *Dagen*, May 4, 2001. The first major step in this direction was taken in 1990 when two San Francisco congregations (St. Francis Church and First United Lutheran Church) defied the Evangelical Lutheran Church of America by ordaining openly gay and lesbian pastors not on the approved ELCA roster; see W. R. Holmen, "Jeff Johnson, Phyllis Zillhart, Ruth Frost: Lutherans on Trial," Spirit of a Liberal (blog), January 14, 2014, http://www.theliberalspirit.com/cast-of-characters-countdown-jeff-johnson-phyllis-zillhart-ruth-frost.

116. See his book *In the Eye of the Storm: Swept to the Center by God* (New York: Seabury, 2008). On September 23, 2003, Stendahl wrote to Archbishop K. G. [Karl Gustav] Hammar, asking for permission to attend the consecration. In the reply of September 30, written by the archbishop's secretary, Stendahl is not only granted permission, but it also explicitly stated that the archbishop is delighted to give him this assignment and to have him represent Church of Sweden. See Stendahl, Papers, bMS 760.

117. Krister Stendahl, "Can Bishops Tell the Truth as They See It?" in *Christianity in the 21st Century*, ed. Deborah A. Brown (New York: Crossroad, 2000), 184.

118. *Dagen*, April 25, 1985.

119. In 2009 the General Assembly decided that this liturgical order be called "wedding," not merely a blessing.

120. How early was Stendahl reflecting on these issues? In a letter of August 11, 1977, to William E. Lesher, president of the Pacific Lutheran Seminary, Stendahl writes that he finds "the subject of homosexuality…a difficult question and [I] have started to do some readings and some thinking,

but I am hardly ready to write on it at this time. It seems clear to me that the movement by which homosexuals are 'coming out of the closet' is to be greatly welcomed and supported by the churches. I would start from there. That is, I would start from a pastoral concern rather than thinking of the pastoral concern as being the last step in the theological process. I have always felt that Pope John XXIII achieved the renewal of the Roman Catholic Church by giving the pastoral questions the higher priority and relegating the questions of Canon Law, etc. to a lower position in the total life and thinking of the Roman Church. I think that is the easiest way to understand the positive developments in Vatican II. I hope to come back to this matter in not too distant a future." This letter can be found in Stendahl's Papers, bMS 760.

121. *Tidningarnas Telegrambyrå*, September 21, 1984. When asked about extremism in other religious traditions, he responded that "there are cardsharpers in all religions."

122. Birger Gerhardsson, *Fridrichsen, Odeberg, Aulén, Nygren: Fyra teologer* (Lund: Novapress, 1994), 18.

123. Anton Fridrichsen, *Fyrahanda sädesåker: En kommentar till Evangeliebokens högmässotexter*, ed. Birger Gerhardsson (Stockholm: Svenska kyrkans diakonistyrelses bokförlag, 1958). See, e.g., pp. 95, 134, 164, 182, 184, 194–95, 197, 201, 210, 219, 240, 242, 244, 246, 263, 294, 301, 347, 351, 379, 387–88, 408–9, 415, 421, 423, 424, 425, 426, 491, 520, and 569–70.

124. Brita Stendahl, *Sabbatsår*, 50.

125. Stendahl, "Vad jag har lärt mig om judendomen mellan 1951 och 1991," 16.

126. *Svenska Dagbladet*, April 29, 1960.

127. "Teologi till vänster," *Vår Lösen* 57:3 (1966): 131–132.

128. *Svenska Dagbladet*, June 5, 1972.

129. See, e.g., *Tidningarnas Telegrambyrå*, June 7, 1984.

130. Helmut Koester, "Tribute to Bishop Krister Stendahl," *Studies in Christian-Jewish Relations* 4 (2009): 6.

131. *Svenska Dagbladet*, July 13, 1987. The interviewer was Ahmed Rami, who was a radio producer of the program Radio Islam. For this program and its *Wirkungsgeschichte* in Swedish media and at Uppsala University, see Inge Lönning, *Antisemittismen som juridisk, intellektuell og moralsk utfordring: En betenkning om rettssaken mot Radio Islam og debatten om professor Jan Bergmans vitneprov i retten* (Uppsala: University of Uppsala Faculty of Theology, 1994).

132. *Dagen*, February 5, 1985.

133. *Expressen*, April 24, 1984.

134. *Svenska Dagbladet*, November 5, 1989.

135. Krister Stendahl, "Why I Love the Bible: Beyond Distinctions of Intellect and Spirit, an Ever-Transforming Affair of the Heart," *Harvard Divinity Bulletin* 35 (2007): 25. See also, e.g., *Norrköpings Tidningar*, January 29, 1982.

136. Will Joyner, "Krister Stendahl, 1921–2008," *Harvard Divinity School—News and Events*, April 16, 2008, hds.harvard.edu/news/2011/02/07/krister-stendahl-1921-2008#.

137. *Svenska Dagbladet*, May 8, 2008.

138. As an example of a low-key and constructive discussion, see Torsten Kälvemark's article in *Aftonbladet*, March 13, 1988, in which he recommends that Stendahl read Elias Chacour and David Hazard's book *Blood Brothers*.

139. *Dagen*, October 31, 1984.

140. Ibid.

141. *Expressen*, January 14, 1983. See also *Upsala Nya Tidning*, August 3, 1983; *Västerbottens-Kuriren*, August 4, 1983; and *Östersunds-Posten*, August 4, 1983.

142. *Dagen*, February 25, 1988.

143. *Kyrkans Tidning*, May 22, 2008.

144. *Tidningarnas Telegrambyrå*, December 22, 1987.

145. *Tidningarnas Telegrambyrå*, June 7, 1988.

146. *Svenska Dagbladet*, September 25, 1988. Hymn 298:1 in the Hymn Book of 1938 (=Hymn 247 in the Hymn Book of 1986, with minor changes): "Befall i Herrens händer/ din möda och din väg,/ och hur sig världen vänder,/ hans ord i hjärtat äg./ Ty intet ord är givet/ som Herrens ord, så visst./ Det visar vägen till livet,/ det för dig hem till sist."

147. *Kyrkans Tidning* #7 (2002).

148. *Svenska Dagbladet*, April 17, 2008.

149. *Sydsvenska Dagbladet*, April 21, 1991.

150. I am grateful to Gunnel Borgegård for this piece of information. In the 1980s she worked at the Swedish Ecumenical Council, and he chaired its executive committee.

151. *Svenska Dagbladet*, April 21, 1991.

152. *Tidningarnas Telegrambyrå*, August 2, 1991, and *Dagens Nyheter*, August 3, 1991.

153. Krister Stendahl, "Ännu ser vi en gåtfull spegelbild: Teologi som vet sin begränsning," in *Samtal om religionsteologi*, ed. Kajsa Ahlstrand and Håkan Sandvik, Tro & Tanke 2001:3, 67–72 (Uppsala: Svenska kyrkans forskningsråd, 2001).

154. "Krister Stendahl Remembered by David Hartman—2009," YouTube video, 13:51, published by Shalom Harman Institute, March 2, 2016, https://www.youtube.com/watch?v=mhMseRUxjJk.

155. See Paideia: The European Institute for Jewish Studies in Sweden website, http://www.paideia-eu.org/about/mission-statement.

156. Krister Stendahl, "Text and Multiculturalism" (lecture, Hässelby Castle; Stockholm, May 23, 2004). On the expression, "community of communities," in which one cannot take one's own worldview for granted, see also *Dagen*, January 30, 1982.

157. *Kyrkans Tidning*, May 15, 2008.

158. *Dagens Nyheter*, June 10, 1984.

159. *Dagens Nyheter*, June 10, 1984. See also "Why I Love the Bible," 24.

160. Diana L. Eck quoted in Bryan Marquard, "Krister Stendahl; Expanded Scope, Depth of Divinity School," *Boston Globe*, April 17, 2008, archive.boston.com/bostonglobe/obituaries/articles/2008/04/17/krister_stendahl_expanded_scope_depth_of_divinity_school.

161. Susannah Heschel, "Memorial to Krister Stendahl," original manuscript, given to Brita Stendahl.

162. Krister Stendahl, "Biblical Theology, Contemporary," in *The Interpreter's Dictionary of the Bible*, ed. George Arthur Buttrick (New York: Abingdon, 1962), 1:418–32. The text was republished in *Meanings*, 11–44.

163. Krister Stendahl, *Energy for Life: Reflections on the Theme "Come, Holy Spirit—Renew the Whole Creation"* (Geneva: WCC Publications, 1990).

164. Unfortunately, due to illness he was unable to participate in the general assembly; see *Aftonbladet*, February 8, 1991, and *Svenska Dagbladet*, April 21, 1991. When interviewed by Laura Nasrallah, John Stendahl has pointed out that his father's first focus was *Jesus* (thanks to the Pentecostal maid in his parents' home), that he gradually shifted focus to the kingdom of *God*, and with this book he also focused on the works of the *Holy Spirit*. John has said that his father himself reflected on this move, which toward the end of his life was a full circle: during his very last time he returned to the Jesus piety of his youth, quoting both Paul (Phil 1:23: "my desire is to depart and be with Christ") and Jesus himself (he quoted the keyword in John 19:28 and 30 in Greek: *tetelestai*, "it is finished").

165. Stendahl, "Immortality Is Too Much and Too Little."

166. *Harvard Divinity Today* 4, no. 2 (2008): 12.

167. See, e.g., Ps 103:15–16.

168. Stendahl, "Immortality Is Too Much and Too Little," 202. For the importance of the kingdom of God motif in his theology, see also the posthumously published book: Krister Stendahl, *The Roots of Violence: Creating Peace through Spiritual Reconciliation* (Brewster, MA: Paraclete Press, 2016).

II

THE WORK

Institutions and Communities

2

SAYING NO

Krister Stendahl on Scripture and on Leadership

Laura Salah Nasrallah

Krister Stendahl was a scholar with an abundant life. He enjoyed an abundance of professional leadership roles, an abundance of national contexts, and an abundance of conversation partners. Paradoxically, my chapter celebrates this abundance by remembering how Stendahl himself said no, particularly in his roles as New Testament scholar and in his retrospective on his deanship at Harvard Divinity School. Exploring Stendahl's musings on saying no, whether this no emerged from biblical scholarship or from academic leadership, may help us to think about the direction of New Testament scholarship today. Stendahl's noes may also encourage a consideration of how an ethics of saying no might inform our own scholarly endeavors, and our involvement in the academy and in various religious communities.

STENDAHL AND ABUNDANCE

Krister Stendahl came to teach at the Harvard Divinity School in 1954. From March 1968 until July 1979 he was its dean. He returned to his post as professor of New Testament thereafter; and then, from 1984 to 1988, he went on to be bishop of—or, as he insisted, "in"—Stockholm.[1] After Stockholm, Stendahl served as inaugural chaplain at Harvard Divinity School, and then as inaugural holder of the Myra and Robert Kraft and Jacob Hiatt Distinguished Professor of Christian Studies at Brandeis University.[2] Meanwhile, he also participated actively in the World Council of Churches and, from 1994 on, he codirected the Osher

Center for Tolerance and Pluralism at the Shalom Hartman Institute in Jerusalem.[3] Stendahl's work was deeply engaged, ethically and theologically informed by his life as an ordained Lutheran minister, and deeply lived out as professor and then dean at the Harvard Divinity School. His roles as Christian leader and as ordained minister—his pastoral role and his theological insight—undergird his thoughts on Scripture and history, and his decisions about leadership.

While this essay focuses on Stendahl saying no, it could equally well focus on his work in saying yes: yes to abundance, yes to plurality. His introductory essay in *Meanings: The Bible as Document and as Guide* begins, "The longer I have lived, the more I have come to like plurals. I have grown increasingly suspicious of singulars. I have come to question the incessant theological urge toward oneness."[4] This plurality and abundance, Stendahl argued, is baked into Christian tradition. Stendahl emphasized that the title "the Bible," which sounds singular in English, sits on top of the Greek *ta biblia*: the books. He also pointed to his love of the plurality of the Trinity, which he declared "a most daring attempt at not sacrificing richness and diversity on the altars of theoretical monisms of various kinds."[5]

Stendahl's scholarship and his leadership as Divinity School dean emerged from urgent ethical concerns in his own time, the second half of the twentieth century. These presented to him ideas, activities, and political and professional positions to which he wanted to say no. "I was once asked by someone who had looked at my bibliography," wrote Stendahl, "why I had been so preoccupied with two topics: Jews and women. I think, in retrospect, that the answer is not hard to find. The Christian Scriptures contain stuff that has proven calamitous to both Jews and women."[6] In order to counteract such moral and social calamities, Stendahl proposed "a hermeneutics suited for the 'public health' task of theology," a kind of academic blood glucose test by which one could quickly discern if things were going in the wrong direction, if one's biblical interpretation was hazardous to another's health or to yours, deleterious or uplifting of the common good.[7] So too, the current Krister Stendahl Professor of Divinity at Harvard, Elisabeth Schüssler Fiorenza, has written that "the contents of biblical texts should be marked with the label: 'Caution, could be dangerous to your health and survival.'"[8] Stendahl spoke to the same concerns: "I would guess that the last racists in this country, if there ever be an end to such, will be the ones with Bible in hand. There never has been an evil cause in the world that has not become more evil if it has been possible to argue it on biblical grounds."[9] Scholarship in the study of religion as a solution to a public health crisis: this kind of thinking surely resonates today. We could extend it, with Stendahl's approval, to many scriptures in the world more globally.[10]

SAYING NO IN THREE ACTS

Because of Stendahl's evaluation that biblical studies can lead to a public health crisis, his legacy of leadership and scholarship involved saying no. Saying no is also a significant lesson in this world of academic business, of overwhelming data, of needing to know what is urgent among the many urgent calls for political action. Saying no allowed Stendahl to think about his priorities as scholar and as dean, and to encourage others to say no as well. This chapter explores Stendahl's saying no in three "acts."

ACT 1: SAYING NO (AND YES) TO THE BIBLE

In a talk first delivered as the Edward L. Mark Lecture at Harvard-Epworth United Methodist Church in Cambridge, Massachusetts, in 2001, Stendahl spoke about "Why I Love the Bible: Beyond Distinctions of Intellect and Spirit, an Ever-Transforming Affair of the Heart."[11] He offered "five 'no' statements" in order to talk about his love for the Bible. This was odd, as he recognized:

> It is usual when one is describing love to describe it in positive and glowing terms. But my friendship with the Bible gave me the joy, and the courage, to express my love in five statements of "not." The first is...: It is not primarily about me. Second, it is not always as deep as we think. Third, even Paul isn't always totally sure. Fourth, don't be so uptight. And fifth, it is probably not as universal as we think.

Stendahl explained his first no—"it is not primarily about me"— by appeal to autobiography. Speaking of his encounter with the Bible, of his reading Paul and of thinking that Paul's struggles were his own,[12] Stendahl explained that, in time, he realized that Paul's Epistle to the Romans was *not* about himself: "It was about the Jews and the Gentiles and not about me. What an awakening….And, imagine, I read these things during the end of the Second World War, when the camps in Auschwitz and Dachau opened up, and I still thought that Romans was a theological tractate about my soul." These insights echo Stendahl's scholarship elsewhere, which insists that New Testament scholarship break the habit of reading Paul through the eyes of Augustine or Luther, as the story of a Christian convert, or as a commentary on the individual sinner's struggle.[13] These insights also echo Stendahl's lifelong commitment—both in scholarly practices and in face-to-face encounters—of taking seriously the Jewish context of the emergence of what we now call early Christianity. This principle flowed in and out of his involvement in the Shalom Hartman Institute's Osher Center in Jerusalem.[14]

His no to the self had its benefits. "[M]y love for the scriptures led me to ways of reading that were so much less ego-centered," Stendahl wrote.

> The Bible was really not about me. It was about many other things—in the long run, much more interesting things. It was about many things in many distant lands, from many distant ages. I came to read it more and more like a book, perhaps more as a "classic." Now it spoke to me from a great distance, of centuries and cultures deeply different from my own. And it began to be, just by its difference, that the fascination grew, that it had a way of saying to me, there are other ways of seeing and thinking and feeling and believing than you have taken for granted. And it just added to my love.

Stendahl's second point is that "it"—that is, the Bible—"is not always as deep as we think."[15] This insight crackles with Stendahl's humor, as well as his ethics of reading, which were emerging from the idea that egocentrism in biblical studies should be set aside.[16]

Third, Stendahl argued, Scripture isn't always as sure as you think. He sounded a hermeneutical warning, a caution to those of any ideology who think that they can know what the Bible "means." He shaped this thought by reference to Paul's own writings—a Paul, Stendahl opined, who, though arrogant, still distinguished between a "word from the Lord" and a directive of his own.[17] Paul's distinction between bases of authority struck Stendahl as useful in the context of the hegemony of historical criticism (that of the mid-twentieth century, and beyond) and the love of certainty in academic biblical studies, on the one hand, and churches' inclinations to want to fix the meaning of Scripture and to defend their conclusions with the phrase "The Bible says...," on the other. Stendahl insisted otherwise and offered biblical *un*certainty not as a problem, but as an attraction, a seed of love.

Stendahl's fourth no is this: "Not so uptight." Apologetics, he suggested, is an "arrogant activity": those who feel a need to defend the Bible or to defend God may have misunderstood their own powers and role in the world. Stendahl found further support for his views within Scripture itself. He argued about the importance of the fact that the Christian Testament has not *one* Gospel that tells the story of Jesus—a possibility that some second-century Christians, such as Tatian, tried out—but *four* Gospels. Some scholars consider this world of difference packed into the Christian Testament to be a liability, an embarrassment; whole careers have been founded in the attempt to resolve differences between these Gospels, to make one whole and straight story of Jesus. Krister wrote instead,

> And so the four Gospels are wonderful lessons in the fact that God is not pedantic when it comes to telling the story; rather, God wants it told a little different to catch as many aspects as possible. As I like to say, when you have four portraits of somebody you love very much, you don't make transparencies of them and then send the light through—that becomes blur, holy blur because it is the Gospels, but still blur. You look at one portrait at a time. And actually where they are different is usually where the artist has something important to say. If you get the apologetic devil in you, then you get bothered by the richness and by the variation. And the more I have lived with the scriptures, the more loving my feelings for them have become. The more important thing for me is to make them as different as possible, in order to catch as many insights and as many perspectives as possible.

Here and elsewhere, Stendahl spoke from his own location as Christian, as minister, and as biblical scholar, from the site of his own difference, about the danger of thinking "universally": the arrogance of it, the hubris, the loss of particularity, cost too much. For Stendahl, this loss was not only found in the collapsing of the Jesuses of the Gospels into one Jesus. It was also found in the arrogant notion that Christianity is a universal religion.[18]

This is Stendahl's fifth no: "Not so universal." Stendahl wrote, "Jesus said, 'You are the salt of the earth.' But who wants the world to become a salt mine?"[19] In other words, Stendahl insisted that Christians stop trying to convert people, taking the particular flavors of the world and oversalting them into an inedible universal, generic Christianity. Stendahl continued, addressing Christians.

> We are born as a minority religion, as a religion among religions. And we are heirs to the Jewish perspective on these things: that's what I learned from the scriptures. It says, to Israel, that Israel is meant to be a light to the nations. That's what Jesus speaks about: a light to the nations. The Jews have never thought that God's hottest dream was that everybody become a Jew. They rather thought that they were called upon to be faithful and that God somehow needed that people in the total cosmos. What a humility, but we called it tribalism.

In this argument, Stendahl's no to universalism articulates the legacy of his own work. This legacy includes the insistence that the apostle Paul, and Christian origins itself, emerged as an intra-Jewish debate about the inclusion of Gentiles in God's people, about the force of a messianic figure whose coming would not exclude "the nations."

Stendahl's insights led to important scholarly movements, including research on the "New Perspective on Paul," and on "the Radical New Perspective,"[20] which understands Paul as a Jew in the context of Jewish diversity in the first century CE. Stendahl also had an impact on scholarship regarding late antiquity, specifically on the question of whether or when Christians and Jews parted company.[21] Stendahl's early work resonates with such scholarship, exemplified in Daniel Boyarin's analysis of

John 1. Boyarin argues that it is Christians who are "particular"—"tribal," to pick up Stendahl's term—in their recrafting of Jewish midrash regarding Genesis 1. "The particularism of Christology," in Boyarin's phrase, results in the crystallization of the divine Logos, Word, Reason, another form of Sophia or Wisdom, into the flesh of a particular man called Jesus—that is, not in universalism, but in an extreme particularism.[22]

ACT 2: SAYING NO TO A MAJOR SCHOLARLY PUBLICATION

On May 16, 1975, Stendahl, writing from Uppsala, Sweden, penned by hand a pained, three-page letter to David Noel Freedman, general editor of the Anchor Bible Series and professor of Hebrew Bible at the University of California San Diego.[23] The letter is frank, forthright, and written on plain paper, with no letterhead and no titles:

> Dear Noel:
>
> The painful answer is No. It does not work. I must admit and confess that I am incapable of writing a commentary. I have worked hard on it this year which I entered with such hopes. But the more I write the more uncertain I get, and the ideas disintegrate before me. Thus I have come to the point where I must face this failure honestly—in order to save my "sanity." That is too strong a word, I do not feel neurotic about it. But I must make some decision about how to use best whatever gifts I have been given.
>
> This sabbatical has deprived me of the excuse of not having time, leisure, long wonderful days uninterrupted by anything, not even telephone calls. And now I know—as I suspected from time to time but did not know for sure—that I cannot do this commentary.
>
> I need not tell you how badly I feel toward you and about the many times I have held off your question in a hope that I believed was realistic—but it was not.[24]

Stendahl clearly said no. He rejected an invitation from Doubleday to write a commentary on the Epistle to the Romans, offered in 1959, as the letter itself states. This "saying no" is marked by his introspection on its causes:

> As I return to the US in a few weeks I hope that I "re-enter" with a more realistic understanding of what I can and cannot [do]. I guess I have come to the age when I just decide how to use my energies in a manner congenial to me. And as life and perhaps even the Lord has moved with me and in me, I find myself thinking hard on questions of Scripture and Theology and Church and World which absorb me so strongly that I find it impossible to concentrate on masses of the issues entailed in a commentary and as I read what has been done—now last by Käsemann—I am overwhelmed by the task.[25]

Stendahl ended with his characteristic humor: "One should not generalize from one[']s own failures—Paul did, and got great theology out of it, but I am not quite Paul—but my frustrations are perhaps part of a crisis in the type of biblical studies that I learned and still love. But I see new possibilities—without having the power to have it come off." (Included with this correspondence is a letter of August 7, 1975, typed on Doubleday Corporation letterhead, from Robert Hewetson, editor of the Anchor Bible Series, canceling the contract.)

But Paul pursued Krister. Stendahl returns to this issue in his *Final Account: Paul's Letter to the Romans*, a slim, seventy-six-page volume first published by Stendahl's home church, University Lutheran of Cambridge, Massachusetts, in 1993.[26] Stendahl confidently wrote in the preface,

> Romans is Paul's final account of his theology of mission. It is not a theological tractate on justification by faith. It is not a pastoral letter dealing with specific problems in Rome.... Romans is Paul's account of how his mission to the Gentiles fit into God's total mission to the world, the *tikkun*, the mending of the creation (cf. Roman[s] 8:18-25), and hence particularly the redemption of Israel.[27]

Indeed, Stendahl had returned to the Epistle to the Romans over the years, using it particularly for his important arguments about Paul as an apostle who understood himself to be prophetically called (*not* converted) to bring Gentiles into the covenantal plan that God had for the people of Israel.[28] Stendahl went on to insist, "It is important that when we read it we get it right,"[29] immediately following this with the personal reflection: "I have pondered how to do that for more than forty years. I never managed to write the commentary of my dreams. When I tried, I was too overwhelmed."[30]

Final Account takes its form from notes and musings rescued from the tapes of five of Stendahl's lectures—"rescued" is Stendahl's word—by Missy Daniels, who together with Stendahl's wife, Brita, put the book together.[31] Even as he immediately turned to more scholarly matters, for example setting the record straight about his interpretation of whether Paul insisted upon two separate ways to covenantal relationship with God, one for Jews and one for Gentiles, or one way, Stendahl returned at the end of his preface to the issue of writing, and of the production of this and another of his books. "There is much to apologize for on my part in these notes and musings on Romans," he wrote. "My speaking style is so different from my writing style. That is no doubt one reason why it is so difficult for me to transform a transcribed tape into a proper chapter of a book. I have tried many times and have failed."[32] He appreciated the fact that Daniels and Brita Stendahl came to his aid in producing *Final Account*. He noted that Emilie T. Sanders had similarly helped him to transform taped lectures into the manuscript that became *Paul among Jews and Gentiles*. He concluded the preface this way: "It would be arrogant to compare myself with Paul, but there is a slight analogy in his final recognition of his inability to do all that he wanted to do or even what he thought God wanted him to do."[33] Even if Stendahl argued in his letter to Freedman that he was not "neurotic" about abandoning the commentary on Romans, the question certainly haunted him, as did Paul's Epistle to the Romans.

ACT 3: SAYING NO AS DEAN

In a final and brief act, we turn to an interview conducted by Yehezkel Landau in April 2006.[34] In this friendly reflection on his time as dean, Stendahl confessed, "I wanted to control details more than I should have, despite my own prayer for discernment so as to distinguish the important from what only seems so." Stendahl reflected upon the fact that he enjoyed face time with people and that this distracted him from publication.[35] He offered his assessment of what is truly significant in (Christian) religious leadership: "In assessing acts of leadership, the ultimate goal is the Kingdom of God. Compared to that ideal, everything is a failure." The interview raises the question, to what should one say no? To publications? To people? What theological or ethical lodestar directs one to say no?

SAYING NO IN ORDER TO SAY YES

Stendahl's inclination to say no runs throughout his work. Say no to the Christian Saint Paul who exemplifies the introspective spirit of the West, who has come to define the struggling soul in each of us, the torn psychology, and then who forms in us the Paul-as-triumphant-hero.[36] Say no to a biblical scholarship that asserts imperialism over theology, squelching creative, multivocal, and imaginative conversations. Say no to sexism. Say no to anti-Semitism.

These acts of saying no begot the abundance in Stendahl's life—his spirit open to conversation, and perhaps to unexpected conversation partners. These conversations occurred among Jews, Christians, and Muslims at the Shalom Hartman Institute, in Jerusalem, even in the teeth of two lethal Intifadas.[37] These conversations happened in Sweden, even as the ordination of women was debated, and as Stendahl argued that this was a hermeneutical question to which the answer was yes![38] These conversations occurred with the Women's Caucus of Harvard Divinity School.[39] Saying no allowed Stendahl time to say yes to weekly meetings with the Women's Caucus at Harvard Divinity School,[40] and to a speech recognizing the importance of women in Christian ministry and the problems of a sexism undergirded by fear.[41] These last conversations also earned him the *nom de guerre* of "Sister Krister."

This abundance, conditioned as it was by saying no, allowed conversations not only in Jerusalem and Boston, but elsewhere and with others as well. The Lutheran-ordained, bishop-to-be Stendahl accepted an invitation to speak at the Conference on the Charismatic Movement at the Washington Cathedral in 1974, putting him in dialogue with Pentecostals and allowing him to be published alongside Oral Roberts.[42] This availability and openness subvened conversations such as those at a conference with the Latter Day Saints. Stendahl authored an essay entitled "The Sermon on the Mount and Third Nephi in the Book of Mormon," which he delivered at a symposium in 1978 at Brigham Young University. Here he experimented with exegesis of the Book of Mormon.[43]

Stendahl's insistence upon saying no granted him the humility to see Christianity and its Bible—and his love for it—as a peculiar and particular connection that need not be foisted upon other religious peoples but could open conversation with others. This no to various duties, such as commentary writing and other publication pressures, gave Stendahl the time, the moral space, and the mental clarity to attend to the urgent needs of his time. Saying no allowed him to "redeem the time."[44]

Stendahl's thoughts about time and urgency can be found especially in a sermon that he gave on Sunday, March 14, 1965, at Houghton Memorial Chapel of Wellesley College. He called it "The Faith Which Changed God's Plan." The church bulletin for the day contained a printed note announcing that the Rev. Dr. Martin Luther King Jr. asked for a march on that Sunday; and that rides would be provided to march in Boston Common for a 2:00 p.m. memorial service for Reverend James Reeb.[45] Reeb was an ordained Presbyterian minister and a participant in the Southern Christian Leadership Conference. After eating dinner with two other white ministers at an integrated restaurant in Selma, Alabama, Reeb was beaten to death. Among Stendahl's notes for this sermon is a prayer for Reeb's wife and children.

Stendahl's sermon notes for the day are laconic, scratched onto small pieces of paper. Yet they clearly address both the American racism of the day and the church's reading of the day, the Gospel of Matthew's account of the Canaanite woman who requests that Jesus heal her demon-possessed daughter (15:21–28). This mother hears from his lips that Jesus is called not to those of *her* ethnicity, but only to the lost children of Israel. She talks back in a famously difficult passage: "Yes, Lord; yet even the dogs eat the crumbs that fall from their masters' table" (Matt 15:27//Mark 7:28). Jesus then recognizes her faith and heals her daughter. On the first page of his sermon notes, Stendahl wrote,[46] "Shocking to see Jesus as the segregationist, who changes his mind." His notes then continue in a more historical vein:

> How did the Gentiles read this? A Gentile gospel
>
> [The Canaanite woman is] The pioneer (with the centurion) of their faith

The faith that changed the plan of partition
For there now the wall is broken down.

Stendahl's sermon addressed the urgency of the time, and the resonance between what a text means (for the antiracist work of the 1960s) and what it meant (for the ethnic thinking of the first century CE).[47] How, Stendahl wondered, no doubt casting his mind back to his own early research on the Gospel of Matthew, would the Gentiles have heard a gospel in which one's own—someone from the "nations" or Gentiles, not a Jew—was initially rejected by Jesus? Stendahl recognized the embarrassing difficulty of a Jesus who argues for segregation, then changes his own mind. Stendahl's sermon notes continued shakily, with lines crossed out:

> ~~The Time~~
> ~~The signs of the time~~
> The Faith which changed God's plan [this is also the sermon title]
> The cry which broke through

He returned in his next page of notes to the idea of "The Time" (underlining and capitalization his), and he expanded the idea further: "with deliberate speed. How fast is that. God does not stand for patience only but for the Signs of the Time. The revolution." Here Stendahl alluded to the phrase "with all deliberate speed," used in the US Supreme Court ruling of *Brown vs. Board of Education* in 1954. While the legal case insisted that states could no longer support a policy of "separate but equal" education, the phrase "with all deliberate speed" neither encouraged rapid change nor called for the states to enforce such change. The phrase eventually exemplified the deliberate slowness of the transformation of racist legal structures in the United States.[48]

Stendahl had addressed this issue of time and of urgency in an earlier sermon in the same church, dated November 15, 1964. That sermon was titled "Redeem the Time." His sermon notes begin,

> Redeem the Time
> The teaching of Jesus full of words of time. The time is fulfilled. The kingdom is at hand, hence believe the Gospel, and repent. The time has come.

He continued later in his notes,

> Christianity is a sensitivity to time. What is called for *now*: Redeem the time....
>
> —
>
> Supreme Court's "deliberate speed"
>
> ...
>
> The church as the grandmother in her rocking chair during the holy days. Ties with the past
>
> Not bearings for the future
>
> —
>
> The time. Sensitivity to God's will now...to history. The eschatological itch. Thy will be done

Like others of his time, Stendahl brought the eschatological urgency of early Christianity, the idea of an eschatological end of time that is attuned to God's actions in history, to bear upon the crises of racism in the mid-twentieth century United States.

In this sermon, as in his teaching on "New Testament Piety" and his concern with liturgy and the church elsewhere, Stendahl seemed to point to what we would now call "lived religion": community as the locus of transformative practice.[49]

> Singing, etc.
>
> Serious and lighthearted
>
> Civil rights and folksongs[50]

These words that he scratched out resonated with his sermon notes from "The Faith Which Changed God's Plan":

> And yet: the naïve language of worship of prayer
>
> Of devotion of cult of faith
>
> Not the language of philosophy where changes and time counts *[sic]* little
>
> The Time

Stendahl's sermons, as well as his teaching, were deeply taken up in the urgent needs of the moment and in a moral conviction that was expressed in piety, liturgy, song, and sermon. These were urgently needed in times of crisis.[51]

CONCLUSION

In an interview published a year before his death, Stendahl reflected upon his leadership at Harvard Divinity School. He offered the observation:

> As Dean, fund-raising burdens took up time that should have gone toward administering the School. Being a Dean was actually more intellectually challenging than being a professor—in your own field, the agenda is pretty much self-engendered, whereas a Dean must ask all the time: why are we doing what we are doing, and what else should we rather do? That *is* hard thinking.[52]

It was in this interview that he also reflected, "I love to talk to people; some of my time could have been better spent sitting alone and writing something that would last."

Stendahl embraced the "hard thinking" about urgent priorities that was his role as dean. That led to his saying no, for example, to a commentary on Romans. But this reflex also allowed him to consider and to enact other intellectually and religiously charged ways of saying no: especially no to sexism; no to anti-Judaic racism; no to seeing Christianity as a universal and superior religion. His thought, never captured in a magnum opus, was lived out at the intersection of the social, the political, and the religious. He engaged in impassioned and dignified religious leadership in turbulent times in American politics and education, debates that flow into the present. He lived a world of difference, moving from Sweden to the United States and back; living and working in Jerusalem, Israel; engaging during his deanship as the movements for women's rights, civil rights, the call of Dr. King to march, and the anti-Vietnam war efforts swelled in the United States. In the midst of a divinity school that was reaching out to incorporate other religious traditions—even if still in a very Christian model—Stendahl coined the phrase and conceived the idea of "holy envy" as a way to recognize the good in another religion without trying to appropriate it simply for one's own tradition.[53]

In the grip of the exclusion of women from religious leadership, Stendahl worked in the Church in Sweden and on Harvard Divinity's campus to give female leaders a voice.

Stendahl's legacy lives on at Harvard Divinity School, not only in its institutional structures, but also in the spirit of the place. By learning foreign languages, by carefully describing physical artifacts, by spending time with difficult texts from the *Therigatha* to the Talmud to the Koran to Judith Butler, Divinity School faculty and students prepare again and again to listen, to pay attention, to notice and to respect difference, to embrace with humility the limits of our religious traditions, and to sit together alongside those of different religions or those who are "nones."

Standing in the tradition that Stendahl established and in which he participated, students and faculty members become studied resisters, informed activists, careful scholars. Stendahl knew that academia and church alike formed people in practices that prepared them to consider carefully what was difficult to understand—to say no to the idea that Scripture or a religious tradition is "about me," and to turn instead to placing one's own religious love within a broader landscape of history and peoples. Stendahl's legacy encourages scholars and religious people to take care not to be seduced by claims of authority or authenticity or canonicity that do not take seriously the context of those ideas, on the one hand, and the urgent needs of communities today, on the other.

One significant legacy he left, a legacy that hovers at the edge of scholarship and ethics, is his question: To what should we say no?

NOTES

1. See Jesper Svartvik's chapter in the present volume.

2. George H. Williams, *Calm Rising through Change and through Storm: The Contours of Religion and Commitment in an Age of Upheaval and Globalization*, vol. 3 of *Divinings: Religion at Harvard from its Origins in New England Ecclesiastical History to the 175th Anniversary of the Harvard Divinity School, 1636–1992* (Newton, MA: Boston Theological Institute, 2014), 4–7. See Melanie Johnson-DeBaufre and Laura Salah Nasrallah, "Beyond the Heroic Paul: Toward a Feminist and Decolonizing Approach to the Letters of Paul," in *The Colonized Apostle: Paul through Postcolonial Eyes*, ed. Christopher Stanley, 161–74 (Minneapolis: Fortress, 2011).

3. "Krister Stendahl, 86, was HDS Dean from 1968-1979," *Harvard Gazette* (April 17, 2008), https://news.harvard.edu/gazette/story/2008/04/krister-stendahl-86-was-hds-dean-from-1968-1979.

4. Krister Stendahl, *Meanings: The Bible as Document and as Guide*, 2nd ed. (Minneapolis: Fortress, 2008), 1.

5. Ibid.

6. Ibid., 4.

7. As cited in Joseph A. Marchal, "To What End(s)? Biblical Studies and Critical Rhetorical Engagement(s) for a 'Safer' World," *SBL Forum* (June 2006), http://sbl-site.org/Article.aspx?ArticleID=550. See also Stendahl: "The nonapologetic thrust of descriptive biblical theology allows us to face that problem squarely. It suggests a hermeneutics suited for the 'public health' task of theology, that is, a hermeneutic of suspicion, by which the nondesirable side effects, or even effects, of the biblical material can be discerned and counteracted. But such a task requires the honesty of not 'prettying up' the original" (*Meanings*, 11).

8. As discussed and cited in Marchal, "To What End(s)?"; see also Joseph Marchal, "Responsibilities to the Publics of Biblical Studies and Critical Rhetorical Engagements for a Safer World," in *Secularism and Biblical Studies*, ed. Roland Boer (Oakville, CT: Equinox, 2010), 101–15. Schüssler Fiorenza, like Stendahl, works at the intersection of biblical studies, theology, and ethics. Some of her recent work demonstrates ways in which the very field of biblical studies needs to transform; see for example Elizabeth Schüssler Fiorenza and Kent Harold Richards, eds., *Transforming Graduate Biblical Studies: Ethos and Transformation* (Atlanta: Society of Biblical Literature, 2010). See also Stendahl, *Meanings*, 2, regarding his goal that biblical scholars not engage in "imperialism over theology." We find an echo of this phrase at the end of his "Biblical Studies in the University," in *The Study of Religion in Colleges and Universities*, ed. Paul Ramsey and John F. Wilson (Princeton, NJ: Princeton University Press, 1970), 39; originally prepared in 1968 for a conference at Princeton University celebrating the retirement of George F. Williams. There, Stendahl wrote, "It is my guess that we shall overcome the silent presupposition in the biblical theology of the last generation—a presupposition I would describe as *Im Anfang war der Text*. The imperialism of the biblical theologians is gone, and we shall rather recognize that among its many assets the community, the church also has its Scriptures. The normative questions of how the church lives with its Scriptures will loom large and remain more open than heretofore. Authority is only one aspect; creativity in interpretation is another."

9. See Krister Stendahl, "Ancient Scripture in the Modern World," in *Scripture in the Jewish and Christian Traditions: Authority, Interpretation, Relevance*, ed. Frederick E. Greenspahn (Nashville: Abingdon, 1982), 205. As cited in Marchal, "To What End(s)?"

10. See Stendahl, "Biblical Studies in the University" and his mention of the peculiarity of his falling in love with his Scripture, the Bible, without having explored other religions' scriptures: in "Why I Love the Bible: Beyond Distinctions of Intellect and Spirit, an Ever-Transforming Affair of the Heart," *Harvard Divinity Bulletin*, 35 (2007), https://bulletin.hds.harvard.edu/articles/winter2007/why-i-love-bible.

11. All citations below are from the version published in *Harvard Divinity Bulletin* 35 (2007); the essay can also be found in *Meanings*, 2nd ed. Details about its context of delivery, and situating the essay within Stendahl's larger career, are found in *Meanings*, 245. To hear the essay read by Stendahl's son, the Rev. John Stendahl, go to https://hds.harvard.edu/news/2014/01/21/john-stendahl-reads-why-i-love-bible-video.

12. This identification with Paul is a recurring theme in Stendahl's writings; see, e.g., a letter to Noel Freedman, discussed below, and also in his *Final Account: Paul's Letter to the Romans* (Minneapolis: Fortress, 1995).

13. Krister Stendahl, "The Apostle Paul and the Introspective Conscience of the West," *Harvard Theological Review* 56 (1963): 199–215 and also in his *Paul among Jews and Gentiles and Other Essays* (Minneapolis: Fortress, 1976).

14. Stendahl's early work was concerned to explore how early Christians used the Jewish Scriptures and how the New Testament relates to the Dead Sea Scrolls. See *The School of St. Matthew and Its Use of the Old Testament*, ASNU 20 (Uppsala: Almqvist & Wiksell, 1954); *The Scrolls and the New Testament* (New York: Harper, 1957); see also his programmatic essay "Biblical Studies in the University."

15. See also *Final Account*, 4, for a specific example of misguided exegetical "depth" that leads to misinterpretation of Romans, in Stendahl's opinion.

16. Stendahl, "Why I Love the Bible."

17. "I think he was the last preacher in Christendom who had the guts to say that," wrote Stendahl.

18. Stendahl, *Meanings*, 241–43; on the pitfalls of Christianity as a universal religion. He emphasizes here, in "Why I Love the Bible," and elsewhere the importance of understanding Christian origins as a minority

religion thinking in universal terms—a theological and political notion that has very different effects than a majority religion asserting its "universal" status.

19. Stendahl, "Why I Love the Bible."

20. See John Marshall's chapter in this volume.

21. See, e.g., Adam H. Becker and Annette Yoshiko Reed, eds., *The Ways That Never Parted: Jews and Christians in Late Antiquity and the Early Middle Ages*, Texte und Studien zum Antiken Judentum 95 (Tubingen: Mohr Siebeck, 2003).

22. Daniel Boyarin, "The Gospel of the Memra: Jewish Binitarianism and the Prologue to John," *Harvard Theological Review* 94 (2001): 284.

23. Stendahl to David Noel Freedman, May 16, 1975, in unprocessed Krister Stendahl archival materials, Harvard Divinity School.

24. As Paula Fredriksen has helpfully noted (personal communication), no less a light than Augustine, too, demurred to essay a commentary on this letter of Paul's. Speaking of his efforts to do so in 394/95, Augustine said that he was "discouraged by the magnitude and labor of this task," *Retractationes* 1.25 (24).

25. Stendahl to David Noel Freedman, May 16 ,1975.

26. The 1993 volume had a print run of one hundred numbered and signed copies and was intended to raise funds for the church, as do all subsequent royalties from the Fortress Press publication. *Final Account*, xii.

27. Stendahl, *Final Account*, ix.

28. Stendahl, *Paul among Jews and Gentiles*.

29. Ibid., ix.

30. Ibid., x.

31. Ibid., x.

32. Ibid., xi.

33. Ibid., xi.

34. Yehezkel Landau, "An Interview with Krister Stendahl," *Harvard Divinity Bulletin* 35 (2007), https://bulletin.hds.harvard.edu/articles/winter2007/interview-krister-stendahl.

35. Landau, "An Interview."

36. Stendahl, "The Apostle Paul and the Introspective Conscience"; also published in *Meanings*.

37. In writing about Holy Week, Stendahl offers, "Responsible preaching—and Bible reading—cannot be achieved by painting Judaism, its piety and leaders, in ever more ugly and unsympathetic colors, as if the glory of Christianity would thereby shine the brighter. Anti-Semitism," he wrote, "must be uprooted from celebrations of Holy Week." See his *Holy Week*,

Proclamation: Aids for Interpreting the Lessons of the Church Year, Series A (Philadelphia: Fortress, 1974), 5.

38. Krister Stendahl, *The Bible and the Role of Women: A Case Study in Hermeneutics,* trans. Emilie T. Sander, Facet Books Biblical Series 15 (Philadelphia: Fortress, 1966), originally published in Swedish in 1958 as an essay, with the title *Bibelsynen och kvinnan.*

39. Alice Hageman, "Foreword," in *Sexist Religion and Women in the Church: No More Silence!*, ed. Alice Hageman in collaboration with the Women's Caucus of Harvard Divinity School (New York: Association Press, 1974). See also Stendahl, *Bible and the Role of Women*, and Stendahl's reflections in the 1984 preface to *Meanings* (2nd ed.; xi): "It also hits me hard that I have thought of myself as sensitive to the question of inclusive language. After all, I began to write on the themes of *The Bible and the Role of Women* (Philadelphia: Fortress, 1966) in the early 1950s. Now I see that inclusive language did not enter my consciousness until I was awakened by the women of the Harvard Divinity School in the 1970s."

40. As mentioned in the "Foreward/Forward!" of Hageman, *Sexist Religion and Women in the Church*, 11. The Women's Caucus effected the invitation of various female speakers; the volume itself includes a chapter by Mary Daly.

41. Krister Stendahl, "Enrichment or Threat? When the Eves Come Marching In," in *Sexist Religion and Women in the Church*, 117–23; regarding women and contraception see his "Biblical and Theological Basis for Christians Concerned about the Family" (speech, The Family Life Conference, Denver, November 13–16, 1978), Harvard Divinity School Archives, 12: He cites Phyllis Trible's scholarship and states, "And what is the real crown of creation? It is the creation of Eve."

42. The speech from January 19, 1974, is published as "The Charismatic Movement and the New Testament," in *What the Spirit Is Saying to the Churches*, ed. Theodore Runyon (New York: Hawthorn Books, 1975), 17–28.

43. Stendahl, *Meanings*, 99.

44. Eph. 5:16; see also below discussion of Stendahl's sermon of the same title.

45. Bulletin and sermon notes in Harvard Divinity School archive, unnumbered boxes.

46. Spelling errors have been corrected.

47. On "means" and "meant," see especially Stendahl, *Meanings*, 1–3; see also 14–16, which emerge from a dictionary entry on "Biblical Theology,

Contemporary," in *Interpreter's Dictionary of the Bible*, ed. George Arthur Buttrick (Nashville: Abingdon, 1962), 1:418–32.

48. The work of exposing these racist structures, as well as their ongoing effects, continues today. To cite one example, see Michele Alexander, *The New Jim Crow: Mass Incarceration in an Age of Colorblindness*, rev. ed. (New York: New Press, 2012).

49. See also Stendahl, *Holy Week*, 53–57, especially:

> "The Passion is not geared toward a pilgrimage along the *via dolorosa*, where we would identify in our sinfulness with the various actors in the drama, or where we would be stirred in our sympathy for the man of sorrows as if he were a tragic hero. To be sure he does not need our sympathy or our tears. Nor are we invited to imitate his humility and obedience. Our imitation would be arrogant, for we are not primarily followers, we are the beneficiaries, the heirs, the recipients of his mighty glorification on the cross
>
> Now above the Cross, the trophy,
> Sound the loud triumphant lay:
> Tell how Christ, the world's Redeemer,
> As a Victim won the day.
>
> (SBH 61, one of the oldest passion hymns, from the sixth century)
>
> ...We are invited to see, and the response almost has to be in song and poetry. To attach moral lessons would be self-centered and rash or premature."

50. 1964 sermon notes. Harvard Divinity School archive.

51. Note, however, the critique of Harvard Divinity School student leader Stephan Hornberger, as cited in Williams, *Calm Rising*, 48n82.

52. Landau, "An Interview."

53. See A-J. Levine's chapter in the present volume.

3

FROM HOLY ENVY TO HOLY CRITICISM

Im lo 'achshav, eimatai? (If Not Now, When?)

Amy-Jill Levine

Krister Stendahl wrote two articles that changed the ways that I, as a naive undergraduate, understood the New Testament. "*Quis et Unde*? An Analysis of Mt. 1–2" locates Jesus within a Jewish context and shows how Matthew responds to questions about Jesus's messianic qualifications.[1] "The Apostle Paul and the Introspective Conscience of the West" makes clear, inter alia, that for Paul the law is a positive gift from God and not the curse that Augustine, Luther, and much of today's church have made it seem.[2] Both essays emphasize the importance of recognizing the Jewish contexts of Jesus and of Paul. They also demonstrate that one need not construct a negative Jewish background in order to promote Jesus and Paul. These two points—the embeddedness of the Christian message in Judaism and the avoidance of false witness—remain issues to this day.

Over half a century after *Nostra Aetate* and the numerous Protestant statements that followed in its wake, Jewish-Christian dialogue has made enormous progress. That Jesus was a Jew is no longer surprising news. Recognition that the Shoah was carried out primarily by Christian perpetrators influenced by centuries of anti-Jewish and then by anti-Semitic teachings has prompted much-needed changes in Christian liturgy, art, and exegesis. In turn, Jewish organizations and consortia have celebrated these changes, even as they too have come to recognize the

Jewishness of Jesus. Conversation has moved from hatred to wariness to friendship to what the good Bishop called "holy envy."

With this respect in place, we can now move from holy envy to holy criticism, or what Leviticus 19 calls *tochecha*, "rebuke." The goal is not to censor. It is rather to help us to see through each other's eyes and to realize that, however unintended, hurt is still hurt. This essay first tracks the major participants in Jewish-Christian interfaith dialogue, and then turns to areas where participants could facilitate improvement in sanctioned teachings. I take as my test cases teachings by Roman Catholics, by Evangelicals, and by liberal Protestants (United Methodism, Presbyterian Church [USA], Evangelical Lutheran Church in America, American Baptists). I then turn to the need for conversation between Jewish official bodies and representatives of Messianic Judaism, with focus on Hashivenu and the Messianic Jewish Rabbinical Council (MJRC), whose representatives are already in conversation with Roman Catholic and Protestant representatives.

THE CONVERSATION PARTNERS

The first type of conversation, which takes place among the religious professionals with institutional backing, produces position papers: the Pontifical Biblical Commission's "The Jewish People and Their Sacred Scriptures in the Christian Bible" (2001); the Institute of Christian and Jewish Studies in Baltimore's "*Dabru Emet*: A Jewish Statement on Christians and Christianity" (2000); the Christian Scholars' Working Group on Jew and Judaism's "A Sacred Obligation" (2002); the Vatican's Commission for Religious Relations with the Jews "The Gifts and Calling of God Are Irrevocable: A Reflection on the Theological Questions Pertaining to Catholic Jewish Relations" (2015); the Center for Jewish-Christian Understanding and Cooperation's "To Do the Will of Our Father in Heaven: Toward a Partnership between Jews and Christians" (2015), and so on. Complementing such efforts are national church statements and pronouncements by the International Council of Christians and Jews (ICCJ). These papers evince both knowledge of and respect for the other's traditions. Generally, they accentuate the positive, latch onto the affirmative, and make the expected points for interreligious harmony: for example, Jews are not Christ-killers; supersessionism/

replacement theology and Marcionism are illegitimate; Jews and Christians, both living in eschatological expectation, can work together.

The second type, the academic symposium, typically produces essay collections that are not for either the faint of heart or those weak in technical terminology. These include the edited collections *Christianity in Jewish Terms* (2000),[3] *Christ Jesus and the Jewish People Today: New Explorations of Theological Interrelationships* (2011),[4] *Juden und Christen im Dialog* (2016),[5] and numerous others. The essays respond to theological, soteriological, and ethical issues. Is the Torah Judaism's "incarnation"? Can we speak of "anonymous Christians" (so Karl Rahner)? What does it mean to find Jesus in the pages of the "Old Testament"? Is the Mosaic covenant still valid? Is Paul to be seen within Judaism (variously defined) or against it? How does the church respond to Auschwitz, or the synagogue to the cross? These works all expand the academic dialogue, but they rarely find their way into the pulpit or onto the bima.

Programs sponsored by centers for Jewish-Christian relations on college campuses attract religion majors, the theologically curious, and students with positive religious formation, whether from youth groups or day camps. Along with dinners and speakers, such centers often tap into social programs. Conversation is generally of the show-and-tell model, and it often involves pizza, veggies, soda, and lemonade. Critique is rare and, as is the case with other interreligious groups, conservative students—for whom the only reason to engage in interreligious dialogue is to convert the "other"—rarely show up.

Finally, Jewish-Christian conversation takes place among friends, whether in church or synagogue or in a private home. Often such conversations are formed and maintained by individuals invested in avoiding religious ignorance and, thus, prejudice. They may discuss books such as James Carroll's *Constantine's Sword* or films such as Mel Gibson's *The Passion of the Christ* or current difficult issues (abortion, homosexuality, the Middle East, etc.). Again, the focus is on peace and on information, rather than on raw questioning.

Not a few such groups have disbanded in recent years over the inability to conduct a mutually respectful conversation regarding Israel/Palestine. Moreover, as Islam has become an increasingly popular topic, centers and groups previously invested in Jewish/Christian dialogue have expanded to include Islam or other traditions. The National Conference of Christians and Jews (NCCJ) in the 1990s became the National Conference for Community and Justice. (A keyword search on their website for *Jews, Judaism, Christians,* and *Christianity* yielded a maximum of four hits; *racism* yielded several pages.) The Baltimore Institute for Christian-Jewish Studies (ICJS) is now the Institute for Islamic-Christian-Jewish Studies (the acronym has remained the same). The International Council of Christians and Jews is increasingly running "Abrahamic faith" initiatives in order to include Islam. Jewish/Christian dialogue fades to secondary importance.

Increasingly entering, or at least seeking to enter, these groups are Messianic Jews. They often find the doors shut. Messianics are not welcome in most synagogue contexts, where the vast majority of (nonmessianic) rabbis consider them to be apostates. In turn, Christian groups need to determine whether Messianics belong *qua Jews* in their churches. Churches tend to follow Ephesians 2:14–15 ("in his flesh he has made both groups into one and has broken down the dividing wall, that is, the hostility between us. He has abolished the law with its commandments and ordinances, that he might create in himself one new humanity in place of the two, thus making peace") and not Romans 11:18 (the separate Jewish and Gentiles branches share a common root but remain mutually distinct). Hence, Catholic and Protestant individuals and bodies are in formal conversation with Messianic Jews; nonmessianic Jews are not.[6] This lack of intra-Jewish conversation creates a disjunction in Jewish-Christian conversation. To many Christians, Jewish claims of "holy envy" or "we respect your views" ring hollow when the Jews making these claims reject Messianic Judaism.

Each of these gatherings has the opportunity to create structural changes that will have broader impact. All four forms of conversation can move from position papers to the implementation of actual liturgical and educational changes. More, they can rely on the trust that holds participants together to move not only into holy envy, but also into holy criticism. They can correct the unfortunate teachings that still appear on the websites of major denominations. They can push for the official bodies to address the difficult question of Messianic Jews. They can advance discussion.

ROMAN CATHOLIC COMMENTARY

There are individuals whose jobs entail participating in Jewish-Christian conversation. The International Jewish Committee on Interreligious Consultations (IJCIC) "serves on behalf of, and as an instrument of, its constituent member organizations to maintain and develop relations with the Vatican's Commission for Religious Relations with the Jews, the Orthodox Christian Church, the World Council of Churches, and other international religious bodies."[7] The website speaks primarily of meetings with Vatican bodies, as is consistent from IJCIC's origins as the International Catholic-Jewish Liaison Committee.[8] The "Resource" page includes two articles on Jewish/Orthodox Christian conversation, several additional essays on Jewish/Catholic relations, and a link to the International Council of Christians and Jews.[9] A search for *Protestant*, *Lutheran*, and *Presbyterian* yielded no results; *Anglican* yielded two links, from 2009 and 2010, to "Statements of the Anglican-Jewish Commission of the Archbishop of Canterbury and the Chief Rabbinate of Israel."[10]

The IJCIC's counterpart is the International Catholic-Jewish Liaison Committee (ILC), which was "created in 1971, formalizing the establishment of the official relationship between the Holy See and the worldwide Jewish community. The ILC is the official forum for ongoing dialogue between the Holy See's Commission for Religious Relations with the Jews and the International Jewish Committee for Interreligious Consultations (IJCIC)."[11] It was the Pontifical Commission for Religious Relations with the Jews that issued, in December 2015, the renunciation of evangelizing Jews: "The Catholic Church neither conducts nor supports any specific institutional mission work directed towards Jews."[12]

The meetings of these groups—Buenos Aires (2004); Cape Town (2006); Budapest (2008); Paris (2011); Madrid (2013); Warsaw (2016)—are splendid occasions for dialogue, and dinners.[13] Yet most Jews and Christians have never heard of these organizations, nor can they name their members or determine the means by which appointments to serve are made.

The International Council of Christians and Jews "serves as the umbrella organization of 40 national Jewish-Christian dialogue organizations worldwide."[14] The US organization connected to the ICCJ is the

Council of Centers on Jewish-Christian Relations (CCJR), which primarily represents university-based programs. Like IJCIC/ILC gatherings, the ICCJ meets in global settings, presents papers, gives awards, celebrates achievements, and has nice dinners.

All these groups are in excellent positions to enhance their current practices.

They might start, for example, with providing the major spokespeople for the Christian traditions, from the Vatican to the World Council of Churches, with a list of trigger terms. The point is not censorship, but respect. Keyword searches (*Pharisees, Jesus and women, purity, Samaritan, outcast, religious leaders*, etc.) reveal the abiding problems. Students at CCJR schools might be tapped to do website searches. Lay dialogue groups can contribute alternative articles. Academics can explain why the statements are incorrect. Religious professionals can speak to their colleagues to get the statements removed.

For example, Pope Francis continues to make comments that have been construed as anti-Jewish. The Vatican Radio records for morning Mass at Casa Santa Marta (May 11, 2015) the pope's comment that "publicans and sinners draw near to Jesus—'that is, the excluded, all those that were outside,'—and the Pharisees and the scribes complained....The attitude of the Scribes and the Pharisees is the same, they exclude. [They say,] 'We are perfect, we follow the law.'"[15] In *Commonweal*, Philip Cunningham documented additional comments that the pope's critics have flagged, including claims that the temple priests displayed "arrogance and tyranny toward the people," and that they "remade [the law] many times: so many times, to the point that they had arrived at 500 commandments. Everything was regulated, everything!" and accusations that the Pharisees "thought they were pure because they observed the law, but they did not know mercy."[16] Peter M. J. Stravinskas notes that in the pope's "first homily to the cardinals after his election," he "declared that anyone who does not pray to Christ prays to the Devil! On other occasions, he has replaced 'Devil' with 'idols.'"[17]

The pope does not intend his comments to be anti-Jewish. The problem is that they nevertheless introduce or reinforce anti-Jewish stereotypes. They are easily prevented. Any of the major Jewish organizations can offer a prophylactic list to the Holy Father and to other clergy to prevent such unfortunate representations.[18]

PROTESTANT CONSTRUCTIONS OF AN EVIL JUDAISM

Protestant/Jewish dialogue is less advanced than is the Catholic/Jewish version, but on the formal level it is equally poised to correct similarly uninformed or unthinking statements.[19] The Jewish-Evangelical Dialogue, which has been meeting annually for about a decade, brings together representatives from *Sojourners* and *Christian Century*; members of World Vision and the National Association of Evangelicals; faculty from Wheaton, Gordon Conwell, and Fuller with Reform, Conservative, and Modern Orthodox rabbis based in major cities, representatives from the ADL, AJC, JCPA, APN, New Israel Fund, the Jewish Federation of Chicago, and an occasional academic. Everyone can schmooze, deliver papers, learn about each other, and have dinner together. Members can rely on friends to speak up, privately, when coreligionists say something unfortunate.

Despite such gatherings, mistakes continue because tone deafness does as well. For example, in February 2014, *Sojourners* published an article in which well-known Evangelical Brian McClaren described Pharisees as "rich and successful people who lived in fancy houses and stepped over their destitute neighbors who slept in the gutters outside their gates! Proud people who judged, insulted, excluded, avoided, and accused others!"[20] He then listed as among the saved

> the very people whom the Pharisees despised, deprived, avoided, excluded, and condemned! Heaven's gates opened wide for the poor and destitute...the sinners, the sick, and the homeless...even the prostitutes and tax collectors! In other words, all the people the Pharisees were careful to avoid were exactly the ones who would someday be welcomed into heaven! Imagine how this overturning of traditional language of hell must have shocked everyone—multitudes and Pharisees alike.

Aside from his mistaken classification of Jews ("multitudes and Pharisees alike") as having a hateful soteriology that associated wealth with righteousness and poverty with sin, the saddest part of this article was the failure of the journal, from its acquisitions editor to its typesetter to its proofreader to its publisher, to catch these errors and falsehoods. Ten years earlier, the journal had published similar mischaracterizations of Pharisees, and then ran an article correcting the problem. The dialogue has not led to the necessary changes.[21]

A quick search in *Christianity Today*'s articles unearthed similar problems. Plug in *Pharisee* and find "The Love Shack," an interview with Paul Young by member of the Evangelical-Jewish Conference Mark Galli (March 2013), in which Young states, "I grew up fundamentalist, evangelical, Protestant. Those are my roots, and they are good roots. But it means the Pharisees are my people. I grew up with an image of God that was not helpful…."[22] Similarly, Paul Bane writes, in a 2016 piece entitled "I am a Pharisee!," that "the mind in its arrogance sets up the proper parameters of knowledge to achieve salvation. I as a Pharisee know the way."[23] Bane now identifies himself as a "recovering Pharisee," as if Pharisaism were a disease from which detoxification were required.

The World Council of Churches, especially since the appointment of Clare Amos, has substantially decreased the number of its anti-Jewish commentaries.[24] But some stereotypes do continue. The keywords, including *Samaritan, outcast*, and *Pharisee*, also continue to summon problematic comments. For example, WCC general secretary Rev. Dr. Samuel Kobia, preaching in 2009 on the Good Samaritan, trots out the tired, and incorrect, claims, from "More knowledgeable exegetes refer to the various laws and hygienic codes [hygienic codes??] that would have to be broken for priests and Levites to engage in road-side rescue work," to the claim that the lawyer "may have had a narrow understanding of who his neighbor was."[25] The parable provides no explanation for the actions of the priest and the Levite.[26]

The question, "Who is my neighbor?," is a valid one, even for churches, which keep membership rolls and which, in some cases, restrict access to the sacraments. Rev. Kobia misses the point that Leviticus, which the lawyer cites, goes on to mandate love also for the stranger. The sermon's mention of Anne Frank—"On Friday, the day before yesterday, this nation observed what would have been the eightieth birthday of Anne Frank; it is an occasion to remember the attempts that were made to aid those whom the Nazis were determined to destroy, as well as to regret that many such attempts fell short"—does not resolve the problem of insensitivity to Jews and Judaism. Fully to acknowledge the responsibility of Christians would require moving from "attempts made" and "attempts that fell short" to recognizing that churchgoing Christians made up the bulk of the perpetrators. Similarly, seeking to eliminate the stigma associated with AIDS/HIV, the WCC speaks of "the Pharisaic face that, from its position of authority, thoughtlessly points an accusing finger and condemns those living in these circumstances as impure and reprehensible sinners."[27]

A quick search on the sites for the United Methodist Church, the Presbyterian Church USA, the Evangelical Lutheran Church in America, and the American Baptists, yielded the expected denunciations of anti-Judaism and of anti-Semitism, notes interfaith celebrations (e.g., Thanksgiving services, food drives), and offers up the same old anti-Jewish teachings.

The website of the United Methodist Church yielded thirty-nine results for the search *Judaism*. The second listing is to the Book of Resolutions, which offers the 2016 "United Methodist Guiding Principles for Christian-Jewish Relations."[28] This terrific statement includes, "We do not believe that earlier covenantal relationships have been invalidated or that God has abandoned Jewish partners in covenant," and "As followers of Jesus Christ, we deeply repent of the complicity of the church and the participation of many Christians in the long history of persecution of the Jewish people." It also affirms, "The church has an obligation to correct erroneous and harmful past teachings and to ensure that the use of Scripture, as well as the preparation, selection, and use of liturgical and educational resources, does not perpetuate misleading interpretations and misunderstanding of Judaism." In another excellent posting, the Rev. A. W. "Bill" Martin Jr. advises pastors "*Leave Jesus in Judaism*....Keeping Jesus in his context of first-century Judaism...means identifying places within the New Testament itself that separate him from his Jewish context. It means, in other words, never turning Jesus into a Christian theologian."[29]

The UMC does not, however, always honor this obligation. A quick search using the keywords *women* and *purity* quickly yielded three postings that promote a Jesus proactive on women by presenting his Jewish context as unremittingly sexist. The mildest one offers, "Jesus, by treating women with dignity and respect, challenged the conventional sexism of his day."[30] Continuing this theme, Joy J. Moore, associate professor of homiletics and Christian ministry at Wesley Seminary (Indiana Wesleyan University) writes,

> In the context of first century Judaism, a directive to let women learn was not only countercultural, but a revolutionary notion....Whereas previously tradition forbade women from even being taught the scriptures, this text grants women the opportunity to learn in the same manner as men who previously had little knowledge of a subject.[31]

Ignoring learned Jewish women from Tobit's grandmother Deborah to the Maccabean mothers to the patrons of the Pharisees (*t. Demai* 2.16–17), Rev. Dr. Moore also missed the New Testament witnesses to learned Jewish women: Anna in the temple (Luke 2) and the bent-over woman in the synagogue (Luke 13:10–17). While some rabbis sought to bar women from learning, these sources are relatively late (e.g., *b. Kiddushin* 30a, a fifth- to sixth-century text) and can be taken to indicate that women were in fact learning. Earlier materials, such as *M. Sotah* 3.4, quote Ben Azzai as mandating, "A man is required to teach Torah to his daughter." The Tosefta (*Bava Metzia* 1.6, cf. *b. Pesachim* 62b) quotes Beruria, the wife of Rabbi Meir, pronouncing halakhic teachings. The better comparison of rabbinic restrictive teaching is not to Jesus or to Paul, but to the church fathers, who are not the most progressive speakers on feminist concerns. Nor is it appropriate to pair a negative teaching from one tradition to a positive teaching from another.

Finally, Steve Harper, the dean of Asbury Theological Seminary (Orlando), insists that "the silence of women [in the Corinthian congregation] was a carry-over from the synagogue."[32] To the contrary, it is more likely that the role of women as primary in the Pauline churches—from Phoebe the deacon and Junia the apostle (Romans 16) to the work of Euodia and Synteche in Philippi (Phil 4:3)—was carried over from Diaspora synagogues. As Tal Ilan notes, "Inscriptional evidence indicates that some women, like men, held office and carried titles such as *archisynagogos* (head of synagogue), *presbyter* (elder), or *mater synagogos* (mother of the synagogue)."[33]

The Presbyterian Church (USA) website "Interfaith Toolkit: Engage Your Neighbors" links readers to a 1987 document entitled, "A

Theological Understanding of the Relationship between Christians and Jews."[34] Its seven theological affirmations include the "acknowledgment...that Jews are in covenant relationship with God," "a determination by Christians to put an end to the 'teaching of contempt' for the Jews," and a rejection of supersessionism: "Christians have not replaced Jews." The paragraph on the teaching of contempt defines the problem:

> To this day, the church's worship, preaching, and teaching often lend themselves, at times unwittingly, to a perpetuation of the "teaching of contempt." For example, the public reading of Scripture without explicating potentially misleading passages concerning "the Jews," preaching which uses Judaism as a negative example in order to commend Christianity, public prayer which assumes that only the prayers of Christians are pleasing to God, teaching in the church school which reiterates stereotypes and non-historical ideas about the Pharisees and Jewish leadership—all of these contribute, however subtly, to a continuation of the church's "teaching of contempt."

The site, however, is not easily searchable. Looking for *Judaism*, I found about 4,100 hits.[35] The first hit is "Academic Bible—Early Judaism: TheThoughtfulChristian.Com," which leads to a bibliography of "Old Testament" books including Michael D. Coogan and Mark S. Smith's *Stories from Ancient Canaan*, 2nd ed., which is a translation of Ugaritic tales. Conflation of "Judaism" with "ancient Israel" or the "ancient Near East" is a minor, but correctable problem. The next several pages led to more books. A more concentrated search, for *Jesus and Judaism*, led to 31,800 hits; still not helpful if one wants to find specific examples.

The *women/Jesus/purity* search yielded expected results: a 2013 piece on "Empirical Hermeneutics" offered the results of a study of John 4 (Jesus and the Samaritan woman), describing how a group of Hindu transsexuals in India "certainly understand the cultural rejection of the Samaritan woman by the Jews."[36] One would never know from this posting that enmity between Jews and Samaritans was mutual; that religious difference (rival temples, Torahs, priesthoods, sacred space...) is not the same thing as prejudice against a minority group; or that Jesus is hardly an example of multicultural sensitivity, given that he tells the Samaritan woman, "You worship what you do not know; we worship what we know, for salvation is from the Jews" (John 4:22). Mapping contemporary justice issues onto the New Testament, such that "Judaism" becomes the cultural problem and Jesus the solution, can only lead to anti-Jewish prejudice.

A check for commentary on Mark 7//Matthew 15, the Syro-Phoenician/Canaanite woman, quickly returned a publication by the Office of Ecumenical and Interfaith Relations, Worldwide Ministries Division: *Respectful Presence: An Understanding of Interfaith Prayer and Celebration from a Reformed Christian Perspective, a Document Commended to Congregations and Governing Bodies of the Presbyterian Church (U.S.A.) by the 209th General Assembly* (1997). In this otherwise helpful document are standard misperceptions of Jewish purity laws: "When the woman [widow of Zarephath] told the prophet about the death of her son, Elijah did not argue with her about Israel's religious codes of purity that would have required him to keep a physical distance."[37] There is *no reason* why Elijah would have brought purity codes into the conversation; to suggest that he would indicates at best a misunderstanding of the codes and, more likely, a negative view of a Jewish law that would find purity more important than saving a life.

From the Evangelical Lutheran Church of America (ELCA), a search for *Judaism* yielded an uncountable (or at least uncounted) number of hits. The 2002 "Talking Points: Topics in Christian-Jewish Relations; Law and Gospel," prepared by the Consultative Panel on Lutheran-Jewish Relations of the Office of Ecumenical and Inter-Religious Relations[38] helpfully states,

> We are often surprised, then, to find that Jews embrace the Law more as a gift than as a demand. Thus, the Psalmist explains, "O, how I love thy Law [Torah]" (Psalm 119:97), and the rabbis emphasize that Israel received the commandments (*mitzvot*) not to be condemned but "to live by them" (Leviticus 18:5)—"live" and not die. The Israelites do not receive the law in order to earn God's favor; they were saved from bondage in Egypt before they ever came to Mt. Sinai to

> receive the Torah. So they are already God's people when God gives them the Torah to know how to live out their divine calling.

When it comes to specifics, the Lutherans also offer a negative view of Judaism in order to produce a Jesus immediately relevant to twenty-first-century issues. Speaking to the issue of sex slavery, Matthew S. Rindge offers a 2010 essay entitled "Mark's Gospel, Social Outcasts, and Modern Slavery."[39] His thesis is that, in contrast to Leviticus 13, 15, 21, and 23 (which Rindge presumes to be in place in first-century Galilee), Jesus "restores the outcasts" to the community. The outcasts include the hemorrhaging woman (although Rindge does not note that she touches Jesus; Jesus does not touch her, Matt 9:20–22; Mark 5:25–34; Luke 8:43–48); a paralytic (who is "cast into" a home by his friend and thus hardly "cast out"; Matt 9:2–8; Mark 2:3–12; Luke 5:18–26); a dead girl (whose father pleads for her, and so is not cast out but mourned; Matt 9:18–19, 23–25; Mark 5:22–23, 35–43; Luke 8:41–42, 49–56); and two blind men (who appear in public; Matt 9:27–31, cf. 20:30–34; Mark 8:22–26 and 10:46–52; Luke 18:35–43).

Rindge's move is a common one: Purity laws create outcasts, and Jesus "removes the cause of their social exclusion, thereby restor[ing] the socially marginalized into society...the outcasts to the community." One problem is that, with the possible exception of the person with leprosy, no one is "cast out." The second problem is that Jesus is *restoring people to states of ritual purity*, and so *reinforcing* the purity laws, not dismissing them. When purity laws are read as harmful and Jesus is seen as rejecting them, a negative view of Jewish (and indeed of Muslim, Hindu, and Buddhist) practice is introduced. The third problem is forgetting that, for Jews in antiquity, impurity was a normal condition that *everyone* moved into and out of. Jewish purity laws erected no caste system; they described a temporary condition, not an abiding status.

This same theme of exclusionary purity rules is sounded in "Christian Eye for the Queer Guy," a 2005 entry by Michael Stolzfus.[40] Here again we read of "grace so powerful that it cannot be contained by traditional purity regulations," as if purity regulations are to the modern ELCA what "the law" was to Luther (on his less cheerful days). Stolzfus tells us that in the parable of the Good Samaritan, "Neither the Pharisee nor the

Levite helped the injured man...because their conventional purity codes and ritual regulations prevented them from touching unclean bodies." Not only does he misread the parable (the first passerby is a priest, not a Pharisee), but he also misses the *mitzvah* of attending to corpses. This queer reading takes Jesus out of "a life blinded by conformity to narrow contemporary religious and cultural purity" even as it sees Paul as interested in the "shattering of purity barriers." In so doing, it first mischaracterizes both Jesus and Paul, and then demeans and ultimately erases Jewish identity markers. It is thus ultimately not a queer reading at all, but a quite mainstream, historically uninformed, moralizing liberal Protestant one.

From the *Journal of Lutheran Ethics*, Brian A. F. Beckstrom contributes, "Blessed Are the Undocumented? A Reflection on Matthew 5:1–12."[41] Here we find the familiar stereotype that Jews favor the rich and that Christians speak on behalf of the poor: "In a culture where the prosperous and socially respectable were considered the sole recipients of God's favor, Jesus make the point of saying that...the meek, the sad, downtrodden, etc. are included." Beckstrom has apparently missed the Torah, in which God's special protection is extended to the poor, the widow, the orphan, and the stranger (e.g., Lev 19), and in which Jews are required to provide support to these whom God loves, as well as the entire Prophetic corpus with its condemnation of the rich, the psalms of lament, and all postbiblical Jewish literature.

The Board of Directors of American Baptist International Ministries of the American Baptist Churches USA issued in September 2014 "Resolutions on Anti-Semitism and Anti-Muslim Prejudice."[42] Anticipating that the same negative stereotypes found in the other denominational websites would be on this site as well, I did a search for *Jesus and women* and, indeed, found the same stereotypes in place. In her Bible Study on Women in Ministry, ABCOM Advocate for Women in Ministry Rev. Dr. Susan E. Crane writes, "First century Jewish men did pray daily, 'Blessed art thou who hast not made me a Gentile...an uneducated man (slave)... a woman," for "Gentiles, slaves and women did not have the privilege of studying Torah and being part of the covenant community."[43] Such comments would have surprised Queen Helena of Adiabene, who converted to Judaism. They would have surprised Mary and Anna and the widow in the temple, and the bent-over woman in the synagogue. They also would surprise historians, who are appropriately wary of reading a rabbinic prayer back into a first-century context.

Similarly, in her Bible study on Junia, Rev. Dr. Crane tells us that

> by the time of Jesus, these [Old Testament purity] laws were used to treat women as unclean and keep them out of the sanctuary. Women were rarely educated in the Law of Moses and were part of the covenant community only through their husbands or fathers....After the fall of Jerusalem [in 586 BCE] and the Exile, attitudes toward women became highly restrictive, based on priestly interpretations of the Law of Moses, especially the purity laws.

Following this stereotype of what had once been called (disparagingly) "Late Judaism," which allowed Christian readers to distinguish (good) Old Testament Judaism from (bad) Second Temple Judaism, Rev. Dr. Crane cites Luke 10:38–42 to insist that "sitting at the feet of Jesus was a radical thing for a woman to do."[44]

This study misses so much. It insists, for example, that "women were not permitted to attend festivals when ritually unclean,"[45] but it misses the fact that the same purity laws applied to men—and especially to priests. The stereotypes, weakly supported by comments from Josephus and Sirach, pile up: "Women were not to speak with strangers or be seen in public with men; women had to be double-veiled outside their homes; women were little more than slaves."[46] Attempting to reclaim 1 Timothy 2 for women, Crane again uses Judaism as a foil: "Jewish women were not allowed to study Torah at the synagogue or Temple, but Paul realized the danger of not educating Christian women in the faith."[47] Speaking for Junia, Crane asserts, "At the synagogue...girls sat with their mothers behind a screen."[48] One wonders how Jesus saw the bent-over woman: X-ray vision is a power ascribed to Superman, not to Jesus. For this site, first-century Judaism serves as the negative contrast in order to claim Jesus for (modern constructions of) women's equality within the church.

A search for *Jesus* and *outcast* yields the expected stereotypes as well. "Jews considered gentiles as but dogs," asserted General Secretary A. Roy Medley in a July 10, 2014, general meeting.[49] Missing are the converts to Judaism, from Helena to Nicolaus the proselyte from Antioch

(Acts 6:5), the Gentiles worshiping in the Jerusalem temple (John 12:20), the numerous God-fearers (all through Acts), as well as that centurion who built the synagogue in Capernaum and on whose behalf the Jewish elders speak (Luke 7:1–10).

There is no reason for these stereotypes to be promoted in the second decade of the twenty-first century. It is true that the websites are not redolent with anti-Jewish teachings, and representatives of these organizations may well accuse me of hunting for needles in the website haystack. Yet it was quite easy to find the stereotypes: they are not new. Purity, women, universalism versus particularity, the law and the temple—these remain the negative contrasts used for promoting women's rights, social justice, and now gay rights, immigration reform, and the elimination of human trafficking. I suspect that were I to continue to look, the problems would only proliferate.

If the church has to create a negative image of Jesus's Jewish context in order to find a Jesus who speaks to contemporary issues, then the church is bearing false witness.

MESSIANIC JUDAISM

The sites for official Jewish bodies such as the Anti-Defamation League (ADL), the American Jewish Committee (AJC), the Jewish Council for Public Affairs (JCPA), and the Conference of Presidents of Major American Jewish Organizations (COP) as well as for national groups such as the Orthodox Union (OUA), Conservative, Reform, and Reconstructionist movements, have less to say about the tenets of Christianity, given that Christians do not appear in Jewish Scripture or liturgy. These groups also have, by and large, rejected earlier Talmudic and medieval castigations of church teaching. Aside from the several "feel good" pieces (e.g., joint social justice/*tikkun olam* programs; trips to Israel) and the expected critiques when an ecclesiastical body or representative thereof says something inappropriate about Jews and Judaism (as well as, sometimes, a critique of Israeli policy), there is little engagement with Christian thought. Yet on the Messianic Jewish question, the rhetoric can bleed over into problematic wording.

One example demonstrates the point. The Committee on Jewish Law and Standards (CJLS) of the Conservative Movement, in October 2012, published with a vote of eighteen in favor, none opposed, and two abstentions, "The Status of 'Messianic Jews.'"[50] The statement begins with the historical notice of how the Catholic Church and various Protestant groups subjected Jews to "intense missionary activity," and follows that fact with references to the Jews for Jesus, an intensely missionary group. Already the deck is stacked, for today, not all Messianic Jews engage in missionary work. The failure to recognize distinctions among Messianic Jews is comparable to a failure to recognize distinctions among Christian bodies: Catholics are not Baptists, and Jews for Jesus do not hold the same tenets as those involved in Post-missionary Messianic Judaism. The pronouncement concludes that "'Messianic Jewish' sects, by their belief in Jesus as Messiah, as one of a trinity, as 'the son of God,' and as the one who leads to salvation, have crossed the redline and have become a Christian sect in everything but name. As such, members of any such group are apostates as surely as are Jews who have converted to Christianity or to any other religion but do not pretend that they are still Jews," and who have "demonstrated a negative attitude, not to say contempt, for Judaism." By contrast, "today we consider Christians neither apostates nor pagans but members of a legitimate religion."[51]

The text then devolves into what could be considered an anti-Christian view: "A 'Messianic Jew' is not simply an apostate, but rather an apostate who has undergone a period of indoctrination into a cult-like organization." Our Catholic, Evangelical, and liberal Protestant friends by no means see their traditions as "cult-like organizations," but that is how some of them will hear this response.

The Messianic Jewish Rabbinical Council (MJRC) drafted in May 2013 a formal response that challenges the historical claims of the Conservative statement regarding the *Birkat ha-Minim* (benediction against the heretics),[52] and the early separation of Jews and Christians into distinct categories. It notes the ongoing Jewish identity, including Jewish practice, of MJRC members, and explains their distinction from Jews for Jesus and other evangelizing groups.[53] Members of the MJRC are in formal conversation with the Roman Catholic Church and the Anglican Church of North America. Telling Christian bodies to stop talking to Messianic Jews is not the role of the Jewish community. Engaging Messianic Jews who insist on maintaining their Jewish identities, who continue Jewish orthopraxy, and who have some historical arguments in support of their claims, *is* the role of the Jewish community.

It does seem odd to me that we Jews are more comfortable with Jews who become Christian than with Messianic Jews who seek to maintain Jewish identity. It does seem odd to me that we Jews would reject the child of a Jewish mother, who keeps more of the traditions than the average non-Orthodox Jew, but who also holds Jesus to be the Messiah, while we express little to no critique of the secular Jew, with name-change, rhinoplasty, and a Judaism based more on bagels than on *brachot*. It does seem odd to me that we would refuse admittance to our day schools children of Messianic couples, or want them simply to practice "Christianity," and thus deprive from these children one means of appreciating their own Jewish identity.

If, for example, Conservative, Reform, and Reconstructionist traditions can override centuries of condemnation of same-sex relations, could they not at least speak with Messianic Jews who are fully invested in their own Jewish identity and practice? If, for example, the Reform movement can override centuries of determination of Jewish identity by maternal descent, could they not speak with Messianic Jews who are halakhically Jewish according to the matrilineal principle? And if we are to be honest in Jewish-Christian dialogue, then at the very least, Jews who reject the Messianic as a fellow Jew should first have a conversation with the people they reject and with the Christians who see nothing inappropriate in Messianic worship systems.

Times, I think, have changed. If we can move from holy envy to holy critique, we can move from damnation to dialogue.[54] More, we can learn from each other, for learning is what actual dialogue should produce. Christians need not construct a negative image of Judaism in order to make Jesus look relevant or inspirational. He can do this quite well on his own, from within his embeddedness in his Jewish tradition.

As Krister Stendahl insisted: Do not compare the best of one's own tradition with the worst of someone else's. Jews need not eschew anything having to do with Jesus, any more than we would eschew a study of the Dead Sea Scrolls, Josephus, or Philo. He too is part of Jewish history, and he has wisdom, *Jewish* wisdom, worth knowing. One does not need to worship the storyteller to appreciate the stories that he told, or indeed, the stories told about him. For Messianic Jews, who are halakhically Jewish, we (non-Messianic) Jews should recognize that they *want* to retain their Judaism. Surely they should be encouraged to do so, rather than pushed away with both hands. Again, Stendahl offers his wisdom: When studying someone else's religion, ask the practitioners. In turn, Christians who support Messianic congregations should recognize that they are promoting a theology that most Jews would find entirely appropriate *for Christians*, but not for fellow Jews.

There are no easy solutions to the various issues roiling all of these manifold Jewish-Christian relations. But refusing to have the conversations in the first place will not move us forward.

NOTES

1. In *Judentum, Urchristentum, Kirche: Festschrift für Joachim Jeremias*, ed. Walther Eltester (Berlin: Töpelmann, 1960): 94–105.

2. *Harvard Theological Review* 56 (1963): 199–215.

3. Edited by Tikva Frymer-Kensky, David Novak, Peter Ochs, David Fox Sandmel, and Michael Signer (Boulder, CO: Westview Press).

4. Edited by Philip A. Cunningham, Joseph Sievers, Mary Boys, and Hans Herman Hendrix (Grand Rapids, MI: Eerdmans).

5. Edited by Birgit Jeggle-Merz and Michael Durst, *Theologische Berichte* 36 (Fribourg, CH: Paulusverlag).

6. See, e.g., details of the Helsinki Consultation, http://helsinki consultation.squarespace.com; see also Mark S. Kinzer, *Searching Her Own Mystery: Nostra Aetate, the Jewish People, and the Identity of the Church* (Eugene, OR: Cascade Books, 2015).

7. http://ijcic.org.

8. When accessed on October 11, 2017, the home page, under "Press," lists twenty-two links, twenty-one of which concern the Vatican.

9. http://www.jcrelations.net/Home.112.0.html?L=3.

10. At http://ijcic.org/statements.

11. See Joint Declaration of the Commission for Religious Relations with the Jews, Warsaw, April 2016, http://www.vatican.va/roman_curia/pontifical_councils/chrstuni/relations-jews-docs/rc_pc_chrstuni_doc_20160404_riunione-varsavia_en.html.

12. Most Jews (who heard of this statement) were pleased; Jews for Jesus, an evangelizing group, along with other more conservative Christians, rejected the claim. See James Carroll's "Pope Francis and the Renunciation of Jewish Conversion," *New Yorker* (December 16, 2015), http://www.newyorker

.com/news/news-desk/pope-francis-and-the-renunciation-of-jewish-conversion.

13. For details of each meeting, see http://www.vatican.va/roman_curia/pontifical_councils/chrstuni/sub-index/index_relations-jews.htm and follow the links.

14. http://www.iccj.org.

15. Pope Francis Homilies: "The Christian Includes; Pharisees Exclude," *America Magazine*, November 5, 2015, https://www.americamagazine.org/issue/pope-francis-christian-includes-pharisees-exclude.

16. Philip A. Cunningham, "Is the Pope 'Anti-Jewish'? No, but Here Is Why His Critics Think So," *Commonweal* 144, no. 9 (May 19, 2017): 19, https://www.commonwealmagazine.org/pope-'anti-jewish'.

17. Peter M. J. Stravinskas, "Papal Anti-Judaism?," *Catholic World Report*, March 14, 2017, http://www.catholicworldreport.com/Item/5495/papal_antijudaism.aspx. See also Matthew Schmitz, "Rabbi Objects to Pope Francis's Anti-Jewish Rhetoric," *First Things*, March 16, 2017, https://www.firstthings.com/blogs/firstthoughts/2017/03/rabbi-objects-to-pope-franciss-anti-jewish-rhetoric.

18. For a study addressing problematic notes to the New American Bible Revised Edition (NABRE) on the website of the US Conference of Catholic Bishops, see Amy-Jill Levine, "Nostra Aetate, Omnia Mutantur: The Times They Are a Changing," in *Righting Relations after the Holocaust and Vatican II: Essays in Honor of John Pawlikowski*, ed. Elena Procario-Foley and Robert Cathey (Mahwah, NJ: Paulist Press, 2018).

19. See, for case studies, Jonathan Frankel and Ezra Mendelsohn, eds., *The Protestant-Jewish Conundrum: Studies in Contemporary Jewry*, vol. 24 (Oxford: Oxford University Press, 2010).

20. Brian McClaren, "Beyond Fire and Brimstone," *Sojourners*, February 2014, 16–20, http://sojo.net/magazine/2014/02/beyond-fire-and-brimstone.

21. See details in Amy-Jill Levine, "Quit Picking on the Pharisees!," *Sojourners*, March 2015, 26–29. The journal invited me to contribute the essay after it received several criticisms by its Christian readers of McLaren's article. The title was supplied by the editors; the original was "Maligning the Pharisees Once Again."

22. Paul Young, "The Love Shack," *Christianity Today*, March 4, 2013, http://www.christianitytoday.com/ct/2013/march/love-shack.html.

23. Paul Bane, "I am a Pharisee!," *Mindful Christianity Today*, Feb. 17, 2016, http://www.mindfulchristianitytoday.com/i-am-a-pharisee.

24. See Amy-Jill Levine, "With Friends Like These...," in *The Misunderstood Jew: The Church and the Scandal of the Jewish Jesus* (New York: HarperCollins, 2006), 167–90.

25. Samuel Kobia, "...and Who Is My Neighbor?" Opening sermon at World Council of Churches conference, Doorn, Utrecht, June 14, 2009, https://www.oikoumene.org/en/resources/documents/general-secretary/sermons/and-who-is-my-neighbour.

26. See Amy-Jill Levine, *Short Stories by Jesus: The Enigmatic Parables of a Controversial Rabbi* (New York: HarperOne, 2014), 22–117.

27. Doupe, Andrew, "Partnerships between Churches and People Living with HIV/AIDS Organizations," World Council of Churches, January 1, 2005, https://www.oikoumene.org/en/resources/documents/wcc-programmes/justice-diakonia-and-responsibility-for-creation/health-and-healing/hivaids/wcc-statements-and-studies/partnerships-between-churches-and-people-living-with-hivaids-organizations.

28. http://www.umc.org/what-we-believe/united-methodist-guiding-principles-for-christian-jewish-relations.

29. A. W. Bill Martin Jr., "Commentary: Preaching Tips for New Clergy," http://www.umc.org/news-and-media/commentary-preaching-tips-for-new-clergy.

30. United Methodist Church, "Book of Resolutions: Every Barrier Down; Toward Full Embrace of All Women in Church and Society," adopted 2008; amended and readopted 2016, http://www.umc.org/what-we-believe/every-barrier-down-toward-full-embrace-of-all-women-in-church-and-society.

31. Joy J. Moore, "Commentary: Women in Ministry," http://www.umc.org/what-we-believe/commentary-women-in-ministry.

32. Steve Harper, "Commentary: The Ordination of Women," http://www.umc.org/what-we-believe/commentary-the-ordination-of-women.

33. Tal Ilan, "Post-Biblical and Rabbinic Women," in *Jewish Women: A Comprehensive Historical Encyclopedia*, ed. Paula E. Hyman and Dalia Ofer (Jewish Women's Archives and Shalvi Publishing, 2006), CD-ROM, https://jwa.org/encyclopedia/article/post-biblical-and-rabbinic-women.

34. Presbyterian Church (USA) "A Theological Understanding of the Relationship between Christians and Jews," GA *Minutes*, 1987, 417–24, https://www.presbyterianmission.org/wp-content/uploads/christiansjews1.pdf.

35. https://www.pcusa.org/search/?criteria=Judaism.

36. Jerry L. Van Marter, "Empirical Hermeneutics: Dutch Scholar Employs Intercultural Contextual Bible Study to Explore How Study of

Scripture Produces Transformation," *Presbyterian News Service*, June 4, 2014, http://www.pcusa.org/news/2013/6/4/empirical-hermeneutics.

37. Worldwide Ministries Division Presbyterian Church (USA), "Respectful Presence: An Understanding of Interfaith Prayer and Celebration from a Reformed Christian Perspective; A Document Commended to Congregations and Governing Bodies of the Presbyterian Church (USA) by the 209th General Assembly (1997)," 24, http://www.pcusa.org/site_media/media/uploads/interfaithrelations/pdf/respectfulpresence.pdf.

38. ELCA Consultative Panel on Lutheran-Jewish Relations, "Talking Points—Topics in Christian-Jewish Relations: Law and Gospel," September 1, 2002, http://download.elca.org/ELCA%20Resource%20Repository/TP3_Law_And_Gospel.pdf?_ga=2.88399455.515167279.1494874790-200062273.1494873747.

39. Matthew S. Rindge, "Mark's Gospel, Social Outcasts, and Modern Slavery," *Journal of Lutheran Ethics* 10, no. 6 (June 2010), http://www.elca.org/JLE/articles/291?_ga=2.105837763.1352928997.1494874071-200062273.1494873747.

40. Michael Stolzfus, "Christian Eye for the Queer Guy," *Journal of Lutheran Ethics* 5, no. 8 (August 2005), http://www.elca.org/JLE/Articles/646?_ga=2.124910158.515167279.1494874790-200062273.1494873747.

41. Brian A.F. Beckstrom, "Blessed Are the Undocumented? A Reflection on Matthew 5:1–12," *Journal of Lutheran Ethics* 10, no. 12 (December 2010), http://www.elca.org/JLE/Articles/240?_ga=2.108093954.1687925305.1494876105-200062273.1494873747.

42. "International Ministries Issues Resolutions on Anti-Semitism and Anti-Muslim Prejudice," *American Baptist News Service*, September 29, 2014, http://www.abc-usa.org/2014/09/29/international-ministries-issues-resolutions-on-anti-semitism-and-anti-muslim-prejudice.

43. Susan E. Crane, "Bible Study on Women in Ministry," http://www.abc-usa.org/wp-content/uploads/2012/07/BIBLE-STUDY-ON-WOMEN-IN-MINISTRY-for-ABWIM-Resource-List.pdf. Originally published as "Mentoring Women in Ministry: 'Follow Me, as I Follow Christ!,'" *American Baptist Women in Ministry Sunday Celebration*, March 19, 2006, 39, citing *Palestinian Talmud Ber.* 136b, quoted by Aida Besancon Spencer, *Beyond the Curse: Women Called to Ministry* (Nashville: T. Nelson, 1985), 64.

44. Susan E. Crane, *Junia: A Bible Study and Storytelling Resource for the Church* (Valley Forge, PA: Interim Ministries-ABC/American Baptist Women in Ministry, 2005), xiv, http://www.abc-usa.org/wp-content/uploads/2012/07/Junia.pdf.

45. Ibid., 20.

46. Ibid. On p. 62, Crane asserts that "it was against the Law for a woman to speak to a man in public."

47. Ibid., 43.

48. Ibid., 62.

49. A. Roy Medley, "BWA Assembly Blog 5—'But Now,'" http://www.abc-usa.org/2014/07/10/bwa-assembly-blog-5-but-now-a-message-by-dr-medley.

50. Kassel Abelson and Reuven Hammer, "The Status of 'Messianic Jews,'" December 2012, https://www.rabbinicalassembly.org/sites/default/files/assets/public/halakhah/teshuvot/2011-2020/abelson-hammer-messianic-jews.pdf. An earlier statement appeared in 1978.

51. Ibid.

52. See the study by Ruth Langer, *Cursing the Christians? A History of the Birkat HaMinim* (New York: Oxford University Press, 2012).

53. Obtainable by request from the MJRC (my gratitude to Mark Kinzer for alerting me to this text).

54. See Jennifer M. Rosner, "Messianic Jews and Jewish-Christian Dialogue," in *Introduction to Messianic Judaism: Its Ecclesial Context and Biblical Foundations*, ed. David J. Rudolph and Joel Willitts (Grand Rapids, MI: Zondervan, 2013), 145–55.

III

THE WORK

Scholarship

4

INSPECTING *THE SCHOOL OF ST. MATTHEW*

George J. Brooke

INTRODUCTION

From the 1960s through the 1980s, everybody's New Testament monograph was obliged to have a chapter on the Dead Sea Scrolls, not least because scholars increasingly recognized that the Jewishness of the Jesus movement and the Jewish roots of much of the New Testament writings needed reconsideration in light of them. Krister Stendahl contributed greatly to how such engagement might be undertaken, not least in his landmark study *The School of St. Matthew*.[1] But things have changed and it is worth asking to what extent much of the comparative material offered in *The School of St. Matthew* still holds. This essay, however, is not an evaluation of Stendahl's detailed proposals.[2] Rather, in light of what is now known about the Dead Sea Scrolls, it is an attempt to engage with some of the larger framing issues to which Stendahl's important work on Matthew contributed so much.

On the one hand, the pendulum in New Testament and early Christian studies has swung back in favor of the examination of the non-Jewish Greco-Roman and imperial contexts of the New Testament and other texts. For some, this makes it increasingly obvious that there is still a need and a place for explicit reference to Jewish contexts and concepts as well.[3] But it is also important to recognize, on the other hand, that the study of the late Second Temple–period Jewish texts has shifted toward a much more nuanced view of how their Jewishness should be described and assessed. That view involves reconsidering how even Hebrew, Aramaic, and Greek collections of texts such as those from the caves at and near Qumran must be understood as part of a complex cultural mix in which traits from both East and West jostled together in ways that we do not yet fully appreciate. As a result, the Dead Sea Scrolls can indeed still contribute to the appreciation of the Gospel of Matthew, not so much through being representative of that Gospel's Jewish "background," but through being one of the best surviving examples from Judea in the two centuries before the fall of the temple that illustrates the cultural complexity of that time and place.

Stendahl was among the first to pay detailed attention to the Dead Sea Scrolls when studying the New Testament, particularly on the use of the Jewish Scriptures in Matthew's Gospel. He did that, naturally, in the context of the scholarship of his time, though characteristically he also significantly reshaped that scholarship. Notable, too, was his choice to work in English rather than in German or in French. He was in the vanguard of those Scandinavian scholars who, though trained in German and other scholarship, had decided, perhaps in the light of the Second World War, to shift their publications to English. His training in and critical appreciation of German scholarship was thorough, so that he was able to act as a bridge between North European scholarly endeavors and the emerging Dead Sea Scrolls scholarship that was from early on dominated by English. (This was so perhaps because it was to the American School in Jerusalem that those Syrian monks had brought the four scrolls in the possession of Athanasius Samuel.) The breadth and rigor of Stendahl's annotations, the detail of his analysis, and the freshness of his topic gave his work an immediate international authority.

One of the ways in which Stendahl inadvertently reflected German scholarship was in his standing as a New Testament scholar. In North America, and naturally in Israel, nearly all Dead Sea Scrolls scholarship has been undertaken by scholars trained in Old Testament or in Hebrew Bible. By contrast, in Germany until recently, nearly all Dead Sea Scrolls work has been undertaken by scholars of the New Testament.[4] So Stendahl was an early bridge in at least two respects: connecting Northern European scholarship with North American, and connecting New Testament scholarship with Old Testament.

Multilayered and multifaceted, Stendahl's work on Matthew's Gospel concentrates especially on the reconsideration of its explicit quotations of Scripture. In some respects, it confirms what was long known, namely, that the fulfillment quotations exclusive to Matthew among the

Synoptics can be broadly understood as having a different textual character from those that are shared in one way or another with other Gospels. The strength of Stendahl's analysis of the distinctive fulfillment quotations continues to rest in the way that it resisted a single-point explanation, not least because something like a scribal school was involved. Therefore, any evaluation of his analysis, even today, has to consider several issues. I will reflect on four of them, the first more extensively than the other three: first, the Matthean fulfillment quotation proof texts (*Reflexionzitate*); second, the nature of scribal practice in late Second Temple Judea; third, the character of the interpretation of authoritative texts among the communities associated with the sectarian scrolls from the caves at and near Qumran; fourth and finally, the status of Qumran (or of the movement of which it was a part) *as* a school.

THE MATTHEAN FULFILLMENT QUOTATION PROOF TEXTS (*REFLEXIONZITATE*)

The Dead Sea Scrolls have provided us with a wealth of textual forms of those writings that would eventually become canonical for both Jews and Christians. Describing and assessing the plurality of textual forms is ongoing. Some scholars have stressed the essential stability of the Hebrew witnesses; others, myself included, have preferred to acknowledge their variety in the precanonical period. Different theories have been proposed to explain that variety: multiple families, multiple editions, multiple social contexts. In the end, each scriptural book has its own story to tell. It is against this backdrop of textual plurality that New Testament scholars who study the scriptural quotations in the New Testament must work, not least since this textual plurality includes evidence of the early revision of Greek translations toward one form or another of the Hebrew.

For Stendahl's text-critical work on Matthew's fulfillment quotations, it remains the case that these text forms differ, at least in some degree, from those in the rest of the Gospel, for which the Gospel for the most part follows some form of the LXX. Stendahl's variegated insight was that some of the fulfillment quotations are derived from one or more sources with a particular textual character, while others suggest that some member of the scribal school, or perhaps "Matthew" himself (meaning the principal author-redactor of the Gospel), intervened with some form of received text for particular theological purposes, or even made fresh translations from the Hebrew.

The variety of scriptural text forms among the Dead Sea Scrolls was only partially known to Stendahl as he worked on his thesis, but it is a phenomenon that raised an intriguing set of possibilities for him.[5] In light of the complete publication of the so-called biblical scrolls, much now remains to be done to see whether it yields new information to explain the various readings in the Gospel's fulfillment quotations (and, indeed, to explain the readings of other quotations).

To my mind, Stendahl's textual analysis displays several important aspects. Chief among them is a topic that the vast majority of subsequent students of these quotations have largely passed over. In his analysis, Stendahl makes use of the full range of versions, including the Jewish Aramaic targumim and the Peshitta (Syriac Christianity's Aramaic version of the Old Testament).[6] In a way that Stendahl could not have known at the time—not even when he published the second edition of his study in 1968—it has become apparent that variants from Qumran are reflected later, and sometimes uniquely, in the Peshitta. In other words, this later Christian Aramaic translation preserves pre–first-century Jewish textual variants.

We have major and minor examples of this. The most famous macro example concerns the preservation of Psalms 154 and 155 in 11QPs[a]: they are known elsewhere only in the Syriac tradition. It is becoming increasingly evident that, not infrequently, the Peshitta preserves many more earlier Palestinian readings than previously thought. Stendahl anticipated this, despite his favoring Alexandrinus (the MS with the earliest full version of the Alexandrian textual family of the Bible) as reflective of early Palestinian readings. A fine example of such discernment is his view that Matthew 12:19, using *erisei* ("to wrangle or contend") when quoting Isaiah 42:2 (MT: "he will not cry nor lift up his voice") most likely reflects a text also represented in the Peshitta's *nryb* (in place of MT's *nṣ'q*). For Stendahl, "the school of Matthew might have been acquainted with an Eastern Aramaic Targum to Isaiah, where the word *nryb* was used, and this they rendered in accordance with Western Aramaic understanding."[7]

Stendahl continued his comments on Matt 12:19 as follows: "They were not 'mistaken'; they knew exactly what they were doing. A proceeding of this kind was neither unusual in a milieu where different languages and dialects were used, nor was it felt to be unjust."[8] Scholars have frequently held single textual variants of the kind attested in Matthew 12:19 to reflect errors in transmission. But we now know of multiple examples where variants, possibly originally appearing as exegetical marginal glosses, have been later incorporated into the scriptural text.[9] Many of Stendahl's proposals engage astutely with such possibilities. Scribes through those means sought to enhance the text's vitality and relevance.

Furthermore, Stendahl was fully justified in his appeal to the possibility of early Palestinian textual forms of prophetic books. His use of the Minor Prophets Scroll from Naḥal Ḥever to undergird such an approach has been more than vindicated. Through that scroll, we now know that the revision of the Greek text occurred in Judea at a relatively early stage in the first century CE, and quite possibly even before that.[10]

Stimulated in large measure by Stendahl's work, Matthean scholarship on the fulfillment quotations has flourished. Robert H. Gundry was among the first to challenge Stendahl's view that the fulfillment quotations can be isolated as a separate group within Matthew's overall use of Scripture. Gundry asserted rather that little difference distinguished the text forms of the fulfillment quotations and the scriptural citations of the Sermon on the Mount. And he also insisted that allusions—not only quotations—should also take their place in the discussion.[11] Wilhelm Rothfuchs, attempting to further Stendahl's argument, urged that the Gospel's christological agenda—namely, that Jesus fulfilled the criteria of Scripture and, thus, the hopes of Israel—outweighed the precise intricacies of how Scripture was handled. Rothfuchs proposed that Matthew himself concocted the fulfillment formula and then applied it to received traditions.[12]

George Soares Prabhu asserted that citational text forms were the result of Matthew's own translation activity from the original Hebrew, rather than his (or his school's) selection of one variant reading over against another.[13] Stendahl had proposed the same in some instances but resisted the idea as an overall explanation for the shape of the Gospel of Matthew's genealogy and birth narrative. Jean Miler has challenged the source analysis that underpinned Soares Prabhu's translation theory, proposing instead that each fulfillment quotation both serves to make a point within its immediate context, and also connects with other parts of the Gospel.[14] Marten Menken's comprehensive work has generally adopted the same approach as Gundry's, dealing with each quotation in turn and prescinding from singling out the fulfillment quotations as representative of a Matthean school's techniques.[15] Other voices, too, whether challenging or affirming, have joined in this enriching conversation.[16]

In my opinion, the principal reactions to Stendahl's analysis themselves fall short of the high standards that Stendahl set, not because they are necessarily incorrect, but because they tend to take a single perspective and to assess everything else in that light. At least part of the ongoing success of Stendahl's variegated approach, which proffered so much, is evident in the way that only two out of the twelve studies in the volume edited by Thomas Hatina engaged with the quotations in Matthew 1—2. (One attempted to frame Matthew's use of Isa 7:14 in 1:23 as mythologizing; the other considered the same theme for the citations in Matthew 2, from history to myth and back again.[17]) In addition, even Ulrich Luz, in his commentary's excursus on the fulfillment quotations, describes Stendahl's contribution as "problematic" on two grounds.

In my opinion, Luz somewhat misrepresents Stendahl's proposals. They are not as "problematic" as he believes. First, Luz claims that Stendahl obscurely represents the relationship between the author of the Gospel and the "school" that he proposes as the setting for the production of the Gospel text. Second, Luz argues that Stendahl depends overmuch upon Matthew's knowledge of multiple versions. Because Matthew generally takes over citations from Mark unaltered, Luz prefers to understand that the distinctive citations in the fulfillment quotations come from a pre-Matthean tradition.[18]

New information since Stendahl first wrote (and even since his second edition of 1968) has become available; but Stendahl's approach, once adjusted in light of such recent knowledge, offers a frame of reference that still stands strong.[19] Errors or inadequacies of detail notwithstanding, he offers a fruitful direction of thinking.

An example of such thinking can be seen in Stendahl's fairly standard initial comment on Matthew 2:23, identifying its unidentified source as Isaiah 11:1 (Hebrew *nṣr*) and acknowledging that this means that Matthew must have been working in two languages, Hebrew and Greek. In subsequent comments, Stendahl develops his idea, seeing a reference to a Nazirite in Matthew's allusion, which perhaps stems from Judges 13.[20] Eugene Ulrich has proposed that Matthew's allusion testifies to a variant of 1 Samuel 1:11 or 1:22 ("I will offer him as a nazirite for all time"). 1 Samuel 1:11 is now presented on the basis of 4QSam[a] in NRSV as, "Then I will set him before you as a nazirite until the day of his death."[21] It is precisely this kind of evidence that seems to vindicate Stendahl's approach, even though he himself introduced a more interpretive element to account for *The School of St. Matthew*.

With Stendahl, I am of the opinion that there is no need to argue as Luz has done for a series of stages in order to explain what is taking place in the fulfillment quotations, since that falls back onto a single-point approach for each stage. Rather, depending upon what was needed at each turn, Matthew was able to engage with the Scriptures in terms of variant forms or in terms of exegetical adjustment, even fresh translation, perhaps worked out in a "school" context. In concluding his comments on the highly distinctive composite quotation in Matt 2:6, Stendahl remarks, "It may seem strange that Matthew could put such a reading into the mouths of the scribes, but the insight we have received into Jewish interpretation of the Scriptures through the scrolls of the Qumran sect will make this less offensive."[22] Just so.

THE NATURE OF SCRIBAL PRACTICE IN LATE SECOND TEMPLE JUDAISM

Scribes, I have implied, did not work exclusively as passive copyists in late Second Temple times. The canonical period, and the preferences and practices of later times for which there is more secure evidence, can too easily be retrojected. But the New Testament scholar knows that scriptural quotations in the various New Testament and early Christian texts reflect an intriguingly wide range of data that cannot all be explained as errors, as failures of memory, or as retrospective exegetical adjustments by early Christian authors. Scribes are agents, not just passive media.

The Dead Sea Scrolls have stimulated extensive interest in the roles of scribes in Israelite and Judean culture from First Temple times onward.[23] The varieties of scribal identification and practice have been noted several times. In the Qumran context, there are likely to have been at least three kinds of scribes, though the technical designation "scribe" (*spr*) is hardly used at all. First, there would have been wise teachers, or *maśkîlîm*, as represented elsewhere by a figure like Ben Sira: those would have been men of letters whose primary engagement with texts was oral, as was standard in the ancient world.

The role of such a scribe is depicted in Sirach 38:24—39:11. Ben Sira is a work that has survived in the Qumran caves and was certainly known to this sectarian movement. Much has been written on the role and status of the scribe as depicted in this text. Recently, Arie van der Kooij has highlighted how Ben Sira seems to have understood himself as a scholar and an official, perhaps with some political role. He might also have been a priest, though that remains uncertain.[24] We should probably distinguish the office of scribe as might be fulfilled by someone such as Ben Sira, from the technical practice of writing. Some among the sectarian movement might have indeed aspired to the eminence of teacher and scribe such as Ben Sira. The same may be said for Matthew and his circle.

Such wise scribes were concerned with the dissemination of knowledge of various kinds. There was a need for the transmission of priestly craft.[25] Some aspects of priestly lore were no doubt highly technical, involving mathematics for astronomical calculations and the determination of key calendrical events. In addition, there was a wide range of other scientific knowledge of which there is some evidence in the compositions that have come from the caves at and near Qumran, including medicine (4Q266 frg. 6, i), physiognomy (4Q186), as well as some aspects of divination (4Q321). Wider fields of knowledge in antiquity were known about in the sectarian movement.[26]

A second type of scribe would have been those well-educated and literate workers with manuscripts who were responsible for the transmission of compositions containing such knowledge as teacher-scribes might require in the curriculum. Chief among their responsibilities would be the transmission of the scriptural texts in all their precanonical variety. At Qumran it is most likely that the particular but not entirely consistent scribal practices that have been identified by Emanuel Tov are representative of the existence of a scribal school, perhaps not unlike that envisaged by Stendahl for Matthean circles.[27] But more than the evidence of particular scribal practices, it is the attitude of such scribes that is important. We can see very clearly that, perhaps through interaction with the teacher-scribes, they did not consider themselves as mere copyists, but as active participants in the transmission process in both minor and sometimes major ways. It is probably the case that special care was taken in the production of scrolls with deluxe features,[28] but even those manuscripts represent a stage in the transmission of the text with variant readings.

Third, there would have been those scribes trained with additional specialist skills for working with various kinds of text, several of them scriptural. For example, some scrolls contain certain distinctive elements, such as the divine name written in paleo-Hebrew letters.[29] It is possible that paleo-Hebrew generally was written by a specialist scribe with expertise in that alphabet; such scribes would have been responsible for the penning of some whole manuscripts in paleo-Hebrew.[30] In addition, some sectarian compositions are penned in cryptic alphabets.[31] Furthermore, one of the surprising features of the collection of manuscripts as a whole is the set of tefillin that have come from Cave 4 in particular.[32] The professional expertise required for writing these small slips in micrography is remarkable. And in a world charged with the presence of spirits and demons, protection is needed and it is likely that certain texts, such as 11Q11, were produced for apotropaic or quasi-magical purposes: 4Q341 may even be a scribal exercise concerning such things.[33] It is likely, then, that Qumran or the movement of which it was a part had a specialist set of scribes who knew how to present authoritative texts in various ways, some of which required adjustment as they were written out in new copies.

Overall, consideration of the kinds of scribes, and attention to some of their general and specialist skills, provides a thoroughgoing analogy for what Stendahl feasibly envisaged for Matthew and his colleagues.

THE CHARACTER OF INTERPRETATION OF AUTHORITATIVE TEXTS

What did the process of interpretation look like? Concerning the scrolls found in the caves at and near Qumran, many detailed observations have been made over the years on the possible ways in which the details of prophetic and legal texts were provided with both their implicit and explicit exegesis. I have observed in more than one place that, at least in the so-called continuous Pesharim, the scriptural text seems to exercise more control over the *pesher* than is necessarily the case in the Matthean fulfillment quotations.[34] How then should we nuance our definition of "midrash *pesher*" vis-à-vis those quotations?[35] Stendahl seems to me to be on the right road when he considers that the results of the scriptural interpretation represented not least in Matthew's fulfillment quotations relied upon some sort of communal interactions, and was not simply the work of some single author.

In searching for some emic categories for describing what might have been taking place in the Qumran context, I have come back often to a passage to which many Scrolls scholars have appealed when considering the study of the Scriptures, namely 1QS 6:6–8:

> And in the place in which the Ten assemble there should not be missing a man to interpret the law (*dwrš btwrh*) day and night,[36] always, one relieving another. And the Many shall be on watch together for a third of each night of the year in order to read the book (*lqrw' bspr*), explain the regulation (*ldrwš mšpṭ*), and bless together (*lbrk byḥd*).[37]

James VanderKam has commented,

> The sectarian literature indicates that the members of the community engaged regularly in the study of the scriptures (for example, 1QS 6:6–8), but their diligent exegesis almost certainly did not make them unique in their time. Their distinctive attribute was, in their considered opinion, possession of the correct interpretation of the scriptures that they and their Jewish opponents agreed were important and applicable to present concerns.[38]

The interpretation of scripture was a form of lifelong communal learning. Members of the community, probably but not necessarily in every instance male, are described as involved in some kind of educational process for long periods of the night. That well-known text in the Rule of the Community seems to describe what is to take place.

Three significant aspects characterize this process. In the first place, the group will have read together some text, probably a scriptural one. I have argued elsewhere that such reading was likely to have interacted with the written text.[39] That is, the text would not just have been read aloud, but also in some sense performed: rhetorical recitation would affect a particular meaning. Furthermore, such reading was probably not straightforwardly a word-for-word precise presentation, but an active participation by the reader with the text, involving glossing of various kinds, both major and minor, such as can be found in the manuscript evidence itself, and which is best known from the traditions of scriptural rewriting that have come to light.

The reading of the text was followed, secondly, by engaged communal interrogation of the text, what is labeled as *drš*. We do not know precisely what kind of oral process was involved, nor whether any kind of written record of such a study session was ever made. Scholars debate whether *drš* means "study" or not. Overall, I side with those who understand *drš* as akin to searching a text through rigorous examination. Such might be the basis of sound investigative study by research—a somewhat anachronistic rendering of the verb as "study" implies a school activity that might be more passive than active. Johann Maier is probably correct in understanding the activity of *drš* in the sectarian compositions as investigative and interrogatory, rather than as an umbrella term for study as such.[40] Such "searching" was a mixture of recalling the authoritative interpretations of earlier members of the congregation, perhaps even what was supposed to derive from the Teacher of Righteousness himself, together with offering fresh insights that would then be scrutinized orally by fellow seekers. Perhaps it was in those settings that extrapolations of scriptural laws were created and then put in written form as new statutes (e.g., concerning the Sabbath: CD 10:10–14; 10:21–12:2, 12–15).

Those innovations are dressed in scriptural terminology to indicate something of their status, not in order to deceive the reader or hearer, but so that the reader or hearer could appreciate all the better the ways in which Torah was being extended or brought into the present. This was not an invention of the sectarians, but was a method already discernible in various ways in such compositions as the Book of Jubilees or the Temple Scroll. Though the implication is that it was portions of the Law that formed the regular basis of such study, it is just as easy to suppose that sections of the prophets were also interrogated. The results of such searching for understanding might be represented in written form in the

Pesharim, the prophetic commentaries. The Pesharim suggest that in the reading of the prophetic text, minor adjustments were made that both facilitated and anticipated some aspects of the interpretation that followed. Matthew, too, presents the results of some earlier interpretation, but particularly the scriptural examinations of his own context.

The third ingredient of the study session was "blessing." In my opinion, such activity was more than a rote (re)presentation of some liturgical formula. More likely, the activity of blessing also involved some creative, performative interactions with known formulae. For example, several of the blessings that survive among the compositions on the manuscripts from the Qumran caves are variations on the Aaronic benediction from Numbers 6.[41] Although there might be some communal prayers of blessing, perhaps learned by heart and recited together from memory, one can readily imagine that rather than giving a fixed or set blessing, the president of the session might orally improvise on a known blessing formula to create a benediction specific for the moment. In fact, it is likely that blessings need to be considered as performative speech acts of some kind, bringing into actuality what they state when pronounced.

These three activities—reading, searching, blessing—all aspects of the study of Scripture, should not be understood as applying only to a sectarian group resident at Qumran. As John Collins has argued,[42] the *yaḥad* consisted of multiple communities. The passage in the first cave version of the Rule of the Community implies that an assembly of at least ten men was needed for the activities described to take place. Although any one of those ten or more men might conceivably undertake any of the activities of reading, searching, or blessing, given the hierarchical character of the community reflected in the Cave 1 version of the Rule of the Community, it seems more likely that only certain members of the community exercised those roles. One might easily imagine something similar occurring in Matthew's community, though perhaps the activity of interpretation was of a less intense scale. If Matthew were part of such a group in which scribes were members, the texts of Scripture could have been engaged in multiple ways, whether in Hebrew or in Greek; and a school could have indeed helped produce the revised scriptural quotations now especially evident in some parts of the Gospel.

QUMRAN AS A SCHOOL

Stendahl spoke of a "school." Can more be said in light of what we know about Qumran or the movement of which it was a part, about whether Qumran might be a suitable model for what Stendahl might have envisaged? I will offer some few comments on literacy and on Qumran more generally.[43]

All recent students of literacy in Jewish and Christian groups of the late Second Temple period and beyond are dependent on the landmark but largely synthetic work by Catherine Hezser.[44] For the sectarian movement visible in the principal compositions found in Qumran's caves, two further specialist studies have advanced the discussion. First, for Philip Alexander, "the Community at Qumran was literate on any definition of that term."[45] Alexander has argued cogently that manuscripts were indeed produced at Qumran, though the remaining evidence might indicate production on only a small scale. Some of the materials for manuscripts were likely produced locally; equally likely, many of the scribes were trained elsewhere. Disputes among archaeologists and others notwithstanding, there is no adequate reason for supposing that the Qumran site might not make a suitable setting for sectarian activities, especially educational ones, notably those of a tertiary kind such as might inform the fresh reading of authoritative texts.

Thus, for Alexander, the scrolls from Qumran provide clear evidence of community literacy, but several of the features of the Qumran evidence, such as the quantity of manuscripts, the likely skills and the status of its scribes, and the linguistic expertise of community members should be used with caution in establishing the nature and extent of such activity. "The members of the Community came having already acquired at least basic Hebrew. They probably learned the distinctive Qumran style of Hebrew, not by formal study of the language, but by studying intensely the sectarian classics, by hearing sermons and above all by praying the sectarian prayers and participating in the great sectarian liturgies."[46]

Second, André Lemaire has insightfully commented that the evidence from the Qumran caves most likely coheres with other forms of contemporary Judaism.[47] He has also proposed that teaching and learning processes at Qumran and elsewhere were probably primarily oral, though some explanation also has to be given of the presence of texts in paleo-Hebrew and in Greek in the collection. The principal component of the curriculum among members of the movement was the Torah; and that curriculum was delivered primarily by priests or specially trained laypeople. There is enough evidence to indicate communal activity at Qumran that involved debates and discussion about authoritative compositions, their performance, and their copying.

Alexander and Lemaire seem to agree that the finds from the caves at Qumran evince a form of oral and written textual culture among the movement responsible for collecting the scrolls together. However, both of them indicate that the evidence should not be overread by giving a privileged place to scribes and to writing. Such insights it seems to me are largely justifiable, and suggest that the Qumran community can be appropriately compared to that of Matthew.

Qumran seems to reflect both oral and written literacy. Can we then assess whether it represents a "school"? For Alexander, "Qumran did function as a kind of school in which a body of knowledge was studied and passed on, but from an educational standpoint it must be classified as a tertiary institution. It did not contain children, but only adults, who had their basic education elsewhere."[48] As noted previously, study was a considerable part of the sectarian's way of life. Inasmuch as some of the space at the Qumran site was given over to the production of manuscripts and the writing of texts, the site was at least providing resources, many of which could have been used in didactic or pedagogical settings, both at Qumran and elsewhere. However, in addition, there was a larger meeting room, sometimes demarcated as a dining area, where apart from common meals there could have been assemblies for study purposes. Perhaps that was where the sessions mentioned in the Rule of the Community took place (1QS 6:8).

Defining the function of the Qumran site has proved problematic. The debates have largely resulted from readers of the site wanting to impose a single explanation for all that took place there. However, because of the size of the site, beyond that of a standard semifortified farmhouse, and because of the character of its buildings, it is most likely that during the major period of its occupation the site served several purposes.[49] Among those purposes would be communal storage, and the production of manuscripts and pottery. It seems that there were also spaces for communal gatherings, among which could have been the very kind of study activities around authoritative texts, both scriptural and communal ones, that could have been responsible for transmitting and taking advantage of variations between texts, which could have promoted new readings, all based upon a sophisticated set of hermeneutical principles.

Three matters underline that some of the activities at Qumran might permit us to identify the site as a school. First, it is most likely that the site of Qumran and the manuscripts found in the caves should not be separated from one another. The extensive use of terms such as teacher (*môreh*) and wise instructor (*maskîl*) in the principal sectarian compositions indicate that adult or continuous education was a significant part of the ethos of those who lived and worked at Qumran. Second, the presence of inkwells at the site and the overwhelming predominance of literary compositions among the manuscript finds from the Qumran caves is indicative of the production at Qumran of at least some literary texts, perhaps especially those reflecting a distinctive scribal practice, including various sectarian compositions with their widespread and variegated use of scripture. Third, if such a text as 1QS 6:6–8 is indicative of communal activity at Qumran, then at least some of the occupants of the site seem to have attempted to live out a daily pattern of life that included extensive study.

Overall, it is not necessary to say that Qumran was only a school. It was probably not exclusively the residence of a master and his disciples. However, it is highly likely that there was educational activity embedded in the regularities of the spiritual lives of its residents. Was Matthew's context something similar? It seems unlikely that Matthew lived and worked in a group that was as exclusive as those reflected in the evidence from Qumran, but the presence of the modes of activities and the types of engagement with received scriptural traditions in all their variety is entirely feasible. Stendahl's insights are, in my opinion, largely vindicated.

CONCLUSION

Examining Stendahl's *School of St. Matthew*, I have come to the general conclusion that his book is in good working order. Perhaps more nuance is required concerning the relationship between the Gospel's author and the school, the group of colleagues with whom he interacted or perhaps led. But in light of the four points considered here, it is indeed possible to imagine that the distinctiveness of the Matthean fulfillment quotations is best understood as the product of a Judean or other school context. Such a context accommodated the textual variety of the

Scriptures. And such variety could have been reflected in various ways, rather than in terms of a single point of reference, from variant reading to exegetical adjustment (even to larger schemes of exegetical rewriting), the texts of Scripture and the work of their transmitters would have provided the resources that Matthew needed. Furthermore, scribes came in various guises: Matthew probably envisaged himself as one with multiple competencies, some more general and educative, others more specialist and refined; but he was probably not a master of all the various data that the fulfillment quotations in particular seem to reflect.

The New Testament writings, not least the Gospel of Matthew, all variously participate in the kinds of interpretation that are discernible in the Qumran sectarian texts and in other Jewish (and even non-Jewish) compositions of the time. The Qumran community can indeed be described in part as a "school" without distorting the evidence or removing it from its wider Hellenistic environment: from curriculum to pedagogy, just the kinds of things that are required for a *Sitz im Leben* such as Stendahl provided for the Gospel of Matthew, are apparent at Qumran. Stendahl's *School* has passed its inspection, it seems, with flying colors.

NOTES

1. Krister Stendahl, *The School of St. Matthew and Its Use of the Old Testament*, ASNU 20 (Uppsala, Almqvist & Wiksell, 1954). Reprinted with a "Preface to the Second Edition" (Philadelphia: Fortress, 1968).

2. Stendahl included a long list of reviews of the first edition in the second edition, p. xv.

3. See, e.g., J. Andrew Overman, "Problems with Pluralism in the Second Temple Judaism: Matthew, James, and the Didache in Their Jewish-Roman Milieu," in *Matthew, James and Didache: Three Related Documents in Their Jewish and Christian Settings*, ed. Huub van de Sandt and Jürgen K. Zangenberg, SymS 45 (Atlanta: Society of Biblical Literature, 2008), 259–70. Having stressed Matthew's overriding concern with Torah interpretation, Overman writes, "While Matthew does not mention Roman and Roman realities explicitly…he does address issues that we can recognize as related to Roman imperial realities" (p. 262).

4. There have been notable exceptions in both arenas: Raymond E. Brown and Joseph A. Fitzmyer in North America; and Odil Hannes Steck and

Armin Lange in Germany—though both eventually found positions in German-speaking areas outside Germany itself.

5. The groundbreaking initial insights of Dominique Barthélemy were published in 1953: "Redécouverte d'un chaînon manquant de l'histoire de la Septante," *Revue Biblique* 60 (1953): 18–29. Stendahl refers to this study.

6. Two recent surveys do indeed engage with the versions but in ways that tend to marginalize their evidence: Marten J. J. Menken, *Matthew's Bible: The Old Testament Text of the Evangelist*, BETL 173. (Louvain: Peeters, 2004); and Craig L. Blomberg, "Matthew," in *Commentary on the New Testament Use of the Old Testament*, ed. Gregory K. Beale and Donald A. Carson (Grand Rapids, MI: Baker Academic, 2007), 1–109.

7. Stendahl, *The School of St. Matthew*, 112.

8. Ibid., 112.

9. An example can be seen in the reading of *ywmm* for *ywm* in 4QGen[g] for Gen 1:5 (as also in the Targumim and Peshitta); the addition of a single *mem* disambiguates the meaning of "day," enabling a distinction between "day" (*ywm*) as a twenty-four-hour period and "daytime" (*ywmm*) as distinct from "night" (*lylh*).

10. See now Anneli Aejmelaeus and Tuukka Kauhanen, eds., *The Legacy of Barthélemy: 50 Years after Les Devanciers d'Aquila*, De Septuaginta Investigationes 9 (Göttingen: Vandnhoeck & Ruprecht, 2017).

11. Robert H. Gundry, *The Use of the Old Testament in St. Matthew's Gospel with Special Reference to the Messianic Hope*, NovTSup 18 (Leiden: Brill, 1967).

12. Wilhelm Rothfuchs, *Die Erfüllungszitate des Matthäus-Evangeliums: Eine biblisch-theologische Untersuchung*, BWANT 88 (Stuttgart: W. Kohlhammer, 1969).

13. George M. Soares Prabhu, *The Formula Quotations in the Infancy Narrative of Matthew: An Enquiry into the Tradition History of Mt 1–2*, Analecta Biblica 63 (Rome: Biblical Institute Press, 1976). The discussion of the fulfillment quotations by Richard B. Hays, *Echoes of Scripture in the Gospels* (Waco, TX: Baylor University Press, 2016), 105–109, is disappointingly and largely uncritically dependent on Soares Prabhu.

14. Jean Miler, *Les citations d'accomplissement dans l'évangile de Matthieu: Quand Dieu se rend présent en toute humanité*, Analecta Biblica 140 (Rome: Editrice Pontificio Istituto Biblico, 1999).

15. See especially Menken, *Matthew's Bible* (n6).

16. Jean Miler, *Les citations d'accomplissement*, 60, writes of the fulfillment quotations, "The text form is more probably dependent on

hellenistic traditions and translations and may illustrate an awareness of the debates concerning scriptural interpretation in Hellenistic Judaism."

17. M. Anthony Apodaca, "Myth Theory, Comparison and Embedded Scripture Texts: Ibn Ishāq's Biography of Muhammad and the Mythologizing Function of Isaiah 7.14 in Matthew 1.23," and Thomas R. Hatina, "From History to Myth and Back Again: The Historicizing Function of Scripture in Matthew 2," in *Biblical Interpretation in Early Christian Gospels*, vol. 2, *The Gospel of Matthew*, ed. Thomas R. Hatina, LNTS 310 (London: T&T Clark, 2008), 14–29, 98–118.

18. Ulrich Luz, *Matthew 1—7: A Commentary* (Minneapolis: Augsburg Fortress 1989), 160.

19. As I argued in George J. Brooke, "Aspects of Matthew's Use of Scripture in Light of the Dead Sea Scrolls," in *A Teacher for All Generations: Essays in Honor of James C. VanderKam*, vol. 2, edited by Eric F. Mason et al., JSJSup 153 (Leiden: Brill, 2012), 821–38.

20. Stendahl, *School of St. Matthew*, 103–4, 198.

21. MT reads, "Then I will give him to the Lord all the days of his life." See Eugene C. Ulrich, "The Qumran Biblical Scrolls: The Scriptures of Late Second Temple Judaism," in *The Dead Sea Scrolls in Their Historical Context*, ed. Timothy H. Lim et al. (Edinburgh: T&T Clark, 2000), 78–79.

22. Stendahl, *School of St. Matthew*, 101.

23. For the Gospel of Matthew, David E. Orton, *The Understanding Scribe: Matthew and the Apocalyptic Ideal*, JSNTSup 25 (Sheffield, UK: Sheffield Academic Press, 1989), still repays study, notably in his discussion of "Scribes and Qumran Literature" (121–33).

24. Arie van der Kooij, "Scholars and Officials in Early Judaism: The Sôfer of Jesus Ben Sira," in *Septuagint, Sages, and Scripture: Studies in Honour of Johann Cook*, ed. Randall X. Gauthier, Gideon R. Kotzé, and Gert J. Steyn, VTSup 172 (Leiden: Brill, 2016), 190–204.

25. See, e.g., Henryk Drawnel, "Priestly Education in the 'Aramaic Levi Document (Visions of Levi)' and 'Aramaic Astronomical Book' (4Q208–211)," *Revue de Qumrân*, 22 (2006): 547–74.

26. See, e.g., Philip S. Alexander, "Enoch and the Beginnings of Jewish Interest in Natural Science," in *The Wisdom Texts from Qumran and the Development of Sapiential Thought*, ed. Charlotte Hempel, Armin Lange, and Hermann Lichtenberger (Louvain: Peeters, 2002), 223–43; reprinted in Jonathan Ben-Dov and Seth Sanders, eds., *Ancient Jewish Science and the History of Knowledge in Second Temple Jewish Literature* (New York: New York University Press and Institute for the Study of the Ancient World, 2014),

25–49. The other articles in the volume and the bibliography are all worthy contributions along the same lines.

27. Note the landmark study by Emanuel Tov, *Scribal Practices and Approaches Reflected in the Texts Found in the Judean Desert*, STDJ 54 (Leiden: Brill, 2004), and the issues raised against seeing too much uniformity in such a school by Eibert J.C. Tigchelaar, "Assessing Emanuel Tov's 'Qumran Scribal Practice,'" in *The Dead Sea Scrolls: Transmission of Traditions and Production of Texts*, ed. Sarianna Metso, Hindy Najman, and Eileen Schuller, STDJ 92 (Leiden: Brill, 2010), 173–208.

28. See Tov, *Scribal Practices*, 125–30.

29. Note the remarks of Al Wolters, "The Tetragrammaton in the Psalms Scroll," *Textus* 18 (1995): 87–99.

30. See Tov, *Scribal Practices*, 238–48.

31. Though largely deciphered long ago, considerable work remains to be done on the manuscripts penned in cryptic alphabets; see, e.g., Asaf Gayer, Daniel Stökl Ben Ezra, and Jonathan Ben-Dov, "A New Join of Two Fragments of 4QcryptA Serekh haEdah and Its Implications," *Dead Sea Discoveries* 23 (2016): 139–54.

32. On the tefillin see the descriptions in Yehudah B. Cohn, *Tangled Up in Text: Tefillin and the Ancient World*, Brown Judaic Studies 351 (Providence, RI: Brown University Press, 2008).

33. See George J. Brooke, "4Q341: An Exercise for Spelling and for Spells?," in *Writing and Ancient Near Eastern Society: Papers in Honour of Alan R. Millard*, ed. Piotr Bienowski, Christopher B. Mee, and Elizabeth A. Slater, LHBOTS 426 (London: T&T Clark, 2005), 271–82; and Joan E. Taylor, "4Q341: A Writing Exercise Remembered," in *Is There a Text in This Cave? Studies in the Textuality of the Dead Sea Scrolls in Honour of George J. Brooke*, ed. Ariel Feldman, Maria Cioată, and Charlotte Hempel, STDJ 119 (Leiden: Brill, 2017), 133–51.

34. E.g., George J. Brooke, "Shared Exegetical Traditions between the Scrolls and the New Testament," in *The Oxford Handbook of the Dead Sea Scrolls*, ed. Timothy H. Lim and John J. Collins (Oxford: Oxford University Press, 2010), 571–78.

35. Stendahl, *School of St. Matthew*, 193.

36. On "day and night" for continuous rehearsing and reflecting on the law, see also Josh 1:8 and Ps 1:2.

37. Florentino García Martínez and Eibert J. C. Tigchelaar, trans., *The Dead Sea Scrolls Study Edition* (Leiden: Brill; Grand Rapids: Eerdmans, 2000), 1:83.

38. James C. VanderKam, "To What End? Functions of Scriptural Interpretation in Qumran Texts," in *Studies in the Hebrew Bible, Qumran, and the Septuagint Presented to Eugene Ulrich*, ed. Peter W. Flint, Emanuel Tov, and James C. VanderKam, VTSup 101 (Leiden: Brill, 2006), 305.

39. George J. Brooke, "Reading, Searching Blessing: A Functional Approach to Scriptural Interpretation in the יחד," in *The Temple in Text and Tradition: A Festschrift in Honour of Robert Hayward*, ed. R. Timothy McLay, LSTS 83 (London: Bloomsbury, 2015), 142–47.

40. Johann Maier, "Early Jewish Biblical Interpretation in the Qumran Literature," in *Hebrew Bible/Old Testament: The History of Its Interpretation*, vol. 1, *From the Beginnings to the Middle Ages (until 1300)*, ed. Magne Sæbø (Göttingen: Vandenhoeck & Ruprecht, 1996), 113.

41. See Bilhah Nitzan, *Qumran Prayer and Religious Poetry*, trans. Jonathan Chipman, STDJ 12 (Leiden: Brill, 1994), 145–71.

42. John J. Collins, *Beyond the Qumran Community: The Sectarian Movement of the Dead Sea Scrolls* (Grand Rapids, MI: Eerdmans, 2010).

43. For more detail on the topic of education see George J. Brooke, "Aspects of Education in the Sectarian Scrolls from the Qumran Caves," in *Jewish Education from Antiquity to the Middle Ages: Studies in Honour of Philip S. Alexander*, ed. George J. Brooke and Renate Smithuis, AJEC 100 (Leiden: Brill, 2017), 11–42.

44. Catherine Hezser, *Jewish Literacy in Roman Palestine*, TSAJ 81 (Tübingen: Mohr Siebeck, 2001); there is no distinct treatment of the scrolls from the Qumran caves, but their evidence is integrated into an overall perspective. See also Hezser, "Private and Public Education," in *Jewish Daily Life in Roman Palestine*, ed. Catherine Hezser (Oxford: Oxford University Press, 2010), 465–81.

45. Philip S. Alexander, "Literacy among Jews in Second Temple Palestine: Reflections on the Evidence from Qumran," in *Hamlet on a Hill: Semitic and Greek Studies Presented to Professor T. Muraoka on the Occasion of His Sixty-Fifth Birthday*, ed. Martin F.J. Baasten and Wido Th. Van Peursen, OLA 118 (Louvain: Peeters, 2003), 5.

46. Alexander, "Literacy among Jews in Second Temple Palestine," 23.

47. André Lemaire, "Lire, écrire, étudier à Qoumrân et ailleurs," in *Qoumrân et le Judaïsme du tournant de notre ère: Actes de la Table Ronde, Collège de France, 16 novembre 2004*, ed. André Lemaire and Simon G. Mimouni, Collection de la REJ 40 (Louvain: Peeters, 2006), 63–79.

48. Alexander, "Literacy among Jews in Second Temple Palestine," 14.

49. For a balanced survey of several possibilities see Eric M. Meyers, "Khirbet Qumran and its Environs," in *The Oxford Handbook of the Dead Sea Scrolls*, ed. Timothy H. Lim and John J. Collins (Oxford: Oxford University Press, 2010), 21–29.

5

THE INFLUENCE OF "THE INTROSPECTIVE CONSCIENCE" ON THE NEW PAUL(S)

John W. Marshall

INTRODUCTION

Scholars have chosen such terms as *seminal*, *influential*, *famous*, and *pioneering*[1] to describe Krister Stendahl's 1963 article, "The Apostle Paul and the Introspective Conscience of the West."[2] Steven Westerholm, while striving to refute Stendahl, asserts that "no article published in the twentieth century on a New Testament topic garnered more attention, provoked more debate, or exercised greater influence" than Stendahl's essay.[3] On the basis of this article, and Stendahl's 1976 elaboration of it,[4] James Dunn called Stendahl "the father of the new perspective."[5] Such influence is rare: at article length, nothing has changed the game like Stendahl did. Stendahl's foray into the question of what moved Paul, what we inappropriately impute to him, and what a renewed and more fully historicized understanding of Paul might look like has been a course-changing stone dropped into the stream of twentieth- and now twenty-first-century scholarship on the purposes, the mission, and the enterprise of the apostle Paul.

The purpose of this essay is to chart that new course with specific attention to the influence of Stendahl's intervention. This essay also seeks to situate Stendahl's work in relation to its predecessors and, in addition to charting its aftermath, to reflect on what it left undone. It also will consider the ways in which Stendahl's most radical interpreters—

and here "radical" genuinely refers to the root, namely the roots of Stendahl's intervention into the interpretation of Paul—have advanced the insights of Stendahl as "the father of the [radical] new perspective."

THE ARGUMENT

The argument of "The Introspective Conscience" is worth recapitulating. The article falls into four parts: (1) introductory matters; (2) the influence of Luther's agenda on the study of Paul; (3) Paul's own treatment of sin and especially of his own sin; and (4) the perils of modernizing Paul.

Stendahl commences by suggesting that Paul's status as "a hero of the introspective conscience" is a symptom of a false hypothesis of contemporaneity that can deeply distort the reading of the historian, the theologian, the psychologist, or even of the average reader who attempts to understand the New Testament.[6] Stendahl's worry concerns not just an oversimplified (and intrinsically anachronistic) equation of Paul and the twentieth-century reader, but also a four-point continuum of Paul, Augustine, Luther, and the modern reader. Contrary to the tortured introspection that he understands as prototypically Lutheran, Stendahl sees Paul as equipped with a "robust" conscience. Stendahl sets Paul's robust conscience—his understanding that he was "as to righteousness under the law, blameless" (Phil 3:6)—in relation to a revised understanding of the role of the law in Judaism and in relation to the concerns driving Paul's entire enterprise, namely the relation of Jews and Gentiles to salvation. His introductory section concludes by noting that the Reformation slogan *simul iustus et peccator* does not constitute "the center of Paul's conscious attitude to his personal sins."[7] This opening move displays the large topics that Stendahl attempts to rethink simultaneously: (1) the strong likelihood that centuries of obligatory relevance may have distorted Paul and occluded his robust conscience; (2) that "Jew" and "Gentile" are the proper categories for understanding Paul's enterprise; (3) that the law in Judaism did not function with the crushing force that it holds for Lutheran theology's law-grace dichotomy.

As Stendahl's argument proceeds, the first two topics receive influential subsidiary developments. Regarding the first topic, Stendahl argues that Romans 7 functions as an exploration of law rather than as an account of Paul's own conscience. Regarding the second, Stendahl emphasizes that Paul's reception of the gospel and his purpose in preaching, as narrated in Galatians 1:11–17, fit the model of a prophetic "call" rather than a religious "conversion" (i.e., from Judaism to Christianity). Stendahl effects his intervention into the first topic most thoroughly, but his influence on the interpretation of all of these issues has been defining and substantial.

After his first six paragraphs introduce his topic and concerns, Stendahl spends the next ten elucidating the shape and the influence of Luther's question, derived from Irish monasticism: "How can I find a gracious God?"[8] He tracks the formation of this orientation toward Paul from Augustine through to its existentialist philosophical formulation in Bultmann, and illumines the ways that it affects later understandings of Paul's teachings on justification by faith. Stendahl notes that Paul formulated this phrase in order to answer a question different than that of the Irish monastics, namely "the question about the place of Gentiles in the Church,"[9] a question that lost its force and relevance as Christianity became a more fully non-Jewish entity in the West.[10] In short, the situation that Paul had addressed through this formulation had passed, and Paul's meaning, read within a later and fundamentally different context, was transformed.

For twelve more paragraphs, after he introduces Romans 1—3 on page 208, Stendahl develops his account of Paul's robust conscience, with particular attention to contrasting Paul's self-estimate with traditional readings of Romans 7. He chronicles the transformation of the historical Paul's confident self-understanding to the later theological tradition's anthropology of depravity. The final six paragraphs of the essay defend the historical contingency of human ideologies and foci, and reiterate the peril of modernizing.[11] In contrast, Stendahl narrates a process of theological development of "Sacred History," which he sees as the true framework of Pauline theology. Paul's readers, he urges, need to acknowledge that later theological work can differ from "the Pauline original."[12]

INFLUENCES AND FORMATION

Stendahl recounts that in the 1950s, in the course of his work as a chaplain hearing student confessions, he began to perceive "the gap between Paul's thinking about Jews and Gentiles and the introspective Lutheran interpretation."[13] The first version of "The Introspective Conscience" appeared in Swedish,[14] and took English form as a plenary lecture delivered to the American Psychological Association.[15] The *Journal for the Scientific Study of Religion* prevailed upon Stendahl to publish a two-and-a-half-page summary of his lecture, which Stendahl described as "half-baked" and the editorial preface described as "explosive."[16] Stendahl also gave a version of the paper in March 1963 to the Harvard Roman Catholic-Protestant Colloquium. Finally, the paper reached the light of day in the *Harvard Theological Review* in 1963.

Beyond the article's dedication to Henry J. Cadbury and its citation of his work,[17] several earlier treatments of Paul contributed to "The Introspective Conscience." Stendahl explicitly acknowledges his debt to Johannes Munck's *Paulus und die Heilsgeschichte*.[18] Munck too had emphasized call, and its attendant psychological dimensions, though without the same opposition to conversion that Stendahl highlights. Munck also brought into focus Paul's role as apostle to the Gentiles. While Stendahl makes no reference to William Wrede and only one to Albert Schweitzer, both of these scholars preceded Stendahl in decentering a putative "doctrine" of justification by faith in Paul's thought. On this topic, Wrede's words particularly anticipate Stendahl's critique: "The Reformation has accustomed us to look upon this as the central point of Pauline doctrine: but it is not so." Instead, Wrede continues, it is a "polemical doctrine [*Kampfeslehre*]" that "only appears where Paul is dealing with the strife against Judaism."[19] Wrede was also prescient of Stendahl's psychological insight:

> It is quite possible that Paul underwent depressing experiences of this kind in his striving after salvation, and to this extent his picture may include an element of personal experience. But that does not prove in the least that just before his conversion his soul was full of this one feeling. His own assertion that as a Pharisee he had lived irreproachably in the Law does not support this notion—the less, as his conversion was before his eyes as he wrote. The truth is, the soul-strivings of Luther have stood as model for the portrait of Paul.[20]

Wrede does not build from these observations the same paradigm-shifting case that Stendahl mounts, but he stands as an important predecessor.

Stendahl also positioned himself within an important, though not in his time dominant, trajectory of understanding Judaism. In relation to the third large topic that Stendahl engages, regarding the picture of Judaism within which a historical interpretation of Paul must take place, he acknowledges the previous works of G. F. Moore, H. J. Schoeps, and W. D. Davies as well as of J. Munck. Thus when Stendahl writes, "It is pointed out that for the Jew the Law did not require a static or pedantic perfectionism but supposed a covenant relationship in which there was room for forgiveness and repentance and where God applied the Measure of Grace,"[21] he has phrased forcefully and directly a view that had been brewing slowly throughout the twentieth century and that reached an important culmination in the 1970s with the work of E. P. Sanders.[22]

1960S REACTIONS

The first reactions to Stendahl were appreciative, but they did not fully comprehend the significance of Stendahl's complex of arguments.[23] Then in 1969, Ernst Käsemann undertook an extensive counterargument to Stendahl's article.[24] Käsemann did not engage Stendahl closely, but argued that Stendahl had placed "salvation history" (*Heilsgeschichte*) at the center of Paul's thinking whereas, Käsemann insisted, justification (*Rechtfertigung*) stood as the apostle's primary commitment.[25] For English readers, Stendahl's emphasis might not be as clear as it was to Käsemann. Stendahl's claim that he has found "the framework of 'Sacred History'...to be that of Pauline theology" that "opens up a new perspective for systematic and practical theology," coupled with his reliance on Munck,[26] set Stendahl on the wrong side of a divide that Käsemann understood to have profound theological and political consequences. Käsemann suggested that salvation history, and theology of history more generally, was what had led German New Testament scholars to provide cover for Nazi eschatology. A theology of proclamation, he argued, had immunized his generation against "a conception of salvation history which broke in on us in secularized and political form with the Third Reich and its ideology."[27]

It is a painful irony that deep concern to avoid readings of history that abetted the horrors of Nazism—a concern felt strongly by both men—drove Stendahl and Käsemann to polemic against one another. It is also worth noting that Käsemann's counterarguments are overwhelmingly theological rather than historical. In the words of N. T.

Wright, Käsemann "lapsed into a dogmatic polemic."[28] This characterization may be unkind without being inaccurate.

Given his political concerns, Käsemann undertook an examination of Paul's "doctrine of justification" that, nearly a half-century later, reads jarringly:

> It has rightly been repeatedly noticed that the apostle's message of justification is a fighting doctrine, directed against Judaism [German: *antijudaistische Kampfeslehre*]. But to go on to say that, since this is so, it holds a subordinate place in Paul's theology, is an assertion which divides modern Protestantism inevitably and finally from the Reformers' interpretation of Paul and hence from the Reformation itself.[29]

Käsemann goes on to admit that "the doctrine undoubtedly grew up in the course of the anti-Jewish struggle [German: *antijudaistichen Kampf*] and stands or falls with this antithesis."[30] This sounds as if Protestantism and anti-Judaism are necessarily and eternally wed. Clearly, for Käsemann, three commitments precede his historical-critical act of reading: the unity or unanimity of Luther and Paul; a naturally antagonistic relationship between Christianity and Judaism as a framework for reading Paul's letters; and a general anti-Jewish struggle as the basic conflict and context of Paul's work. For Käsemann, Paul's driving question is a universal and timeless—"How can I find a gracious God?"[31]—rather than a particular and context specific, eschatological—"How can Gentiles be included in God's salvation of Israel?"

A second early reaction came from N. T. Wright. In his Tyndale House lecture in Cambridge University, "The Paul of History and the Apostle of Faith,"[32] Wright positioned himself as the scholar who could "incorporate the strengths of both parties while avoiding their weaknesses."[33] More polemically, Wright undertook a mission comparable to "Luther's double battle against Rome and the radical reformers."[34] For Wright, Käsemann is (to Käsemann's probable horror) Rome, and Stendahl is (to Stendahl's possible horror) a radical like Müntzer, Grebel, or Simons. Wright affirmed Stendahl's assessment of Paul's robust conscience,[35] and he prefigured Dunn's later argument that Paul had a problem with Judaism, namely its "ethnic pride."[36] Wright's article, and to some extent Wright's entire oeuvre, needs to be seen as a concerted effort to domesticate Stendahl's radical insight and to integrate it into the theological program so characteristic of Käsemann.

In 1976, Stendahl published a slim and eclectic volume that was meant to reinforce the argument of "The Introspective Conscience" while responding to Käsemann.[37] The first part of the work, "Paul among Jews and Gentiles," is organized around a series of five antitheses that distinguish Stendahl's interpretation of Paul from that of Lutheran tradition: call rather than conversion; justification rather than forgiveness; weakness rather than sin; love rather than integrity, and uniqueness rather than universality. Though he moves along a completely different hermeneutical path than that of Marcion, Stendahl too appreciated the rhetorical power of antitheses when attacking an established interpretation. In 1976, Stendahl understood that his thesis was, in his own words, "much more radical" than his critic Käsemann could recognize.[38] This remained true of the appropriation of Stendahl by scholars of the "New Perspective on Paul" that followed.

FEEDING THE NEW PERSPECTIVE

James Dunn's foundational article "The New Perspective on Paul" is popularly thought of as the commencement of the interpretive movement of the same name.[39] Dunn understands himself as building primarily off the work of E. P. Sanders. Dunn's retrospective acknowledges Stendahl and Wright more generously than Sanders had, noting in particular their deployments of the notion of a "new perspective."[40] In Dunn's words,

> If Stendahl cracked the mould of twentieth century reconstructions of Paul's theological context, by showing how much it had been determined by Luther's quest for a gracious God, Sanders has broken it altogether by showing how different these reconstructions are from what we know of first-century Judaism from other sources.[41]

In 1977, E. P. Sanders published the work that, for Dunn and many others, completely changed—or should have changed—the New Testament guild's view of late Second Temple Judaism. In his work on Judaism,

Sanders scarcely referred to Stendahl. In his work on Paul, however, Sanders noted the Stendahl-Käsemann debate and positioned himself, like Wright, as a mediator.[42]

At this point, we should pause to analyze Stendahl's influence by means of the three large topics outlined above, namely (1) Paul's robust conscience (that is, Romans 7 is not autobiographical); (2) Paul's concern with his "call" to preach to Gentiles; and (3) Jewish covenant as religion of repentance and grace rather than of legalism.

Regarding Paul's "robust" conscience, Sanders stands squarely in Stendahl's debt.[43] This is part of a larger movement of revaluing the communitarian dimension of Paul's thinking.[44] A year after *Paul and Palestinian Judaism* was published, Sanders offered an article evaluating the work of Stendahl and W. D. Davies. In this essay, Sanders also stands with Stendahl in removing the individual's justification by faith from the center of Paul's thought.[45] Oddly, Sanders does not treat Romans 7 in this evaluation of Stendahl, nor does his treatment of Romans 7 in *Paul, the Law, and the Jewish People* undertake a dialogue either with Stendahl or with Kümmel.[46] In later work, however, Sanders wrote that "one of the keystones of Bultmann's position—the centrality of 'anthropology' and of Romans 7—was destroyed by Krister Stendahl" in "The Introspective Conscience."[47]

Sanders affirmed and further developed Stendahl's emphasis on Paul's concern with the inclusion of the Gentiles and his call to preach to the Gentiles. Sanders noted that "it is an argument from silence, but nevertheless a striking one, to observe that there is not a single passage to indicate that there was a single Jewish member in any of the churches founded by Paul."[48] Nevertheless, Sanders persists in understanding many of Paul's statements to be about both Gentiles and Jews, treating deictic speech—where "all" or "only" have their reference restricted to a particular context—as systematic universal speech. Moreover, Sanders's work on Paul has a clear commitment to understanding Paul as discussing "universal fact[s]," "universal sinfulness," "the universal human plight," and so on.[49]

On the third topic—a covenant of repentance and grace rather than legalism—Sanders undertook in *Paul and Palestinian Judaism* a massive investigation justifying and extending the insight that Stendahl articulates, though with reference to other scholars rather than to Stendahl, analyzing an immense body of primary literature.[50] Stendahl, in brief, anticipated in a small way what Sanders achieved in a monumental way. On the whole, Sanders acknowledges, but is not fully moved by, the cumulative force of Stendahl's arguments.

By contrast, Wright, as noted above, begins his scholarly interaction with Stendahl by forging a mediating position in Stendahl's debate with Käsemann. This disposition to blunt insights that expose a gulf between historical-critical and ecclesiastical readings is characteristic of Wright. He seems most willing to appropriate Stendahl's claim concerning Paul's robust conscience, but persists in maintaining the notion that "Paul had a problem with Judaism." To this end, he deploys various strategies: Paul, he claims, was critical of Jewish "'national righteousness', a putative Jewish belief that fleshly descent guarantees membership of God's true covenant people";[51] that the continuity of "the pagan world under the power of evil" troubled Paul;[52] or that Paul thought Roman hegemony implied that God has not fulfilled his promises to Israel.[53] Wright is persuaded that Paul did not suffer a paralyzing introspective guilt brought on by an insurmountable "burden" of keeping the law. At the same time, he is committed to the idea that Paul was deeply critical of the Jewish practice of Judaism. Wright is, in fact, more committed to the principle of Pauline dissatisfaction with Judaism than he is to the attribution of any particular criticism of Judaism to Paul. Like Sanders, Wright understands Paul to consistently address "universal sin."[54] Wright remains careful to refrain from caricaturing "legalistic Judaism," though his early work is perhaps clearest.[55]

So much for the first and third aspects of Stendahl's major contribution. Regarding the second—seeing "Jew" and "Gentile" as the proper categories for reading Paul, and seeing Paul's Damascus event as a call rather than conversion—Wright does not fully commit. For Wright, as admittedly for Stendahl, "Christian" plays a synthesizing and superseding role that vitiates Stendahl's and Wrede's insights that Paul's statements about justification were formulated as a solution to the problem of integrating Gentiles into the benefits of God's covenant with Abraham and his descendants.[56]

On the issue of call and conversion, Wright presumes to school Stendahl:

> Krister Stendahl's suggestion that we should think of Paul's "call" as opposed to his "conversion" misses the point. For Paul, the word "call" denoted not merely a vocation to a particular task but also, more fundamentally, the effective call of the gospel, applied by the Spirit to the individual heart and life and resulting in a turning away from idolatry and sin and a lifelong turning to God in Christ in believing allegiance.[57]

In what way Paul, a Jew blameless under the law (Phil 3:6), understood himself to be called to turn away from idolatry is something Wright does not (and perhaps cannot) explain. Committed mediation evidently entails distortion.

James Dunn, in "The New Perspective on Paul" (1983), sought to synthesize the insights of Stendahl's "Introspective Conscience" and of Sanders's *Paul and Palestinian Judaism* into a new reading of Paul unobscured by "Lutheran spectacles"—to see afresh Paul's enterprise as driven by the concern to include Gentiles in God's promises to Israel.[58] For Dunn, Stendahl "cracked the mould" that Sanders went on to break.[59] After Stendahl and Sanders, Paul was never the same for Dunn. A new perspective had been opened on the apostle.[60]

For the perception that the law functioned in Second Temple Judaism as a framework for grace and repentance, Dunn gave full and proper credit to Sanders's magnum opus rather than to Stendahl's brief remarks.[61] Turning to the question of reading Paul, Dunn generously notes how far ahead of the curve Krister Stendahl was in understanding the pernicious power of Luther's crises of introspection when attempting to read Paul historically rather than dogmatically.[62] Dunn adopts Stendahl's view that Paul's notion of "justification by faith" addressed a communal rather than an individual problem.[63] Stendahl also—in coordination with Kümmel—decisively turned Dunn around on the interpretation of Romans 7, moving him away from an autobiographical reading of the text.[64] For his own part, Dunn coins the metaphor that endures as a paraphrase of Stendahl's argument: Luther's spectacles distort a historical-critical reading of Paul.[65]

Dunn also affirmed Stendahl's observation that Paul was "grappling with the question about the place of the Gentiles in the Church and in the plan of God, with the problem Jew/Gentiles or Jewish Christians/Gentile Christians."[66] Calling justification by faith "a polemical doctrine" (echoing

Wrede and Käsemann), Dunn writes that "'justification by faith' was Paul's answer to the question: How is it that Gentiles can be equally acceptable to God as Jews?"[67] More commonly, however, Dunn understands Paul to be struggling on account of his dissatisfaction with Israel or with Judaism, caused by what Dunn characterizes as Jewish "boasting," understanding the covenant as an ethnic privilege.[68] For Dunn, the Lutheran problem of individual pride in works is replaced by a national problem of Israel's pride in covenant.

Like Wright, Dunn seeks to tame the force of Stendahl's contentions. Admitting that Paul's teachings on justification by faith "grew out of his Gentile mission," Dunn insists that "its relevance was not limited to that mission."[69] Similarly, Dunn integrates Stendahl's conviction that the language of conversion distorts Paul's experience as narrated in Galatians 1:11–17, but he suggests that "calling" was part of an experience rightly described as a conversion.[70]

The legacy of "The Introspective Conscience" in the New Perspective and in German studies of Paul remains both significant and ambiguous. Stendahl inspired the polemic of Käsemann, but also the complex appropriations of Sanders, Wright, Dunn, and many others, all of whom tamed the force of his intervention. Still, Stendahl played a key role in resurrecting the generative ideas of Johannes Munck, concerning Paul's focus on community rather than the individual (which Käsemann denigrated when formulated as *Heilsgeschichte*, the title of Munck's German original) and concerning the appropriateness of "call" over "conversion"—by implication to another religion, Christianity—as a mode of understanding the events that Paul narrates in Galatians 1. So also the work of Wrede, concerning the context of the formulation justification by faith in the larger enterprise of integrating Gentiles into the benefits of the covenants made by the God of Israel. Indebted to Kümmel, Stendahl participated in turning the interpretation of Romans 7 away from autobiographical and theologically anthropological modes of understanding. The New Perspective under Sanders, Dunn, and Wright was unable or unwilling to embrace the full force of Stendahl's arguments.

RADICALIZING THE NEW PERSPECTIVE

While the New Perspective has been driven by the tension between conservation and revolution, another trajectory in the reading of Paul has deemed revolution necessary. Named sometimes by means of its early academic proponents (the "Stendahl-Gaston-Gager" reading),[71] by characterizations of "ways" for Jews and Gentiles (the *Sonderweg* reading, the "two covenants" reading),[72] sometimes by descriptions of the eschatological convictions that made such a conception possible (the *Sonderzeit* reading),[73] or by the religious identity by which Paul understood himself (the "Paul within Judaism" reading),[74] the approach has been dubbed by Magnus Zetterholm "the Radical New Perspective."[75] Without pronouncing on which name is proper, I will here, in honor of Stendahl's own description of his argument as "radical," call this trajectory by that name. Scholars participating in this movement have sought to extend insights that lie at the root/*radix* of Stendahl's 1963 intervention into the basis of a renewed and more historically responsible reading of Paul.

Even before N. T. Wright worked in 1978 at Tyndale House in Cambridge to tame Stendahl's insights, Lloyd Gaston presented a paper to the Canadian Society of Biblical Studies in Quebec City in the summer of 1977. Extending Stendahl's insights, Gaston suggested a way of reading Paul that more fully implemented his critique of the traditional interpretation. This is worth noting and recording: the Radical New Perspective is, by this reckoning, an earlier and a more fundamental appropriation of Stendahl's "The Introspective Conscience" than was the New Perspective, whether the latter is dated to Wright (1978) or to Dunn (1983).[76] Thus the Radical New Perspective is not simply *re*active, but also *pro*active.

Three key ideas from Gaston's work and from his colleagues' development of it have driven the Radical New Perspective: (1) Paul's enterprise was fully oriented to Gentiles; (2) Paul himself fully expected an imminent eschatological event; (3) the category "Christian" must be avoided when attempting to interpret Paul within his own historical context. Stendahl's arguments provided a template understanding of Paul that was more radical, and more revolutionary, than the one that Stendahl actually himself undertook.[77]

FULL ORIENTATION TO GENTILES

Scholars of the Radical New Perspective, taking Stendahl's point that Paul was chiefly concerned to integrate Gentiles into the benefits of God's covenant with Israel, understand that Paul saw himself as apostle to Gentiles.[78] Stendahl phrases this process as "the possibility for Gentiles to be included in the messianic community" or "the possibility of Gentiles becoming Christians."[79] From the vantage of the Radical New Perspective, this latter formulation is deeply problematic, because it embodies assumptions that actually work against a historical-critical understanding of Paul. Nevertheless, Stendahl started this ball rolling.

Gaston, extending in 1977 Stendahl's line of thought, commented that "Paul writes to Gentile Christians, dealing with Gentile Christian problems, foremost among which was the right of Gentiles qua Gentiles, without adopting the Torah of Israel, to full citizenship in the people of God."[80] Gaston infers from the identity of this audience that when Paul discusses Jewish law in general or circumcision (for example) in particular, Paul speaks specifically to *how such issues relate to Gentiles*. Thus we do not know from Paul's discussion of the value of circumcision for Gentiles what he thinks of the value of circumcision for Jews.

Combining Stendahl's insight about Paul's context and audience with his conviction that what Paul might have meant is not necessarily what Paul came to mean, Gaston broadened the argument.[81] Stendahl recognized that Paul's discourse cannot be considered ahistorically univocal. Gaston follows this through to see that Paul's pronouncements on topics, such as law, understood by later Christians as universal, are in their original context particular to Paul's address to his Gentile audience. Stendahl's formulation is the slippery slope that Käsemann recoiled from, labeling this view *Heilsgeschichte* and knowing how (in)human and political a hermeneutic of adaptation to current context can be. Though Stendahl and Gaston remained theologically engaged all their careers, they took seriously the human and political character, the contingency in time and place, of the work of a human historical actor like Paul.

This notion of a complete practical and discursive orientation toward Gentiles formed the basis of particular conceptions, such as Gaston's conviction that Torah functioned as an instrument of condemnation for Gentiles, but as an instrument of reconciliation for Jews.[82] This conviction of complete practical and discursive orientation to Gentiles is characteristic of most scholars of the Radical New Perspective.[83]

ESCHATOLOGICAL CONTEXT

Another development of the Radical New Perspective has been to emphasize the eschatological character of Paul's thought. Stendahl focused only minimally on eschatology.[84] Nevertheless, his insight that Paul was "transformed" applies not only to Paul's commitment to a non-Jewish demographic, but also to his being transformatively reinterpreted once second-century Gentile Christians had to meaningfully deal with the obvious lack of any eschatological culmination or return of Christ. If Paul was to retain relevance through the immense changes from the first to the fifth century, he had to be radically and ahistorically reinterpreted.

Gager was the first within the Radical New Perspective to see the fundamental importance of failed eschatology for later Christian interpretations of Paul, though he credits Gaston for the idea.[85] For Gager, eschatology was for Paul an "all-consuming orientation,"[86] and an "intense eschatological mentality underlies his every thought and action." "Paul's preoccupation with the Gentiles remains incomprehensible apart from his eschatological framework."[87] This concern with the eschatological frame of Paul's thought is an important temporal complement to the historicizing impulse. What facilitates an understanding of Paul's enterprise as particular in its audience and in its admonitions and pronouncements is, partially but significantly, Paul's own understanding of himself as living in an extremely special time, the crowded and short span between the resurrection of the Christ and the Christ's return.[88]

NON-CHRISTIAN(ITY)

The combination of two of Stendahl's prime ideas—that Paul focused on Gentiles, and that he was called rather than "converted"—propelled another radical revolution, namely, that that the term and concept *Christian* is itself deeply problematic when questing for the historical Paul. Stanley Stowers was the first to highlight the conceptual problems of the term *Christianity* in a study that attempted to move beyond the New Perspective.[89] Gager, summarizing Stendahl's achievement, extends his teacher's insight thusly: "We should not speak of Paul's conversion as if it implied a transfer out of Judaism; he has no concept of Christianity or of his gospel as a new religion."[90] Given that Stendahl had repeatedly characterized Paul as a Christian, Paul's audience as Christians, and

"Christianity" as a social construct operative in the first century,[91] Gager drew out an implication for which Stendahl's context in the early 1960s could not itself make room. Learning why and how to forsake such a traditional category as Christianity took time and distance. The question of terminology, especially of the appropriateness of the terms *Christian* and *Christianity*, has been an intense focus of reflection and development for scholars of the Radical New Perspective.[92]

Individual articulations of the Radical New Perspective have, of course, offered particular lines of interpretation of Paul's enterprise in keeping with the premises that guide them. The Radical New Perspective continually returns to Stendahl's 1963 intervention for inspiration on how to read the arguments of Paul's texts. How a discipline does so remains both a scholarly and a human problem.

CONCLUSION

Stendahl's "Introspective Conscience" has been changing the course of scholarship on Paul for more than half a century. It generated the New Perspective on Paul, perhaps the most influential current in contemporary Pauline scholarship. Stendahl's article also generated the Radical New Perspective on Paul, which has in turn sought to extend his insights and free them from the curtailments that New Perspective scholars often undertook.[93]

Stendahl inspired the Radical New Perspective, and he saw its early fruits. He was unable to anticipate in his 1963 work the ways in which his thought would be developed by later scholars, but some forty years later, his comment on the back cover Gager's *Reinventing Paul* (2000) endorsed that effort:

> It took the twentieth century to see that Paul meant it when he said that he was Apostle to the Gentiles–and not to the Jews. When that sinks in, one sees a very different Paul. With zest and consistency Gager now presents that picture and tells us why it took so long to hear what Paul once wrote to his Gentile converts.

Stendahl understood that it had taken a century—from Wrede's recognition of the polemical context of Paul's thinking on justification, through his own initial intervention in 1963, to Gager's second effort at a Radical New Perspective in his 2000 publication—for basic insights to sink in. The work continues in the twenty-first century, and Stendahl's mid-twentieth-century synthesis and advancement continues to influence cutting-edge scholarship on Paul.

NOTES

1. N. T. Wright, *What Saint Paul Really Said: Was Paul of Tarsus the Real Founder of Christianity?* (Grand Rapids, MI: Eerdmans, 1997), 190; Terence L. Donaldson, "Paul within Judaism: A Critical Evaluation from a 'New Perspective' Perspective," in *Paul within Judaism: Restoring the First-Century Context to the Apostle*, ed. Mark D. Nanos and Magnus Zetterholm (Minneapolis: Fortress, 2015), 278n2; Ben Witherington, *Paul's Narrative Thought World: The Tapestry of Tragedy and Triumph* (Louisville, KY: Westminster John Knox Press, 1994), 33; and Stanley K. Stowers, *A Rereading of Romans: Justice, Jews, and Gentiles* (New Haven, CT: Yale University Press, 1994), 6, respectively.

2. Krister Stendahl, "The Apostle Paul and the Introspective Conscience of the West," *Harvard Theological Review* 56 (1963): 199–215. Hereafter referred to as "The Introspective Conscience."

3. Stephen Westerholm, "Justification by Faith Is the Answer: What Is the Question?," *Concordia Theological Quarterly* 70 (2006): 197.

4. Krister Stendahl, *Paul among Jews and Gentiles and Other Essays* (Minneapolis: Fortress, 1976).

5. James D. G. Dunn, "The New Perspective: What, Whence, and Whither?," in *The New Perspective on Paul: Collected Essays* (Tübingen: Mohr Siebeck, 2005), 29n109. NB: Revised edition published by Eerdmans, Grand Rapids, MI, 2008.

6. Stendahl, "Introspective Conscience," 199–200.

7. Ibid., 202.

8. Ibid., 203.

9. Ibid., 204.

10. "This problem was, however, not a live one after the end of the first century, when Christianity for all practical purposes had a non-Jewish constituency" ibid., 205. Cf. 207 "...once the original framework of 'Jews and Gentiles' is lost...."

11. Ibid., 214.

12. Ibid., 215.

13. Krister Stendahl, *Final Account: Paul's Letter to the Romans* (Minneapolis: Fortress, 1995), xi.

14. Krister Stendahl, "Paulus och samvetet," *Svensk exegetisk årsbok* 25 (1960): 62–77.

15. For the context in the history of psychology that led a divinity professor to give an invited address, see Pamela E. Klassen and John W. Marshall, "Saint as Cipher: Paul, Badiou, and the Politics of Ritual Repudiation," *History of Religions* 51 (2012): 353.

16. Krister Stendahl, "Working Paper and Notes: The Apostle Paul and the Introspective Conscience of the West," *JSSR* 1 (1962): 261.

17. Henry J. Cadbury, *The Peril of Modernizing Jesus* (New York: Macmillan, 1937).

18. Johannes Munck, *Paulus und die Heilsgeschichte* (Copenhagen: Munksgaard, 1954), trans. by Frank Clarke as *Paul and the Salvation of Mankind* (Richmond, VA: John Knox Press, 1959). See Stendahl, *Paul among Jews and Gentiles*, vi, viii.

19. William Wrede, *Paul,* trans. Edward Lummis (London: Philip Green, 1907), 123.

20. Ibid., 145–46. The German original of the last sentence reads, "Die Wahrheit ist: die Seelenkämpfe Luthers haben für dies Bild des Paulus Modell gestanden." William Wrede, *Paulus* (Tübingen: J.C.B. Mohr, 1904), 83.

21. Stendahl, "Introspective Conscience," 201.

22. Sanders chronicles the inchoate, and sometimes contradictory, trajectory of understanding a more varied view of Second Temple and rabbinic Judaism that also included C. G. Montefiore, S. Schechter, J. Parkes, S. Sandmel, and E. R. Goodenough. See E. P. Sanders, *Paul and Palestinian Judaism: A Comparison of Patterns of Religion* (Philadelphia: Fortress, 1977), 4–12.

23. David Stanley was the invited respondent to Stendahl's 1963 conference presentation of "The Introspective Conscience." Stanley's generally positive response described the project as "accurate," but he really understood only the argument about robust conscience and the repositioning of Romans 7. See "Some Reflections on the Introspective Conscience from New Testament Data," in *Ecumenical Dialogue at Harvard: The Roman Catholic-Protestant Colloquium,* ed. Samuel H. Miller and G. Ernest Wright (Cambridge, MA: Belknap Press, 1964), 257–61. Articles in 1967 by Joseph Fitzmeyer ("Saint Paul and the Law," *Jurist* 27 [1967]: 18–36) and George Howard ("On the 'Faith of Christ,'" *Harvard Theological Review* 60 [1967]: 459–65) offer early positive appropriations of Stendahl's argument.

24. Ernst Käsemann, "Justification and Salvation History in the Epistle to the Romans," in *Perspectives on Paul*, trans. Margaret Kohl (Philadelphia: Fortress,1971), 60–78.

25. Ibid., 60–61.

26. Stendahl, "Introspective Conscience," 95. Note also the original German title of Munck's *Paulus und die Heilsgeschichte*, cited by Stendahl in its English translation, *Paul and the Salvation of Mankind*.

27. Käsemann, "Justification and Salvation History," 64.

28. N. T. Wright, "The Paul of History and the Apostle of Faith," *Tyndale Bulletin* 29 (1978): 64.

29. Käsemann, "Justification and Salvation History," 70.

30. Ibid., 71. In both instances on page 70 and 71, Käsemann uses *antijudaistische* rather than *antijüdisch*. I have not presumed to modify Margaret Kohl's translation, but to be fair to Käsemann, the possibility that he chose *antijudaistische* in order to specify "Judaizing" deserves consideration.

31. Ibid., 74.

32. Wright, "Paul of History and the Apostle of Faith."

33. Ibid., 71. The parties are Stendahl and Käsemann.

34. Ibid., 79.

35. Ibid., 63.

36. Ibid., 65. "If we ask how it is that Israel has missed her vocation, Paul's answer is that she is guilty not of 'legalism' or 'works-righteousness' but of what I call 'national righteousness', the belief that fleshly Jewish descent guarantees membership of God's true covenant people."

37. Stendahl, *Paul among Jews and Gentiles*. The work includes a revised version of lectures he gave 1963 and 1964, reprints of his 1963 essay, the text of an address from 1972 and of a later conference paper published in 1975, as well as a direct response to Käsemann and Bornkamm.

38. Ibid., 130.

39. James D. G. Dunn, "The New on Paul," *Bulletin of the John Rylands Library* 65 (1983): 95–122. The material was first delivered as a Manson Memorial Lecture in Manchester.

40. Dunn, "New Perspective: What, Whence, and Whither?," 6n24.

41. Dunn, "New Perspective on Paul," 100.

42. Sanders, *Paul and Palestinian Judaism*, 436–38.

43. Ibid., 436.

44. E.g., Munck, *Paul and the Salvation of Mankind*, 42 on Romans 9—11.

45. E. P. Sanders, "Paul's Attitude toward the Jewish People," *Union Seminary Quarterly Review* 33 (1978): 175.

46. E. P. Sanders, *Paul, the Law, and the Jewish People* (Philadelphia: Fortress, 1983), 71–80.

47. E. P. Sanders, *Paul: A Brief Insight* (New York: Sterling, 2009), 204.

48. Sanders, "Paul's Attitude toward the Jewish People," 178.

49. Sanders, *Paul, the Law, and the Jewish People*, 35, 72.

50. Sanders, *Paul and Palestinian Judaism*. Sanders introduces the term *covenantal nomism* at the end of his discussion of Tannaitic literature (236) and develops it extensively in his synthesis on Palestinian Judaism (422–28).

51. Wright, "Paul of History and the Apostle of Faith," 65. See also ibid., 71: "We must see justification by faith as a polemical doctrine, whose target is not the usual Lutheran one of 'nomism' or 'Menschenwerke', but the Pauline one of Jewish national pride."

52. N. T. Wright, "The Letter to the Galatians: Exegesis and Theology," in *Between Two Horizons: Spanning New Testament Studies and Systematic Theology*, ed. Joel B. Green and Max Turner (Grand Rapids, MI: Eerdmans, 2000), 217.

53. N. T. Wright, "Paul in Current Anglophone Scholarship," *Expository Times* 123, no. 8 (2012): 378.

54. N. T. Wright, "Justification: The Biblical Basis and Its Relevance for Contemporary Evangelicalism," in *The Great Acquittal: Justification by Faith and Current Christian Thought*, ed. Gavin Reid (London: Collins, 1980), 26, 30; Wright, *What Saint Paul Really Said*, 129; Wright, *Paul: In Fresh Perspective* (Minneapolis: Fortress, 2005), 65, 119.

55. Wright, "Paul of History and the Apostle of Faith," 78. "My case here is simply stated: the tradition of Pauline interpretation has manufactured a false Paul by manufacturing a false Judaism for him to oppose."

56. See Wright, *Paul: In Fresh Perspective*, 36. "This is where the so-called 'new perspective' has made one of its necessary points—that every time Paul discusses justification he seems simultaneously to be talking about Gentile inclusion—but has not, usually, shown how this integrates with the traditional view that he is talking about how sinners are put right with God." Wright's mediating—and vitiating—enterprise is ubiquitous.

57. N. T. Wright, "New Perspectives on Paul," in *Justification in Perspective: Historical Developments and Contemporary Challenges*, ed. Bruce McCormack (Grand Rapids, MI: Baker Academic, 2006), 256.

58. Dunn, "New Perspective on Paul," 99ff.; James D. G. Dunn, *The Theology of the Apostle Paul* (Grand Rapids, MI: Eerdmans, 1998), 501.

59. Dunn, "New Perspective on Paul," 100.

60. Dunn, "New Perspective: What, Whence, and Whither?," 29n109.

61. Dunn, "New Perspective on Paul," 97. Dunn indicates his conviction that no recent studies of Paul "have succeeded in, to use a contemporary phrase, 'breaking the mould' of Pauline studies, the mold into which descriptions of Paul's work and thought have regularly been poured for many decades now. There is, in my judgment, only one work written during the past decade or two which deserves that accolade. I refer to the volume entitled *Paul and Palestinian Judaism* by E. P. Sanders of McMaster University in Canada."

62. Ibid., 98. "As Krister Stendahl warned twenty years ago, it is deceptively easy to read Paul in the light of Luther's agonized search for relief from a troubled conscience."

63. Ibid., 121. "All this confirms the earlier important thesis of Stendahl, that Paul's doctrine of justification by faith should not be understood primarily as an exposition of the individual's relation to God, but primarily in the context of Paul the Jew wrestling with the question of how Jews and Gentiles stand in relation to each other within the covenant purpose of God now reached its climax in Jesus Christ."

64. Dunn, "The New Perspective: What, Whence, and Whither?," 17n76; James D. G. Dunn, "The Justice of God: A Renewed Perspective on Justification by Faith (The Henton Davies Lecture, Regents Park College, Oxford, January 1991)," *Journal of Theological Studies* 43 (1992): 4–5.

65. Dunn, "New Perspective on Paul," 99.

66. Stendahl, "Introspective Conscience," 204.

67. Dunn, *Theology of Paul the Apostle*, 340, cf. 501.

68. Dunn, "New Perspective on Paul," 114, 118. This theme recurs throughout Dunn's oeuvre.

69. Dunn, "New Perspective: What, Whence, and Whither?," 37n151.

70. James D. G. Dunn, *The New Perspective on Paul: Collected Essays* (Tübingen: Mohr Siebeck, 2005), 357–58.

71. Alan F. Segal, *Paul the Convert: The Apostolate and Apostasy of Saul the Pharisee* (New Haven, CT: Yale University Press, 1990), 146.

72. First used perhaps as a label in Reidar Hvalvik, "A 'Sonderweg' for Israel: A Critical Examination of a Current Interpretation of Romans 11.25–27," *Journal for the Study of the New Testament* 38 (1990): 87–107. For a history of the term's earlier deployment and criticism thereof in Mussner,

Gaston, and Gager, see Terence L. Donaldson, "Jewish Christianity, Israel's Stumbling and the *Sonderweg* Reading of Paul," *Journal for the Study of the New Testament* 29 (2006): 28n4.

73. John W. Marshall, "Misunderstanding the New Paul: Marcion's Transformation of the *Sonderzeit* Paul," *Journal of Early Christian Studies* 20 (2012): 1–29.

74. Nanos and Zetterholm, *Paul within Judaism.* See also Pamela Eisenbaum, "Paul, Polemics, and the Problem of Essentialism," *Biblical Interpretation* 13 (2005): 224–38.

75. Magnus Zetterholm, *Approaches to Paul: A Student's Guide to Recent Scholarship* (Minneapolis: Fortress, 2009), 191. Scholars of the Radical New Perspective and their works, many of which follow in discussion below, are no more unified than any other scholarly trajectory, but they possess a coherence in their agreement with key elements of Stendahl's critique and their conviction that moving beyond the New Perspective's appropriation of Stendahl and reading of Paul is a matter of crucial historical-critical responsibility.

76. Sanders, *Paul and Palestinian Judaism,* properly complicates this claim. I have not been able to uncover the prepublication presentation history of the work that underlay this book.

77. In 1963, Stendahl did not see any problem in calling Paul or his Gentile followers Christians, as he was still wedded to a stronger measure of universalism than characterizes the current Radical New Perspective. As for many after him, "Jewish Christianity" seemed a valuable mediating concept. Inasmuch as we accept his endorsement of Gager's *Reinventing Paul* as a considered statement of position, we see Stendahl developing his position further than his 1976 work. For a helpful overview of the Radical New Perspective, see Magnus Zetterholm, "Paul within Judaism: The State of the Questions," in Nanos and Zetterholm, *Paul within Judaism*, 31–51.

78. Stendahl, "Introspective Conscience," 204, 205.

79. Ibid., 206.

80. Lloyd Gaston, *Paul and the Torah* (Vancouver: University of British Columbia Press, 1987), 23.

81. Stendahl, *Paul among Jews and Gentiles*, 125.

82. Gaston, *Paul and the Torah*, 28; John G. Gager, *The Origins of Anti-Semitism: Attitudes toward Judaism in Pagan and Christian Antiquity* (New York: Oxford University Press, 1983), 237–38.

83. For developments of this insight, see Gager, *Origins of Anti-Semitism*, 207; Stowers, *A Rereading of Romans*, 36; Paula Fredriksen, "Jesus

the Jewish Christ," *Studia Theologica—Nordic Journal of Theology* 66 (2012): 6; Paula Fredriksen, "Judaizing the Nations: The Ritual Demands of Paul's Gospel," *New Testament Studies* 56 (2010): 232–52; Caroline Johnson Hodge, *If Sons, Then Heirs: A Study of Kinship and Ethnicity in the Letters of Paul* (Oxford: Oxford University Press, 2007); Pamela Eisenbaum, *Paul Was Not a Christian: The Original Message of a Misunderstood Apostle* (New York: HarperOne, 2009), 60–62.

84. Stendahl, "Introspective Conscience," 210.

85. Gager, *Origins of Anti-Semitism*, 201.

86. John G. Gager, *Reinventing Paul* (New York: Oxford University Press, 2000), 61.

87. Ibid., 62. See also Gager, *Origins of Anti-Semitism*, 201, 208, 226, 259–60.

88. Other scholars who seek to move beyond the New Perspective have also emphasized eschatology, e.g., Fredriksen, "Judaizing the Nations"; Fredriksen, "Jesus the Jewish Christ," 6. Marshall, "Misunderstanding the New Paul," describes his reading of Paul as a *Sonderzeit* reading, to emphasize the eschatological conditions of its plausibility.

89. Stowers, *Rereading of Romans*, 23–24, 241, 251.

90. Gager, *Reinventing Paul*, 45. Albert Schweitzer stands generations ahead of the Radical New Perspective on this insight: "For him [Paul] there was only one religion: that of Judaism. 'Christianity' is for Paul no new religion, but simply Judaism with the centre of gravity shifted in consequence of the new era. His own system of thought is certainly for him no new religion." Albert Schweitzer, *Paul and His Interpreters: A Critical History*, trans. W. Montgomery (London: A&C Black, 1912), 227; cited in Fredriksen, "Jesus the Jewish Christ," 17n16.

91. Stendahl, "Introspective Conscience," 215, 206, 205 respectively.

92. Gaston does not face this question, even as his conviction of Paul's complete practical and discursive orientation toward Gentiles informs the entire Radical New Perspective. Gager moves from cautiously using the concept of "Christian" to fully forswearing it (e.g., op. cit., 258–64). Similarly, Gager moves from dismissiveness about the call/conversion distinction and embrace of the psychology of conversion ("Some Notes on Paul's Conversion," *NTS* 27 [1981]: 697–704), to ambivalence (*Origins of Anti-Semitism*, 209–10) to strong endorsement of the distinction and its significance (*Reinventing Paul*, 53–54). Fredriksen embraces the value of a distinction between calling and conversion and yet could not retire fully the term *Christian* for individuals in Paul's context: "Mandatory Retirement: Ideas in the Study of Christian

Origins Whose Time Has Come to Go," *Studies in Religion/Sciences Religieuses* 35 (2006): 234. At the same time, she demonstrates awareness and appreciation that it does not apply to the very situation to which she applies it, by the next page writing, "Using 'convert' or 'conversion' to describe either Paul or his Gentiles implicitly but necessarily posits that Christianity was already something other than Judaism." She laments her own past calling of Paul's Gentiles as converts: "If we slip into calling them 'converts'—as I, alas, have routinely done—then we confuse the very situation that we are trying to describe." Anders Runesson makes a strong case against "Christianity and Christian as designators of Paul and Pauline Gentiles loyal to Christ." Together with Nanos, Runesson has suggested that "Paul and his communities" have become practitioners of "Apostolic Judaism." See "Inventing Christian Identity: Paul, Ignatius, and Theodosius I," in *Exploring Early Christian Identity*, ed. Bengt Holmberg (Tubingen: Mohr Siebeck, 2008), 72–74.

Likewise, Carolyn Johnson Hodge is steadfast in understanding Paul's audience as Gentiles rather than as "Christians." She points out the tension in Paul's "two kinds of Gentiles," namely the audience and the negative example from which Paul hopes his audiences will distinguish themselves. See "The Question of Identity: Gentiles as Gentiles—but Also Not—in Pauline Communities," in Nanos and Zetterholm, *Paul within Judaism*, 155–59. Hodge's earlier monograph participates in the focus on Gentiles and the attendant abstinence of understanding Paul's audience as Christian and further sharpens the inquiry into the ethnic and gendered quality of these kinship and classificatory concepts (*If Sons, Then Heirs*).

With regard to the concepts *Christian* and *Christianity*, Mark Nanos presents one of the most complex cases within the Radical New Perspective. Nanos argues that Paul remained programmatically Torah observant and instructed the Gentiles to whom he wrote to respect such observance by Jews and to undertake practices that closely—though not completely!—resembled Torah observance by Jews. In his landmark foray into the interpretation of Romans, Nanos tends to use *Christian* as an adjective supporting formulations such as *Gentile Christian* or *Jewish Christian*; that is to say, he overwhelmingly uses *Christian* as an adjective rather than a substantive. Yet occasionally *Christian* and *Christianity* become substantives in Nanos's own discourse (*The Mystery of Romans: The Jewish Context of Paul's Letter* [Minneapolis: Fortress Press, 1996], 68, 72, 108, 116, 144, 159). In later work, Nanos more fully forswears the analytical use of *Christian* and *Christianity*.

Marshall has suggested that the category *Christian/Christianity*, in fact, largely undermines the entire Radical New Perspective ("Misunderstanding the New Paul," 6). More than any other scholar, Pamela Eisenbaum has most fully made abstinence from the conceptions of *Christian* and *Christianity* programmatic for her work (*Paul Was Not a Christian*). It is clear that in our continued reflection on our conceptual apparatus for reading Paul, we need to exercise generosity to those on whose shoulders we stand, who enable us to see what they attempted to discern. We should be fortunate to be in the same generative—and yet vulnerable—position.

93. New Perspective appropriations of "Introspective Conscience" consistently included appreciation and internalization of some of Stendahl's insights. An alternate strategy to trace the article's influence would be to track dedicated opposition to it and endeavors to refute it by traditional scholars of Paul, e.g., Stephen Westerholm, "The 'New Perspective' at Twenty-Five," in *Justification and Variegated Nomism*, vol. 2, *The Paradoxes of Paul*, ed. D. A. Carson, Peter T. O'Brien, and Mark A. Seifrid (Tübingen: Mohr Siebeck, 2001), 1–38; Stephen Westerholm, *Perspectives Old and New on Paul: The "Lutheran" Paul and His Critics* (Grand Rapids, MI: Eerdmans, 2004); Westerholm, "Justification by Faith Is the Answer: What Is the Question?"; Paul C. Maxwell, "Analyzing the Apostle Paul's 'Robust Conscience': Identifying and Engaging the Psychological Concerns of Krister Stendahl's Inceptive Article," *Westminster Theological Journal* 75 (2013): 145–64.

6

PAUL, AUGUSTINE, AND KRISTER ON THE INTROSPECTIVE CONSCIENCE OF THE WEST[1]

Paula Fredriksen

In 1963, in the *Harvard Theological Review*, Krister Stendahl published his renowned essay, "The Apostle Paul and the Introspective Conscience of the West."[2] Its sixteen pages have had an impact on the study of Paul out of all proportion to their length. Krister opened his essay by insisting that ancient people be allowed to be genuinely distant and different from us. More to the point, he urged that Paul not be "modernized" into some historically costumed version of ourselves. People living in different historical epochs, he asserted, are not all "essentially the same." This sounds so commonsensical now. But 1963 was the heyday of psychohistory. Erik Erikson's *Young Man Luther* (1958) was on every college reading list. Ids, egos, superegos; desire and guilt; impulse and suppression: the hydraulics of Freudian personality structure was presumed to be universally operative, constant across all cultures and time periods.

So for Krister, in 1963, to challenge this all-but-universal presupposition about timeless humanity took both imagination and intellectual courage. What Krister asserted was nothing else than a principled stand against anachronism, the naive narcissism of projecting ourselves into everywhere else that we look. Krister's call to thinking critically and historically subsequently resounded, in a formative way, in the work of E. P. Sanders. Sanders's great book, *Paul and Palestinian Judaism*,[3] fundamentally altered the terms of New Testament scholarship. It placed Paul emphatically and positively within his own first-century, Jewish context.

And Sanders especially unmasked the Christian anti-Judaism that has blighted so much New Testament scholarship, especially the scholarship on Paul.[4] Both aspects of Sanders's work cohered closely with Krister's own project, and owed much to it.

But this article of Krister's made three further points. First, Krister insisted upon what he called "Paul's robust conscience" (200; e.g., Phil 3:6). Second, Paul's transformation from persecutor to apostle, Krister urged, should be seen not as a "conversion" so much as a prophetic call or a commission (204). These two insights, first articulated by Johannes Munck, had a huge exegetical impact. Together, they dethroned Romans 7 as a premier self-description by an apostle tormented by his own sinfulness. Luther might have thought of himself, and of Everyman, as *simul iustus et peccator*. Paul, said Krister, suffered no such self-esteem issues. No tortured, introspective conscience ground him down.

As the focus on Romans 7 shifted, so too did reconstructions of Paul's signature theological teaching, bringing us to Krister's third point. Romans, he argued, was *not* a theological exploration of the idea of "justification by faith." Rather, Romans addressed the question of how Christ-following Gentiles—ex-pagan pagans—were to be included in the impending redemption of Israel. Romans' theme, as Krister says elsewhere, was missiology (How are Gentiles to be incorporated into Israel's redemption?) not soteriology (How is the sinner saved?).[5] This reframing of Romans also delivered an exegetical payload. It too relocated the letter's center of gravity away from the tormented "I" of Romans 7 and toward the symphonic eschatology of chapters 9–11. Or, as Krister put it, "Rom 9–11 is not an appendix to chs. 1–8, but the climax of the letter" (205).

"The Apostle Paul and the Introspective Conscience of the West" accomplished so much. Krister essentially recast Paul's temperament. He lifted up Pauline eschatology (about which I will say more, later on). He averred that Paul did not "convert," that is, Paul did not move from one religion (Judaism) to another (Christianity) when he received his apostolic call. He insisted that "justification by faith" was Luther's issue, not Paul's. And between page 204 and page 205 flashed a brilliant intuition. How did Luther's Paul *get* to be Luther's Paul? asked Krister. And he answered: through the work of Augustine of Hippo.

Augustine's *Confessions*, said Krister, both articulated the West's idea of the introspective self and served as its conduit. "The *Confessions* are the first great document in the history of the introspective conscience," he asserted. "The Augustinian line leads into the Middle Ages and reaches its climax in the penitential struggle of the Augustinian monk, Martin Luther, and in his interpretation of Paul" (205). Augustine's Paul shaped, and in a sense caused, Luther's Paul, the conflicted, anxious Paul of Romans 7.

This was a brilliant association of ideas. But could it really be true? Augustine was born in 354. He died in 430, in late Roman North Africa, the Bible Belt of Latin antiquity. Luther was born in 1483, and died in 1546. Over a thousand years stood between Augustine and Luther, and Luther the monk lived in a resoundingly different culture—the penitential, postmedieval, Renaissance culture of sixteenth-century Northern Europe. Augustine's Paul *must* have been different from Luther's Paul. To start with, the two men were not even reading the same Pauline texts. (Luther read Paul in Greek. Augustine read Paul in miserable Latin translation. If Augustine *had* read Greek, the West might have been spared the doctrine of original sin.[6])

Krister (and Erikson) had convincingly portrayed Luther's punishing "introspective conscience." But, with more than ten centuries separating the late Empire from Luther's Europe, could Augustine *really* have experienced the same? And where underneath all of these multiple Pauline personae—the Paul of Augustine, the Paul of Luther, the Paul of Harvard Divinity School in the 1960s, the Paul of Krister—where was Paul the Jew, the *Paul* of history? How did the apocalyptic, charismatic Paul of late Second Temple Judaism become Augustine's Paul, the Christian theologian of grace, of predestination, of original sin?

Pursuing these questions complicated the insights of Krister's article in interesting ways. It turns out that it took Augustine a while to come up with Augustine's Paul. And the key to Augustine's Paul was not the *Confessions*. Nor is the *Confessions*, as Krister had claimed in his important article, "the first great document in the history of the introspective conscience." The key to Augustine's "Lutheran" Paul is the battle of Augustine's anti-Pelagian old age. The *Confessions*, yes, marks a stage along the way. But its introspection is not the haunted critical self-examination of late medieval penitential practices. It is the calm inner gazing of late Roman Neoplatonism.[7]

The foundations of Augustine's Paul were laid not by the Roman orthodox church, but by the heretical church of the Manichees. Augustine spent the formative ten years of his young adult life, roughly from ages nineteen to twenty-nine, as an active and full-hearted heretic. The Paul whom he met in these years was an anti-Jewish, anti-catholic[8] Paul; a Paul who condemned the unelevating Jewish Scriptures, the carnal Jewish law, and above all the bloodthirsty Jewish god, the flawed maker of this flawed universe.[9] Then, at around age thirty, climbing the professional ladder, Augustine made his way from Carthage to Milan. It was there that he returned to catholic Christianity.

More than a decade later, Augustine described the events surrounding that time in his great theological masterwork, the *Confessions*. Between his conversion in 386 and his description of it in 397 lay a period of intensive study of Paul, and particularly of Romans. Augustine returns to this master text of Paul's again and again, not least because the Manichees could so easily use the apostle's rhetorical dichotomies—law and grace, flesh and spirit, Jew and Gentile—to critique at the same time Judaism and catholic Christianity. Judaism was too carnal, said the Manichees, and carnal catholic orthodoxy (which promoted marriage and childbearing, which insisted on Christ's incarnation, and which drew on Jewish Scriptures as the "Old Testament") was too Jewish. Short essays and think pieces tumbled out of him: the transcript of a public debate with a former Manichean colleague, which turned upon verses in Paul (the *C. Fortunatum* of 392); a collection of notes on Romans, and the beginnings of an unfinished commentary (*Propositiones* and the *Inchoata Expositio* of 394/95); a commentary on Galatians (also 394/95); transcripts from clerical workshops on particularly knotty verses that seem to deny human moral autonomy, thus God's justice in punishing sinners (especially qu. 66–68, on Romans 9, of *De diversis quaestionibus*, 395); a brief treatise, completed in fits and starts, on the freedom of the will (*De libero arbitrio*, 388–96).[10]

Augustine bangs his head repeatedly against Romans 9. Why did God love Jacob? Why did he hate Esau? Why does God punish the sinner, if God himself shapes the clay? At stake was *not* the plight of the human sinner. At stake was a morally coherent construction of God—the god truly represented in Jewish Scriptures, the god who gave the law, the god who made the universe and everything in it, and saw that it was good. And no less at stake was finding an anti-Manichaean, truly catholic Paul.

In the years between 396 (his *Ad Simplicianum*, on Rom 7:7–25 and 9:10–29) and 400 (when, perhaps, he finished the *Confessions*), Augustine "found" this Paul. The catholic apostle arrived in tandem with the catholic Augustine, who was also presented, even constructed, in the *Confessions*. This was no accident.[11]

The *Confessions*. Its story is well known. Augustine was beaten as a schoolboy. He stole pears as a teenager. He came to Carthage burning, burning, where a cauldron of unholy lusts leapt and boiled about his flesh. He had the freshman year from hell. He joined the Manichees. He acquired a live-in girlfriend, whom he got pregnant. And he changed faculties from law to philosophy. Poor Monica. But then, Augustine became disillusioned with the Manichees. He moved to Milan; he listened to Ambrose; he read in translation some "books of the Platonists" (*Conf.* 7.9,13).

Through late Platonism, Augustine came to reconceive the problem of evil. Evil is not *something*, an active malignant force, as the Manichees had taught. Evil is no-thing, the *absence* of something: the absence of good, just as cold is the absence of heat. God creates, which means, since God is all good and only good, that what God creates is only good, too. Evil erodes the good, like rust erodes steel. But evil does not *invade* the good, because evil is *not*-good, *not*-being. God creates every thing. But not even God can create *no*-thing.

This is Augustine's account, written in 397–400 in the *Confessions*, of how he was thinking about the problem of evil, preconversion, in cosmopolitan Milan, in the mid-380s. He offers in this work not an "*intro*spective self" so much as a "*retro*spective self."[12] Through his ostensibly historical narrative of his life in the mid-380s, he retrojects his grasp of Plotinus and especially of Porphyry, which, by the late 390s, was both more sure and much better integrated with biblical learning than it actually had been during his stay in Italy.[13]

So much for cosmic evil. But what about personal evil, *willed* evil, also known as "sin"? In the works that immediately followed his conversion back in 386, writing to other learned gentlemen in his Platonic reading group, Augustine had characterized sin as a mistake made due to ignorance. Once you know the right thing to do, you do the right thing—

any philosopher knows this to be the case. If you know the good, you choose it.[14] But back in Africa, he had to speak before much less cosmopolitan audiences. He publicly debated with Manichees, who peppered him with quotations from Paul's letters that seemed to talk about *un*willed sin (as in Romans 7). Augustine's fancy Neoplatonism wasn't working, whether to persuade his audience or to pummel his enemies. In the mid-390s, he starts to study seriously the catholic Paul.[15]

The catholic Paul of the fourth century was better published than is the academic Paul of twenty-first-century critical New Testament scholarship. Only seven letters in the canon—1 Thessalonians, Philemon, 1 and 2 Corinthians, Galatians, Philippians, and Romans—are currently uncontested. Augustine painted his picture of Paul from a richer palette that included the deutero-Pauline letters: 2 Thessalonians, 1 and 2 Timothy, Titus, Ephesians, Colossians. And, unlike us, he could draw uncritically on Acts. In the mid-390s, then, commenting on Romans and on Galatians, Augustine begins to construct a Paul who was—in the words of Titus 3:3—"once foolish, disobedient, led astray, slaves to various passions and pleasures." But God chose him anyway. Thus Augustine in 396, immediately before starting the *Confessions*, commenting again on Romans 9:

> What did Saul want but to attack, seize, bind and slay Christians? What a fierce, savage, blind will was that! Yet he was thrown prostrate by one word from on high, and a vision came to him whereby his mind and will were turned from their fierceness and set on the right way towards faith so that, suddenly, from a marvelous persecutor of the Gospel a more marvelous preacher was made. What then shall we say?…"Is there unrighteousness with God? God forbid!" (Rom 9:16; *Ad Simplicianum* 1.2,22).

This is Paul as the archetypical convert. He serves as the template for Augustine's presentation of himself in the *Confessions*. Augustine too, in book 8, is—as "Paul" described himself in Titus 3:3—"foolish, disobedient, led astray, [a slave] to various passions and pleasures." Augustine explores the terrible emotional and moral paralysis of wanting and not wanting the same thing at the same time. This is the literary perch for his great prayer, *Da mihi castitatem et continentiam, sed noli modo*: "O Lord, grant me chastity and continence—but not yet" (*Conf.* 8.7,17). A child's voice mysteriously chants *Tolle, lege*: "Pick up and read." He seizes a copy of Paul's letters, and happily lands upon Romans 13:14: "Make no provision for the flesh, to gratify its desires." Augustine's will is instantaneously healed (*Conf.* 8.12,29). Book 9: Augustine and his household are baptized. Monica dies. Having framed his story through a complex set of allusions to the divided self of Romans 7, Augustine heads back to North Africa, baptized and celibate, a changed man.

But wait! There's more!—much more, in fact. I have just summed up only the first nine books of Augustine's *Confessions*. But the *Confessions* continues for four more long, complex books. Forty percent of its eighty thousand Latin words still remain, rich discussions of memory, of time, of divine revelation, of text and truth and biblical interpretation.[16] Who writes an "autobiography" that spends its second half on the first chapter of Genesis, and on the relation between time and eternity?

Here, then, is the problem with looking at the *Confessions* as a type of introspective autobiography that sheds light on Luther—which is what Krister, in 1963, had done. The *Confessions* is *not* autobiography. It is a brilliant catholic inflection of late Roman Neoplatonism on the nature of humanity, of the cosmos, and of God. Augustine transposes late pagan philosophy into a Pauline key. Not since Philo of Alexandria had Jews and Greeks, the Bible and Plato, been brought into such intimate contact. And it is all happening in bad Latin editions. (Augustine reads and speaks only his native language. It's not the least American thing about him.)

The question that had driven Augustine's story all along was not, how can the sinner find a gracious god? It was, how can a time-bound, imperfect human being *know* the timeless, perfect God? Augustine answers, through the mind, God's image in us, because God has planted in each soul the desire to know him. ("Our hearts are restless until they rest in you," that is, in God; *Conf.* 1.1,1.) But humans, after Adam, are adrift in time. Unlike God, we have no immediate, perfect knowledge. To know *anything*, we have to interpret. And in an infinitely interpretable universe, what certainty can we ever have? Only such certainty as God imparts (as he had done for Augustine, at the end of book 8, with the counsel to "pick up and read"). The *Confessions*, in short, is not a book about Augustine. It is a book about God and about how we can know

God. Augustine mobilizes the life story in his first nine books, from his vantage in 397, in order to illustrate his larger theological point.[17]

Augustine argues throughout the *Confessions* that the soul—or, more exactly, the mind, that highest part of the soul—is the royal road back to God. As we, through disciplined introspection, transcend levels of human consciousness, we move metaphysically up through the universe, back to the nonmaterial, eternal God, the source both of the soul and of the universe. This is not *self-critical, penitential* introspection. It is *Platonic* introspection, wherein the architecture of the soul resonates with the architecture of the metaphysical cosmos. In a sense, within this system, we touch eternity by thinking about it.[18]

The specifically Christian (and, more specifically, the Pauline) twist introduced by Augustine into this system is about the will. Divided against itself, inherited from Adam across generations, the will cannot will effectively. "The good that I want to do I do not do; and the evil I do not want to do, I do." A person can will to turn to God effectively, says Augustine, only if God first heals the will, if God turns the person toward himself. Romans 7 is Paul's description of anguished Everyman, *before* the reception of grace.[19]

How, then, do we get from Augustine's Paul to Luther's Paul? Here we have to fast-forward some two decades, into the thick of Augustine's battle with Pelagius. Pelagius had held that God's grace strengthens human good will, so that, aided by grace, humanity does what is right. And he cited Augustine's two earlier Romans commentaries while making his case. Furious, Augustine countered that humanity *always* needs God's help, even *after* the reception of grace. No one has any merit on his own: even one's own good works, after conversion, are themselves the work of God.

Augustine proves his point by appealing to Romans 7, which he *now* interprets in an anti-Pelagian way. The tormented "I" of Romans 7, he insists, is *not* just Everyman before the reception of grace. *The "I" of Romans 7 is the Christian Paul, thus Paul even after he had received grace.* The voice of Romans 7, says the anti-Pelagian Augustine, is the voice of Paul who, though Christian, still continues to be torn between flesh and spirit, spirit and flesh. Since they miss the saint's autobiographical reference in these lines, urges Augustine, the Pelagians misread Paul's entire text.[20]

Augustine's anti-Pelagian Paul, the Paul of the dark 420s, is the Paul who approximates Luther's *simul iustus et peccator.*[21] This Paul was *not* the product of the *Confessions*. He was *not* the offshoot of Augustine's own introspective conscience.[22] This Paul is the strategic brainchild of Augustine's toxic rhetoric against Pelagius. If even the sainted apostle, after his conversion, still struggled against the flesh, then clearly Pelagius must be wrong. Augustine must be right. The will, even *sub gratia*, is never, ever "free."[23]

In the long run, it was Augustine's use of his idea of Paul's conversion to frame his own—and vice versa, Augustine's use of his own conversion, as he saw it in 397, to understand Paul's—that had the greatest and most lasting effect on Western tradition. Paul, refracted through Acts and through Augustine's works, stands in that tradition as the prototype of the Christian convert, the great sinner redeemed from the error of his earlier life by a single, dramatic moment of conversion. This idea in turn foregrounds Romans 7, especially as interpreted during the campaign against the Pelagians: Romans 7 is the apostle's self-confession, his description of his own abiding torment despite this abrupt transfer from "sin" (works righteousness or, in short, Judaism) to justification through faith in Christ (grace, or, in short, Gentile Christianity). And it cast a long shadow, passing from Augustine through Luther to Reformation Protestant theology, and thence to modern New Testament scholarship.

Three great Scandinavian scholars, mid-twentieth century, significantly challenged this reconstruction of Christian origins: Johannes Munck, Nils Dahl, and Krister Stendahl. Munck leads the list, with his 1954 publication *Paulus und die Heilsgeschichte* (*Paul and the Salvation of Mankind*).[24] The then-prevailing Tübingen School had pitted Judaism against Christianity, and a conservative, law-observant "Jewish Christianity" of Peter and of James against Paul's law-free gospel. On the contrary, Munck insisted: all of the apostles and Paul as well were convinced that they stood at the edge of the end of time, between Christ's resurrection and his imminent Second Coming ("Christ will return soon," 276). *Eschatology gave rise to mission.* The earliest community saw the gospel message as entirely contiguous with the faith of Israel, and the promise of God's redemption to his people. At the end, "all Israel"—that is, all ethnic Israel—is saved. Munck's argument shifted Romans' center of gravity away from chapter 7 toward chapters 9–11.

What then of "Paul the convert"? Munck urged as well that Paul's "Damascus experience" should be seen not as a "conversion" but as Paul's reception of his prophetic "call." Paul's own description of his experience in Galatians 1:15 echoes the language of Isaiah 49:1–6, when the prophet received his call to preach salvation to the Gentiles, and the language of Jeremiah 1:5 (au. trans.), whom God also knew "before I formed you in the womb...and I appointed you a prophet to the Gentiles." Paul's apostleship *in his own view*, insisted Munck, began with this commission, not with a "conversion" (11–35).

The work of Nils Dahl and of Krister Stendahl variously reinforced Munck's arguments. While Dahl held that *conversion* was the term appropriate to Paul's life-changing experience, he also emphasized that it should not connote a "change of religion." Paul and his fellow apostles, Dahl insisted, remained committed to the eschatological redemption of Israel, and it was *to this end* that Paul engaged in his mission to Gentiles. In this reading, no less than in Munck's, Romans 9–11, with its conviction that "all Israel will be saved" (Rom 11:26), set a plumb line for Pauline interpretation.[25]

Stendahl, in "Introspective Conscience," as we have seen, building upon Munck, also championed "call" over "conversion." Guilt did not explain Paul's gospel. "Paul was equipped with what...must be called a rather 'robust' conscience" (200). "Thus, we look in vain for a statement in which Paul would speak about himself as an actual sinner" (210). Paul saw his mission, and the message of the gospel, as finding a place for the nations within *Israel's* coming redemption. Thus, for Stendahl too, Romans 9–11 is the climax of the letter (205).

I wish I could tell you that the work of these three men forever after changed Pauline studies, but that would not be true. The field is still as energetically divided as ever. Many (probably most) scholars still refer to Paul's call as his "conversion." Some will even insist—despite Munck and, before him, the definitive study by Kümmel[26]—that Romans 7 is confessional, Paul's own self-report. Other scholars, noting that Paul's addressees are predominantly if not exclusively Gentile, suggest that Paul taught "two paths of salvation," Torah for Jews and Christ for Gentiles.[27] And still other scholars remain resolutely supersessionist. For them, Paul really did leave an inferior religion—that is, Judaism, and a law that he knew was a "curse"—for a superior religion, law-free Christianity. (The two most recent defenses of this very traditional view, from 2013 and 2015, are each *very* long: the one from 2013 weighs in at 1,660 pages![28] Maybe that's a good thing, in that the book's very bulk signals that the position itself is getting harder to maintain.)

I number among those scholars who think that Paul and his gospel are best interpreted *within* Judaism.[29] Paul did not know that his letters would one day be used to create what we call Christianity. Three reasons for thinking this way have already been provided by Munck, Dahl, and Stendahl. First, Paul thought of his becoming an apostle as a prophetic call rather than as a "conversion." Second, Paul himself had a robust Jewish identity. And, third, Paul expected the return of Christ, the resurrection of the dead, the transformation of the living, and the establishment of God's kingdom within his own lifetime. It is *history* that looks at the apostles as the church's founding generation. They looked at themselves as history's final generation.

It is on this last point—eschatology—that I, and Krister, will end.

So many things disturb undergraduates in courses introducing the New Testament. They read Matthew and Luke together for the first time, and realize that those Gospels tell two very different birth narratives. They find out that none of the twelve disciples in Mark's Gospel ever understands what Jesus is talking about. They find out that there are four different stories about the resurrection. They find out that Paul teaches the resurrection of a spiritual body (1 Cor 15:44, 50). They find out that Mark's Jesus "cleanses" the temple at the very end of his mission (Mark 11:15–17), but that John's Jesus does the same thing at the very beginning of his (John 2:13–22). Some of these things bother some of them, other things bother others of them. But what bothers *all* of them is a teaching on which Jesus and Paul completely agreed, namely, that God's kingdom was at hand.

In first-century texts, the kingdom of God is not a metaphor for heaven. It is not a coded way to talk about "the church." In first-century Judaism, the kingdom is a historical, empirical event: the defeat of pagan gods; the battle between good and evil (and good wins); the resurrection of the dead; the advent of the Messiah (for those groups who expected a messiah); the turning of the nations to Israel's god; the reassembling of Israel's twelve tribes; the establishment of universal peace. The day *after* the kingdom of God arrived, in other words, would definitely look different than had the day before.

John the Baptizer, in the 20s of the first century, taught that these events were imminent. Jesus of Nazareth, in the late 20s/early 30s of the first century, taught that these events were imminent. And this is what Paul, in the middle decades of the first century, also taught was imminent. That's interesting. Because by the time that we have our earliest evidence for this Christ movement—that is to say, with Paul's letters, mid-first century—the kingdom was already about twenty years late. Today, the kingdom is almost two thousand years late.

And that is exactly what Krister says. This too took moral and intellectual courage, because the delay of the end is something of an embarrassment. Indeed, in the 2,300 pages of those two most recent books on Paul-as-Christian-theologian, their authors do not mention eschatology even once. Exegeting Paul in infinite detail, they manage to neglect to consider that Paul expected the end of the normal world within his own lifetime. Perhaps they did not notice. Perhaps it slipped their minds. Or perhaps they could not address the issue, because the only way to turn Paul into a modern Protestant is to forget what he said about the impending return of Christ.

Bad thinking, and bad theology, made Krister impatient. In *Final Account*, his last book on Romans (orig. pub. 1993), he observes, "If the text says 'now' in the year 56 of the Common Era, where does that leave you and me? It leaves us almost 2000 years later. No kerygmatic gamesmanship can overcome that simple fact" (23). Just deal with it, he urges us. Do not ignore it, or pretend that it does not exist. But do not do bad history, which leads to dishonest theology: acknowledge that "NOW!" is what Paul, mid-first century, proclaimed.

Jewish eschatology matters for Christian theology, not least because it, and it alone, accounts for the Christ-movement's mission to pagans.[30] It was only at the end, taught the prophet Isaiah (66:18–20, cf. Gen 10), that the fullness of the pagans—all seventy of the nations descended from Noah—would turn to Israel's god. It was only at the end that the plenum of Israel, all twelve tribes, would recollect. It was only at the end that "the fullness of the Gentiles and all Israel," as Paul says in Romans 11:25–26 (au. trans.), would be redeemed. If we let go of Jewish eschatology, this embarrassing artifact from the Jewish past, we let go of the only thing that explains Christianity's future. Deal with it, said Krister. Think hard; but think.

Why listen to him? Why not just ignore this embarrassment? Leave it out, and write—or read—the most recent few thousand pages on the Protestant Paul. Again, Krister will have none of it. Such a retreat, he argued, betrays the Reformation. Here is Krister again, on page 72 in *Paul among the Jews and Gentiles*:[31]

> Our study has called us to recognize that when we are involved in...interpretation, we must remember that we should interpret the original....[W]e have lived with a sort of chain-reaction—Augustine touching up Paul,...Pelagius discussing and turning these things around,...the medievalists pushing one way or the other, and then further reactions, moving away from the original....The original is there, and I have tried to point to it. The original is there, and to return to *it* is to be a true son or daughter of the Reformation.

And the point of looking at "the original," of course, is to interpret it as best we can within its own historical context. The Renaissance—with its emphasis on reading originally Greek texts (like Paul's letters) in their original language—not only enabled Luther to ignite the Reformation. It also enabled critical historiography. And critical history writing should *dis*enable anachronism.

I end, then, on the point with which Krister's important article began. Respect difference, please. Let ancient people be ancient people. Do not force them into a false role as modern people, no matter how important they are. They stand with their backs to us, their faces toward the faces of their own generation, the hearers to whom they had to make sense. To do good history, we must attempt to hear them as their own contemporaries first heard them, which is to say, within their own context. That is good history. And to do good theology, exhorted Krister, we must do good history first.

Good twenty-first-century theology is not their responsibility, but ours.

NOTES

1. This chapter is based on a lecture given at Lund University, Sweden, on June 1, 2017, to mark the occasion of my receiving a doctorate

honoris causa from the Faculty of Theology. I warmly thank my Lund colleagues both for this honor, and for the opportunity that they provided me for returning, once again, to Krister Stendahl's luminous essay.

2. *Harvard Theological Review* 56 (1963): 199–215.

3. *Paul and Palestinian Judaism: A Comparison of Patterns of Religion* (Philadelphia: Fortress, 1977).

4. See especially ibid., 33–59 and 434–42, two splendid bibliographical essays.

5. "The primary application of Paul's letter to the Romans is to understand the strange ways of God and the mission of the church. *It is missiology, not soteriology*. Romans is a tractate on mission, not just in terms of outreach, but in terms of how Paul's bringing the message to Gentiles fits into God's total plan." Krister Stendahl, *Final Account: Paul's Letter to the Romans* (Minneapolis: Fortress, 1995), 41 (author's emphasis).

6. I refer here to the notorious Latin rendering of Romans 5:12: ἐφ' ᾧ as *in quo*, meaning "in Adam." For discussion of this verse, and the role that it plays in the development of Augustine's ideas on original sin, see esp. Athanase Sage, "Péché originel: La naissance d'un dogme," *Revue des études augustiniennes et patristiques* 13 (1967): 211–48; Stanislas Lyonnet, "Augustin et Rom 5,12 avant la controverse pélagienne: A propos d'un texte de saint Augustin sur le baptême des enfants," *Nouvelle Revue Théologique* 89 (1967): 842–49; Lyonnet, "Rom. 5,12 chez saint Augustin: Note sur l'elaboration de la doctrine augustinienne du péché originel," in *L'homme devant Dieu: Melanges offerts au père Henri de Lubac* (Paris: Auber, 1963), 1:327–39.

7. How this is so is laid out in the notes of Henry Chadwick's superb edition of the *Confessions* (Oxford: Oxford University Press, 1991). See also below, n17.

8. I write *catholic* with a lowercase *c* to distinguish Augustine's church from that of later Roman Catholicism. In Augustine's period (fourth–fifth century), *catholic* was the self-designation of that sect of Christianity recognized as orthodox by the emperor. In this sense, the cognate churches of the Greek East were also "catholic."

9. For Augustine's Manichaean period, and the view of Paul that he would have imbibed then, Paula Fredriksen, *Augustine and the Jews: A Christian Defense of Jews and Judaism* (New Haven, CT: Yale University Press, 2010), 105–21. This Manichaean Paul was an enduring antitype for Augustine's later constructions of the apostle, one that also spurred him to genuinely positive appreciations of Jews, of Jewishness, and of the continuing law

observance of the whole first, Jewish generation of the church, Jesus and Paul included, ibid., 235–366.

10. This stream of Augustine's early literary production is surveyed in Paula Fredriksen, "Beyond the Body/Soul Dichotomy: Augustine on Paul against the Manichees and the Pelagians," *Recherches augustiniennes* 23 (1988): 87–114, at 89–95.

11. For two overviews of this period of Augustine's life, Peter Brown, *Augustine of Hippo: A Biography* (Berkeley: University of California Press, 2000; orig. pub. 1967), 29–124; with specific reference to the retrospective and philosophical framing of the *Confessions*, Fredriksen, *Augustine and the Jews*, 154–210. On Augustine's construction of his catholic self in the *Confessions* and the ways that his Manichean past determines this construct as its antitype, see especially Jason BeDuhn, *Augustine's Manichaean Dilemma*, vol. 2, *Making a "Catholic" Self, 388–401 C.E.* (Philadelphia: University of Pennsylvania Press, 2013).

12. Paula Fredriksen, "Paul and Augustine: Conversion Narratives, Orthodox Traditions, and the Retrospective Self," *Journal of Theological Studies* 37 (1986): 3–34.

13. For the Pauline substructure of the *Confessions*, esp. of books 7 and 8, consult the commentary by James J. O'Donnell, *Augustine: Confessions*, 3 vols. (Oxford: Clarendon Press, 1992); for the *Confession*'s subterranean "dialogue" with Plotinus and, especially with Porphyry, Henry Chadwick, *Augustine: A Very Short Introduction* (Oxford: Oxford University Press, 1986). In the 380s, Augustine's acquaintance with both bodies of tradition would have been much less secure than it seems in his redescription of this period from the perspective of 397.

14. See especially his facile description of the "wise man's" moral decision making in *De lib. arb.* book 1 (begun in 388, when he was still in Italy).

15. For the way that his debate with Fortunatus in 392 drove home the necessity of getting to (better) grips with Paul's letters, see Fredriksen, *Augustine and the Jews*, 142–182.

16. Paula Fredriksen, *Sin: The Early History of an Idea* (Princeton, NJ: Princeton University Press, 2012), 116–20.

17. For the full argument, see Paula Fredriksen, "The Confessions as Autobiography," in *A Companion to Augustine*, ed. Mark Vessey (Malden, MA: Wiley-Blackwell, 2012), 87–98.

18. The "vast ordered cosmos" of the Neoplatonists, observes Robert Markus, had as its source "the transcendent One, beyond speech and beyond

thought, which communicated itself to beings below it in the infinitely ordered hierarchy down to the lowest levels of the system. The universe was pictured as a sort of cascade of divine light descending from its transcendent origin, dissipating itself gradually in multiplicity, limitation, and ultimately the darkness of non-being. The descending self-communication of the One constitutes a cosmic hierarchy, which provides the soul with the route for its ascent. To liberate itself from the realm of darkness and multiplicity, the soul needs to retrace the universal order, ascending from its place of exile, from its dissipation among material things and multiplicity, to its goal and its true home." *Conversion and Disenchantment in Augustine's Spiritual Career* (Villanova, PA: Villanova University Press, 1989), 14–15; cf. *Conf.* 9.10, the so-called vision at Ostia.

19. See, e.g., *Propp.* 37–46, esp. 44.2: "The man described here [i.e., in Rom. 7:15–16] is under the Law, prior to grace;" cf. Augustine's anti-Pelagian disavowal of this position in *Retractationes* 22 (23), 2.

20. *Contra ii epistolas Pelagianorum* 1.8.13–11.24 (cf. 1.10,22, where he refers to his own earlier, and "erroneous," reading of this passage); *De praedestinatione sanctorum* 1.2.4; 1.4.8.

21. I emphasize "approximates." Augustine's Paul is still not Luther's Paul, nor is Augustine's idea of grace Luther's idea. Augustine is searching for a *just* god, not a "gracious" one. For him, election—that is, the reception of efficacious grace—corresponds to the sinner's *most hidden deserts* (*occultissimis meritis*), invisible to humans but evident to God, who accordingly judges with *occulta iustitia*. Salvation may be an unearned gift (*indebita gratia*), but it is not an arbitrary one. God does judge by "standards of fairness," but these standards are not evident to humans in this life. (Indeed, they are *occultissima, remotissima*). "Faith" for Augustine means believing and affirming that God judges "justly" even though his decisions may make him seem morally opaque to us, *Ad Simpl.* 1.2,16.

In his defense of what he takes to be the Augustinian-Lutheran line, on this point about grace and merit, John Barclay gets Augustine wrong. See John M. G. Barclay, *Paul and the Gift* (Grand Rapids, MI: Eerdmans, 2015), 85–95, interpreting what he takes to be Augustine's views on "incongruous grace"; cf. Fredriksen, *Augustine and the Jews*, 175–89 and 277–86, for Augustine's construction of God's *occulta iustitia* and the "most hidden" *meritis* of the sinner.

22. Cf. Barclay, who imagines Augustine coming to his ideas on grace by "drilling down into the depths of the human psyche," *Paul and the Gift*, 91.

23. Fredriksen, "Paul and Augustine," 25–26; in greater textual detail, Fredriksen, "Beyond the Body/Soul Dichotomy," 105–12.

24. German original, Copenhagen: Munkgaard, 1954; English edition, Richmond, VA: John Knox Press, 1959.

25. See the essays assembled in Nils A. Dahl, *Studies in Paul: Theology for the Early Christian Mission* (Minneapolis: Augsburg, 1977; orig. pub. 1956), esp. "The Missionary Theology in the Epistle to the Romans" (70–94), and "The Future of Israel" (137–58).

26. Werner Georg Kümmel, *Römer sieben und das Bild des Menschen im Neuen Testament. Zwei Studien*, Theologische Bücherei 53 (Munich: Kaiser, 1974; orig. pub. 1929), esp. 117–32.

27. This position is most associated with the work of Lloyd Gaston, *Paul and the Torah* (Vancouver: University of British Columbia Press, 1987) and of John G. Gager, *Reinventing Paul* (Oxford: Oxford University Press, 2000); see also Gager, "Paul, the Apostle of Judaism," in *Jesus, Judaism, and Christian Anti-Judaism: Reading the New Testament after the Holocaust*, ed. Paula Fredriksen and Adele Reinhartz (Louisville, KY: John Knox Press, 2002), 56–76. Stendahl had once been associated with this view, but he himself disavowed it, *Final Account*, x and 7.

28. Barclay's book (n21), is the 2015 publication to which I refer; N.T. Wright's behemoth of 2013 is *Paul and the Faithfulness of God*, 2 vols. (Minneapolis: Fortress). For my review of Wright's book, see the *Catholic Biblical Quarterly* 77 (2015): 387–91.

29. Paula Fredriksen, *Paul: The Pagans' Apostle* (New Haven, CT: Yale University Press, *2017)*, places Paul's activity entirely within his native religious context. For different and differing interpretations of various aspects of Paul's life and work along these same lines, see the essays collected in Mark D. Nanos and Magnus Zetterholm, eds., *Paul within Judaism: Restoring the First-Century Context to the Apostle* (Minneapolis: Fortress, 2015); in Gabriele Boccaccini and Carlos A. Segovia, eds., *Paul the Jew: Rereading the Apostle as a Figure of Second Temple Judaism* (Minneapolis: Fortress, 2016); and in Rafael Rodriguez and Matthew Thiessen, eds., *The So-Called Jew in Paul's Letter to the Romans* (Minneapolis: Fortress, 2016).

30. On this point, which again owes much to Munck, most recently Fredriksen, *Paul: The Pagan's Apostle*, 73–77.

31. Minneapolis: Fortress, 1976.

IV

THE FRIENDSHIP

7

KRISTER STENDAHL AND THE INTROSPECTIVE CONSCIENCE OF A FRIEND

A Personal Appreciation

James Carroll

A simple, clear, and straightforward declaration of scholarly conviction can transform the religious imagination of an era. Almost uniquely, that is Martin Luther's story. And, to a far lesser but still pointed degree, it is Krister Stendahl's. That the shift in consciousness embodied in the latter's work upended a basic understanding of the former's compounds the irony that Stendahl is remembered as a towering Lutheran thinker.

By the later Middle Ages, in Europe, abject human helplessness before a judging God was the ground of an obsessive preoccupation with individual justification. That resulted in self-condemning pieties on the part of ordinary Christians and exploitations of that dread by indulgence-selling prelates—a condition that made an explosive reformation of the Roman Catholic Church all but inevitable. The brackets around the German reformer's thought were *faith alone* and *Scripture alone*, but an ancient dynamic—a damning God and a damned people—was accelerated by Luther, despite himself. Ultimately the spirit of dread from which he sought rescue stamped what followed him, both Protestant culture and Catholic counterculture; and finally, in the twentieth century, it was part of what brought the very structure of Christendom down upon itself.

By then, a new reformation was needed, and Krister Stendahl was one of its prophets. The brackets around his thought, adjusting Luther, were *God's faithfulness* and *Scripture interpreted*. With Stendahl, an essential element of the first reform was itself reformed, generating a positive intellectual current, running below the surface of Christian theology, that has yet to be checked. Instead of 95 *Theses*, Stendahl had a short speech, delivered in 1961 to a meeting of the American Psychological Association, a summary of which was published as what its editors called "an explosive analysis" in a theological journal under the title "The Apostle Paul and the Introspective Conscience of the West."[1] The volume in hand, with numerous authors appreciating that article, is a testimony to its ongoing influence. Indeed, this volume shows how that seemingly modest articulation prompted a major re-envisioning of the Letters of Paul, with profound implications for Christian theology, including a challenge to Christian theology's complicity in the historic secular damning of the Jews known as the Holocaust.

Stendahl touched a nerve with that phrase "the introspective conscience of the West," and he efficiently tracked that dark phenomenon—what he called "evermore introspective awareness of sin and guilt"—to a particular reading of St. Paul through lenses ground in the name of Augustine and polished by Luther. The reading was wrong, Stendahl said. Against a dominant understanding, he asserted that Paul's primary concern was not "justification by faith" as a solution to the obsessive individual's problem of the impossibility of salvation through observance of the law ("works"). Rather, Paul's interest was urgently taken up with the organizationally pressing, if existentially mundane, problem of the way Gentiles could be included in the Christ-believing people of God. After the reformer's reading began to dominate, Stendahl said, Paul's statements were read, instead, "as answers to the quest for assurance about man's salvation out of a common human predicament."[2]

Here is my understanding of Stendahl's insight: Paul proclaims not a doomsday God before whom all fallen humans are unworthy, but a gracious God whose faithfulness to the promise inherent in the very act of creation (not to mention the promise given to Abraham) weighs infinitely more than any imagined "faith" on the part even of a perfectly repentant human. God's faithfulness is what matters: not the believer's faith. The introspective conscience, chilled in the shadow of a dire last judgment and reaching "a theological climax with Luther," as Stendahl said, "and a secular climax with Freud," is an offense against the God whose judgment comes as love.[3] Yes, God is concerned with justice, but for him justice is not contradicted by love, but fulfilled by it.

The intellectual resonance of Stendahl's insight—again, as I understand it—centrally included an undermining of the negative-positive bipolarity traditionally attributed to St. Paul: "Jewish piety as the black background," in Stendahl's words, "that makes Christian piety the more shining."[4] But this hopeless foil against which joy itself is posited informs an entire religious schema: Moses versus Christ; law versus grace; works versus faith; form versus substance; judgment versus mercy; greed versus generosity; ultimately—after Marcion's scriptural dualism took hold in the second century—the God of the Old Testament versus the God of the New Testament. The abstractions of that bipolarity were realized, above all, in a history-laden specificity: the synagogue versus the church. The structure of religious anti-Judaism was generated here and, as carried forward in the history of Christendom, it came to full flower in racial anti-Semitism. To all of this, with his simple idea, Stendahl said no!

Luther's texts,[5] and their world-shaking consequences, cannot be understood apart from the context in which they were produced. That decidedly includes political struggles (the German electors vying for power in the Holy Roman Empire; burghers vying with princes); church crises (the blatant corruptions of the Borgia and Medici popes); recurring plagues and rampant social paranoia (expulsions of Jews and Muslims; establishment of ghettos); the new Atlantic economy (Christopher Columbus, John Cabot, and the European encounter with non-Christian native peoples), the movable type printing press and the rise of common literacy (the triumph of the vernacular over Latin). All these forces, individually and taken together, were the tinder into which Luther dropped his torch.

Stendahl's essay, similarly, struck its fainter but still resonant chord precisely because of the religious and social upheaval that defined the moment in which it appeared. In 1961, the culture that came of Christendom had just committed mass suicide during World War II, with profound, if subliminal consequences for the Western psyche. ("There is but one truly serious philosophical problem," Albert Camus wrote in 1955, "and that is suicide. Judging whether life is or is not worth living amounts to answering the fundamental question of philosophy"[6]). The postwar confrontation with the meaning of the Holocaust, especially for Christian religion, was just beginning (*Jesus et Israël* by Jules Isaac; *The Diary of a Young Girl*, by Anne Frank; Elie Wiesel's *Night*; Rolf Hochhuth's *The Deputy*; the trial in Jerusalem of Adolf Eichmann). The Cold War threat of nuclear conflict was palpable (as Stendahl delivered his remarks to the psychologists, the Berlin Wall had just been erected, and the US-Soviet standoff at Checkpoint Charlie was underway). The election of John F. Kennedy, an Irish Catholic, had just marked the start of a new era of American religious pluralism. Catholics worldwide were preparing for the Second Vatican Council, which Pope John XXIII had pointedly announced on the Feast of the Conversion of Saint Paul. But, after currents stirred by Stendahl's essay began to swirl, not even the conversion of Saint Paul would look the same—and that was the point.

In 1961, I was a student at Georgetown, the Jesuit university in Washington, DC. The phrase "introspective conscience of the West" would have meant nothing to me, yet an introspective conscience defined my every waking moment. If I veer at this point into autobiography, moving this consideration of Krister Stendahl's influence from the level of religious abstraction to a quite particular examination of one man's conscience, evolving across a lifetime, it is not because my case is special, but because it is typical. A broad liberation followed from the theological shift of which this Swedish Lutheran was a universal prophet, and that liberation belongs by now to two generations of Christians, including me. My simple and modest story of faith points to the grandeur of Krister Stendahl's story of faithfulness.

As a young American Catholic, my preoccupation with "justification"—Luther's watchword—seemed to owe nothing to the Protestant culture against which my people had so resolutely stood. Yet, as I would understand much later, the German reformer's dread, tied to a sense of radical unworthiness ("The more we wash ourselves, the more unclean we become"[7]) had its equivalent in the Jansenist doctrine of human depravity ("But I am a worm, and not human"[8]) that had so infected Irish Catholicism. Indeed, with our bodies, wills, and minds at the mercy of "concupiscence," we were all—Protestant and Irish Catholic alike—children of a flesh-hating St. Augustine, who, as our teachers read him, had left that very word to us as the definition of the human condition after the fall. I knew nothing of the theology, but I knew the feeling.

Though reared in a large and happy family in one of Washington's chipper suburbs, I had been a scrupulous child, stamped with a palpable sense of eternity and a constitutional certitude that, for reasons I did not understand, I was at grievous risk of spending it in hell. "I do not do the good I want"—this was surely the first Pauline verse to register with me—"but the evil I do not want to do is what I do."[9] Not incidentally, in his milestone essay, Stendahl identified this verse—and its theological misapplications—as key to the problem he was addressing.[10]

In my case, of course, this moral conundrum was puerile; evil reduced to triviality. When I recited the Act of Contrition on my knees, for example, I routinely repeated the words, "O my God, I am heartily sorry for having offended Thee, and I detest all my sins, because I dread the loss of heaven, and the pains of hell; but most of all because they offend Thee, my God, Who art all good and deserving of all my love." The trouble was that, even when I spoke these words directly into the ear of God—the monsignor's ear, in the shadowy booth of the sacrament of confession—my "robust conscience," to use Stendahl's phrase,[11] told me they were a lie. My only conscious motivation for sorrow was terror at the loss of heaven, period. The punishment of God was as real to me as the sting of the candle flame I dared to touch, while taking the measure of hellfire. Love of God had nothing to do with my compunction. That I claimed it did was yet another sin. Trivial evil is still evil. I remember pushing out through the velvet curtain of the confessional, returning to the open church only to feel, instead of relief at having had my sins forgiven, a fresh rush of doom at having added to them. This happened often.

As I grew older, the manifestations of scrupulosity changed, but not the power of its hold over me. My version of the futility of "works" and "law" as modes of salvation adhered in the fact that, to all appearances, I was a good boy—working hard, obeying every rule. I did as I was told. I served Mass at dawn. I clapped erasers after school. I folded the flag. I rushed to clear the table. I lived to please my parents and found that I could outdo my brothers by amplifying reports of the school day (which taught me, not incidentally, the joy of narrative). Mom and Dad duly praised me for my virtues, and so did the nuns. But inwardly, already, I felt like an impostor. Secretly ensnared by the devil, all feelings of righteousness came larded with shame. I would only later understand the tension between appearance and substance, but already I felt its burden.

One Sunday morning, I suffered a minor nosebleed, and before it was staunched, I had swallowed a bit of blood. It occurred to me that this amounted to "breaking the communion fast"—the strict command to abstain from all food and drink before Mass. I put the qualm aside, and a short while later I received the sacrament. But then the qualm returned, explosively. Blood impurity! I had swallowed! I had violated a primal law. I was convinced that I had committed a sacrilege. When I confessed this "sin" to the priest, I sensed his stifled laughter, which only deepened my sense of unworthiness. Damned if you do—how this cliché hit me—damned if you don't. Damned.

By the time I matured to the point of adolescent longing, I was primed for trouble, and knew to be on the lookout for "bad thoughts." Soon enough, I understood why the operative verb was *entertaining*. When I learned of St. Paul's "thorn in the flesh," I understood it as a matter of his sexual restlessness. Now Augustine's *concupiscence* became a word in my own vocabulary, code for the secret rush of a forbidden interiority—and the secret was I liked it. But did that mean that now I was truly doomed?

At Georgetown, I tried my best to leave such childish preoccupations behind. But it was not easy. At the center of my youthful ambition was the United States Air Force, and as an ROTC cadet, I instinctively put my will to please at the service of martial discipline. Success at the marching drill—where creased trousers, shined shoes, and the crisp movements of the martinet were absolute virtues—was entirely a matter of appearances. I excelled. It did not matter that, as far as I knew, no one in authority disapproved of me. I disapproved of myself. I had efficiently turned my inner life into a dark room with no window, or even door. How to get out? Though the words *justification* and *salvation* existed in a realm apart, release from this anguished insecurity, in fact, was the only meaning they could have had for me.

For a young Mick in that era, there was an ultimate act of "works" and "law;" a purest mode of parent-pleasing that would be Jesuit-pleasing, too; the one sure way out from under eternal doom; a wide-open road to "grace." For years I had been told—blatantly by nuns, more coyly by my parents—that I had a "vocation." I was qualified to be a "fisher of men." Encouraged to consider the priesthood, I'd long thought I was being singled out, but in the hothouse subculture of Irish Catholicism, boys like me were universally recruited for the cloth. Thanks, but no thanks.

In high school, I deliberately avoided all shows of religious ardor but, at home, set apart from my brothers, I still had the aura of the one called. At Georgetown, as a gung ho Air Force cadet explicitly imagining life as a fighter jock, I seemed finally to have eluded the shadow I thought of as God's. But my wholly private preoccupation took on an unexpected public dimension in that era, as the heightened threat of nuclear war began its shift from the Berlin Wall to the Cuban missiles. Nuclear war seemed close. Apocalyptic dread suddenly emerged as a fact of politics, and our corner of Washington, where President Kennedy had been a neighbor, was at its center. The coming war could not have been more vivid to me: an introspective conscience at ground zero. At a favored desk in a window alcove of the college library that year, I found myself looking out at the Washington skyline and seeing its familiar marks—the Capitol dome, the Monument, the Smithsonian Castle turrets—all bursting into flames under the ash of the mushroom cloud. I saw it. I saw it clearly. We were balanced on a knife's edge at the end of history. For once, my inner and outer worlds were a match. Reveries of terror. "The evil I do not want to do...."

One day, the charismatic young Jesuit who taught us algebra invited me to meet him after class. I remember his broad smile and how chalk dust always soiled his cassock. Instead of finally helping me to understand how the square root function is the inverse of the square function, he told me that he'd sensed something special about me. Then he asked if I'd ever considered the priesthood. I was startled. My answer was automatic. "No," I said. And then immediately choked: lying to a priest again.

I began to haunt Dahlgren Chapel late at night, taking odd solace in the darkened space alone. The red light of the sanctuary lamp was my point of focus. On many days, at twilight, I took solitary walks along the Potomac River canal. I became aware of carrying on a compulsive, loop-like inner monologue, talking to myself. Then it dawned on me. Not monologue, but dialogue. The echo I was hearing belonged to someone else, and for a lad like me, the leap was there to be made: Him. At last, I saw the meaning of prayer. I was talking not to myself but to God, and yes, God was talking to me, even if his voice was too faint to be understood. I chided myself. His felt presence (and, yes, it was a decisively male presence) was a mystery-laden boon and should have been enough.

Finally, when I went on that year's mandatory student retreat, I heard the stern retreat master's foreboding exhortation—"Watch therefore, for ye know neither the day nor the hour..."[12]—as addressed directly to me. "The last things" sermon—death, judgment, heaven, hell—was a staple of Jesuit preaching, as I would later learn from Stephen Dedalus at Belvedere ("Last of all, consider the frightful torment of those damned souls...."[13]). But I thought the priest's mortal warning was composed expressly for me. At his vivid evoking of judgment day, I felt seen through and exposed. Judgment day was now.

"I fled Him, down the nights and down the days...." I had come across a mystical poem by a British writer, Francis Thompson, and it spoke for me, in flight from God. "I fled Him, down the arches of the years; I fled Him, down the labyrinthine ways / Of my own mind." The poem's title was "The Hound of Heaven,"[14] and on that retreat I was caught. After the Jesuit's doom-laden exhortation, I fairly crawled into the curtained confessional booth, where I put my misery into whispers, turning at last, to "Thee, my God, Who art all good and deserving of all my love." When I came out of the confessional, I was primed for personal atonement, ready to take my place on the altar of sacrifice—the ultimate enactment of "works." I was relieved at having yielded at last and was aware of what seemed an unprecedented bond with the "Him" who had finally seized me; but I did not recognize it as love. I found myself kneeling below a stained glass window on which were etched the words, "Lord, what wilt thou have me to do?"[15] The question was its own answer. To be saved, I would make of my entire life an act of "works." Only later would I remember that the plaintive questioner, having been miraculously knocked from his Damascus-bound horse,[16] was St. Paul. Later still I would learn that, Catholic or not, my false hope of "works" had come to me through Luther.

That the Catholic religious order I joined, the Paulist Fathers, was dedicated to, and took its identity from, the apostle Paul is the first oddity. That the Paulists, while emancipating themselves from a narrow Pauline triumphalism, emancipated me is the second. And that an instrument of that transformation was an intense first encounter with Lutheran theology under the fresh influence of Krister Stendahl is the third. The story is too complex to do much more than indicate it here. The irony is that exactly when I entered the religious life, seeking release from the burden, yes, of conscientious introspection, the Catholic Church convened the Second Vatican Council, which, across the six years of my theological training, offered just such release.

The Council marked the long overdue end of the Counter Reformation, and at St. Paul's College, the Paulist Fathers' seminary in Washington, the theological curriculum immediately reflected that. As it happened, a Rome-based Paulist priest, Father Thomas Stransky, was a member of the just-created Vatican Secretariat for Christian Unity. His broad-minded influence at the Council would be large, and the Paulists, a liberal American order, would be in the forefront of the reform. At St. Paul's College, the seminary faculty followed Stransky's lead in promoting a new openness to Protestant thought. That was the wedge for the enormous theological liberation that followed, for the Church's unfinished business with the Reformation opened equally into its overdue reckoning with the Enlightenment.

For us seminarians, the intellectual breakthrough was a matter of surprising personal experience. One of our professors, a Paulist named Harry McSorely, having recently received his doctorate from the University of Munich, was one of the first Roman Catholic priests to study Luther from within the Lutheran framework, instead of against it. Our seminary promptly embarked on an unprecedented "dialogue" with the Lutheran seminary at Gettysberg, Pennsylvania. Soon enough, we Cath olics were meeting regularly with Lutheran counterparts, studying Scripture together, but also sharing the startling discovery of the faith's American relevance in those heady days of the minister-led civil rights movement. What we had in common as young religious seekers on the politically charged new frontier weighed far more than the denominational divide that had only a short time before seemed absolute. It was our Lutheran compatriots who, in those seminars, first brought to our attention the new thinking that was shifting the ground under Lutheran attitudes, especially having to do with our own patron, St. Paul.

I am sure that it was during the course of those Lutheran-Catholic dialogue sessions that I first encountered Krister Stendahl's thought. I remember the force with which several Stendahl revelations landed: that Paul's "thorn in the flesh" was not a matter of "concupiscence" but, as Stendahl put it, "presumably some physical handicap."[17] That Paul, insisting that "while we were yet sinners, Christ died for us," clearly affirmed that God's love for us was simply a priori—not dependent on our good behavior, much less on our repentance.[18] That Paul was not reacting against the "legalistic Jew" in favor of the grace-filled "Christian."[19] And, perhaps most momentous of all, that essential understandings of Scripture (and therefore of doctrine) inevitably change through time.[20] Scripture, that is, may be divinely inspired, but, also, it is humanly *interpreted.*

The Lutheran scholar Helmut Koester later summarized the impact of what we novices were struggling to grasp:

> Is it thinkable that Paul, when he speaks of justification by faith alone, is not talking about the salvation of individuals, who are constantly burdened by their conscience, telling them they are unable to fulfill the Law and do the will of God?...Paul is not talking about individuals, but about people and nations, about actions of the God of Israel, who is the God of all nations, and who wants freedom and justice.[21]

Yes, justice. There was Martin Luther, and now there was Martin Luther King. There were our seminar rooms, and there were the streets—the bifurcated locus of our transformation. God's preoccupation, I was beginning to sense, was not with sin and its wages, but with suffering and how to end it.

The full meaning of Stendahl's insight would not become clear to me for some time, although its flash was bright enough to illuminate the shadows cast by piety that transcended narrow Lutheran references. Most particularly, the ground was shifting under what we Paulists had taken to be St. Paul's severe oppositionalism, and that shift opened into a whole new realm of questions. If faith was not the enemy of works, or grace the enemy of law, who knew what other structures of conflict might not fall? Was it possible that the entire economy of salvation—a saving God of mercy over against a damning God of judgment—could be revised? And what would that mean for an encumbered lad like me?

It was an astonishment to take up such questions at that moment, in the company of earnest young Lutherans, who were daring to think critically about their own tradition. Despite our being tutored by Harry McSorely, our professor, they knew more than we did. Had Luther distorted the New Testament's meaning by using his personal antagonism toward the pope and papists (greedy materialists of the first order) as the lens through which to view Paul's tensions with his fellow Jews? Had Luther changed how Paul was read by everyone—and, especially in relation to Jews, was that change for the worse? Had Luther done something similar for the patron of his own religious order, offering a distorted reading of Augustine?

If Lutherans had such basic questions to ask, so did Catholics, especially we Paulists for whom St. Paul was defining. Had we also missed something crucial about the apostle to the Gentiles? All at once, even his "conversion" took on different meaning. January 25 was the feast of the great history-altering Damascus road event, a significance reflected in that decision of Pope John to convene his Council on that date. January 25 was always the occasion of the Paulist Fathers' greatest celebration, our best party. Because of Paul, conversion was a central metaphor for Paulists, self-styled "convert makers." We, too, were apostles, even if our "Gentiles" were the religiously indifferent masses of modern America.

The feast of the "conversion" of St. Paul had such resonance because the assumption was that the real life of the church began when its great persecutor was converted from Judaism to Christianity, when the Jew "Saul" became the Christian "Paul." But what if the name change was only a matter of translation, not transformation—an alteration by the author of the Acts of the Apostles that only rendered the Hebrew name into Latin, as Saul-Paul made his way from Palestine to Rome? As Stendahl taught us, "There is not—as we usually think—first a conversion, and then a call to apostleship; there is only the call to work among the Gentiles."[22]

What if Paul, that is, far from seeing an unbridgeable theological opposition between "faith" and "works," between "grace" and "law," saw instead only resolvable tensions between the people of Israel and those Gentiles who, in Jesus Christ, sought adoption into that people? What if the conflict reflected in Paul's letters—and there is conflict—was not against Israel, but *within* it? Not between "the church" and "the synagogue," but inside the hearts and minds of Jesus people who were struggling to understand exactly what their convictions implied?

Historical criticism helped us understand just then that, in Paul's lifetime, "the church" had not yet come into existence. The Jesus movement was, at most, a nascent sect within Judaism. If Paul was enlightened en route to Damascus, it was for having seen the essentially Jewish meaning of the life and death of Jesus. There was no question of his embracing a new religious identity—"conversion." Nor was there any question of God having broken his promise to Israel, repudiating "the synagogue" in favor of "the church." All of that anti-Israel denigrating came later (after the traumas of the destruction of the temple in 70 CE and the leveling of Jerusalem in 135 CE). Later still, the anti-Israel denigration was squared by Martin Luther, who had his own culturally determined reasons for deploring the Jewishness that he happily imagined Paul repudiating.

I remember vividly the oak-paneled seminar room in St. Paul's College in which one of our Lutheran confreres first broached the question that underlies all of this: What if St. Paul never stopped being a Jew? And if Paul was fully a Jew to the end, was it possible that Jesus himself was also? Was it possible that we had to relearn how to read the anti-Jewish texts of the Gospels themselves? Such were the questions that followed, for us, from Krister Stendahl's pivotal assertion in his "Introspective Conscience" article. Why shouldn't we young Catholics have been transfixed by what these Lutherans were showing us, even if the implications would become fully clear only over the years?

In New England at about the same time, a young Jesuit scholar of my generation was undergoing his own version of the same experience. He was Daniel Harrington, and he eventually became a prominent Catholic expert on St. Paul. "We all have had communal and personal moments when the world seemed to change for us," Harrington wrote much later.

> I can recall vividly my own first reading of Krister Stendahl's famous article on "Paul and the Introspective Conscience of the West" while sitting in the library of Harvard Divinity School in 1965. It changed my outlook on Paul, Augustine, and Luther. It was a thrilling intellectual experience that has stayed with me through the years. So much so that whenever I teach or write about Paul, I recall that moment"[23]

If my own paler version of that experience was less a matter of a "moment" than of a succession of encounters that kept me scrambling in the same era, all bracketed by the illuminations of the Second Vatican Council, the transformation that began then was equally defining for me. In nothing was that more true than in relation to the question of St. Paul's permanent and full and loyal and ever-loving Jewishness. Not withstanding the mythic plea—"Lord, what wilt Thou have me to do?"—that made him patron of my own calling, my dear "convert" was not a convert. That recognition made all the difference, not only for my youthful sense of vocation, but also for the most important moral and intellectual challenge of my lifetime.

Helmut Koester shows that there was a direct line from Stendahl's upending of the faith-law dichotomy to a reckoning with the impact of this theology on historic Christian attitudes toward Jews. Indeed, as it turned out, this was, as Koester says, "the core of Krister Stendahl's increasing concern and active involvement in the question of the reconciliation of Jews and Christians. Thanks to Krister Stendahl," Koester continues, "I have learned that as a Christian I belong to a people that is burdened with the guilt of a long history of the persecution of the Jewish people, culminating with the Holocaust." Here is where the airy abstractions of theology crash-land on the rough ground of history. "His interpretation of Paul's letters has opened the door to a fresh understanding of Jews and Christians as people who both possess the promises of a God who is faithful to his promises and wants peace and justice for all."[24]

Vatican II was nothing if not the Roman Catholic attempt to confront the meaning for theology of the church's failures during the Holocaust. At the most obvious level, that was centrally a matter of doing away with the supersessionist denigration of the living religion of the Jewish people, a purpose that prompted the Council to issue its most important document, *Nostra Aetate*. That declaration was not what it might have been—*should* have been—as a Christian reckoning with ancient anti-Judaism and modern anti-Semitism, yet it stands as a historic marker. Famous as the renunciation of the "Christ-killer" slander, *Nostra Aetate's* equally important assertion is that the covenant God made with Israel, far from being renounced, remains in force. ("The Jews remain very dear to God, for the sake of the patriarchs, since God does not take back the gifts he bestowed or the choice he made."[25])

This simple statement—which echoes Paul's, in Romans 11:28–29—undercuts the either/or bipolarity between an outmoded, rejected "synagogue" and a vital and sacred "church." To dismantle that structure of theology was to dismantle the equivalent structure of the religious imagination that opposed the consuming fire of the Old Testament God to the loving Father of the New Testament. That long-standing structure had pit God-the-mortal-enemy against God-the-great-friend, with Jesus taken to be the saving arbiter between them. Yet the negative-positive charge of that dualism had threatened doom no matter what Jesus was taken to have done. That bipolarity had defined, of course, the "introspective conscience of the West," and it showed up not only in religion, but in culture, ultimately erecting, for example, the murderous structures of white supremacy.

One of the authors at the Council of the transforming *Nostra Aetate* was our own Thomas Stransky, who, by the time of my ordination to the priesthood in 1969 was the president of the Paulist Fathers. Stransky was our prophet and our leader. Our electing this pioneer of interfaith reconciliation as president was a signal of how deeply into our consciousness the pillars of Conciliar reform had been drilled. Indeed, the Paulist Fathers' publishing house, Paulist Press, became the most important English-language tribune of that reform. (That Paulist Press is the publisher of the present volume is a signal of the depth of that commitment.) In those years, we Paulists changed our understanding of our patron (opposed not to Judaism, but, like Jesus himself, to the Imperium of Rome, which killed him), of our mission (from "convert makers" to "ecumenists"), and of the church itself (not "militant" but "pilgrim").

Indeed, the idea of God changed. Recovering the Jewish roots of the faith, we could say with resolute new energy that there is One God (*Shema!*), whose attitude is constant ("God saw every thing that he had made, and indeed, it was very good"[26]). No longer did we need to plead with Jesus to change God's mind from damning us to saving us. It was *our* minds that Jesus came to change, not God's. No longer, therefore, were we at the mercy of the apocalyptic dread of the "last things" and their doomsday Divinity. All at once, the good news was truly good, and it seemed real: the One God is the God of love. God is love, period, full stop.

The impact of such a large religious transformation on institutional Christianity was one thing, but its effect on the consciences of individual Christians has been something else. For Catholics, that change shows up most clearly at Mass, where now almost everyone receives the sacrament of communion as a matter of course, where before the majority declined to approach the communion rail because they had been convinced of their own unworthiness. (What if they had swallowed during a nose-bleed?) But that is over. God-the-enemy is gone.

It has become clear that one main function of the old dread was to keep the laity severely in need of the ministrations of the clergy, and that changed, with consequences inside the church (freedom of conscience for Catholics, too), and outside (all those believers who, freed from fear, could simply yield formal connections to institutions of belief[27]). Like many, my own Catholic story can be summed up as a journey from the Church of Pope Pius XII, that dour figure who embodied the sternness of God (Pius XII's contested role during the Holocaust is related to the doom-laden theology of his era), to the church of Pope Francis, the contemporary apostle of divine mercy (and a figure who has forthrightly acknowledged sins and failures, both the church's and his own). The pontificate of the Argentine pope shows what a church looks like once it has been freed from the "introspective conscience" to become a gratefully, and even a joyfully forgiven people.

Krister Stendahl planted a seed that, along with many others, sprouted into these shoots and blossoms. When I was a Catholic priest, trying to proclaim this good news, I encountered him personally for the first time. The Vietnam War was flaring, and antiwar protests were extreme. I was Catholic chaplain at Boston University when he was dean of the Harvard Divinity School across the river. That he was a well-known figure of humane calm in that tumultuous time (in 1969, he bravely opposed the university's unleashing of police against student antiwar demonstrators) was no surprise to me. I went out of my way to hear him preach, and it was the most natural thing in the world to take him as a model. Later, after I left the priesthood to become a writer (a decision my once introspective conscience would never have let me make), accidental circumstances brought us together as friends. Over many years, we lunched regularly in Cambridge, shared a monthly salon in Boston, walked together in Jerusalem, and welcomed one another into our homes. He was a first reader of much of what I wrote. I often adjusted my schedule to hear him lecture or preach. I remain a Catholic, but he was my personal bishop. When I asked for his blessing, he gave it, pressing my head with his hands. I was privileged to sit with him as he approached death, and his dear family welcomed me into its circle of grief.

I saw up close how the spirit of affirmation that had informed Krister Stendahl's revolutionary theological insight reached, in fact, to the very core of his personality. When that affirmation was, again and again, on offer to me, I knew very well why it was so familiar, so bracing, and so precious. My experience was, to repeat, only an instance of the impact he had on legions: an instance of the profound gift he offered to the church he so loved, and to the era that so changed, for the better, because of him.

NOTES

1. Krister Stendahl, "The Apostle Paul and the Introspective Conscience of the West," in *Paul among Jews and Gentiles* (Philadelphia: Fortress, 1976). First published in English in *Harvard Theological Review* 56 (1963): 199–215.

2. Ibid., 86.

3. Ibid., 95.

4. Krister Stendahl, *Meanings: The Bible as Document and as Guide*, 2nd ed. (Minneapolis: Fortress, 2008), 222.

5. "Luther's literary achievement has no parallels in the whole of human history.…During his thirty-year public career Luther produced 544 separate books, pamphlets, or articles, slightly more than one every three weeks." Alec Ryrie, *Protestants: The Faith That Made the Modern World* (New York: Viking, 2017), 20.

6. Albert Camus, *The Myth of Sisyphus, and Other Essays*, trans. Justin O'Brien (New York: Vintage Books, 1955), 3.

7. Julius Köstlin, *The Life of Martin Luther*, trans. John G. Morris (Philadelphia: Lutheran Publication Society, 1883), 56.

8. Psalm 22:6. The verse came to us with the curl of an Irish accent, capturing the broken spirit of a famine-haunted people. The Great Hunger was yesterday—in my grandfather's lifetime. That trauma lived on in the Irish unconscious as monumental proof of our unworthiness.

9. Romans 7:19.

10. Stendahl, *Paul among Jews and Gentiles*, 78.

11. Ibid., 79.

12. Matthew 25:13, KJV.

13. James Joyce, *A Portrait of the Artist as a Young Man* (Mineola, NY: Dover, 1994), 89.

14. Francis Thompson, "The Hound of Heaven," in *The Oxford Book of English Mystical Verse*, ed. D. H. S. Nicholson and A. H. E. Lee (Oxford: Clarendon, 1917), http://www.bartleby.com/236/239.html.

15. Acts 9:6, KJV.

16. Of course, as I am still instructed, there is no horse in the account in Acts.

17. Stendahl, *Paul among Jews and Gentiles*, 91.

18. Ibid., 89, citing Romans 5:6–11.

19. Ibid., 95.

20. Ibid., 96. Stendahl developed this insight in *Meanings*.

21. Helmut Koester,"Tribute to Bishop Krister Stendahl," *Studies in Christian-Jewish Relations* 4 (2009): 5.

22. Stendahl, *Paul among Jews and Gentiles*, 84–85.

23. Daniel Harrington, "Tribute to Bishop Krister Stendahl," *Studies in Christian-Jewish Relations* 4 (2009): 6.

24. Koester, "Tribute to Krister Stendahl," 5.

25. Second Vatican Council, *Declaration on the Relation of the Church to Non-Christian Religions: Nostra Aetate*, proclaimed by Pope Paul VI, October 28, 1965, http://www.vatican.va/archive/hist_councils/ii_vatican_council/documents/vat-ii_decl_19651028_nostra-aetate_en.html.

26. Genesis 1:31.

27. Thirteen percent of all Americans describe themselves as former Catholics, which is the second largest religious group after Catholics, who make up 22 percent, https://cruxnow.com/church/2015/05/12/pew-survey-percentage-of-us-catholics-drops-and-catholicism-is-losing-members-faster-than-any-denomination/.

BIBLIOGRAPHY

Abelson, Kassel and Reuven Hammer. "The Status of 'Messianic Jews.'" December 2012. https://www.rabbinicalassembly.org/sites/default/files/assets/public/halakhah/teshuvot/2011-2020/abelson-hammer-messianic-jews.pdf.

Aejmelaeus, Anneli and Tuukka Kauhanen, eds. *The Legacy of Barthélemy: 50 Years after Les Devanciers d'Aquila*. De Septuaginta Investigationes 9. Göttingen: Vandenhoeck & Ruprecht, 2017.

Alexander, Michele. *The New Jim Crow: Mass Incarceration in an Age of Colorblindness*. Rev. ed. New York: New Press, 2012.

Alexander, Philip S. "Enoch and the Beginnings of Jewish Interest in Natural Science." In *The Wisdom Texts from Qumran and the Development of Sapiential Thought*, edited by Charlotte Hempel, Armin Lange, and Hermann Lichtenberger, 223–43. BETL 159. Louvain: Peeters, 2002. Reprinted in *Ancient Jewish Science and the History of Knowledge in Second Temple Jewish Literature*, edited by Jonathan Ben-Dov and Seth Sanders, 25–49 (New York: New York University Press and Institute for the Study of the Ancient World, 2014).

———. "Literacy among Jews in Second Temple Palestine: Reflections on the Evidence from Qumran." In *Hamlet on a Hill: Semitic and Greek Studies Presented to Professor T. Muraoka on the Occasion of His Sixty-Fifth Birthday*, edited by Martin F. J. Baasten and Wido Th. Van Peursen, 3–24. OLA 118. Louvain: Peeters, 2003.

Apodaca, M. Anthony. "Myth Theory, Comparison and Embedded Scripture Texts: Ibn Ishāq's Biography of Muhammad and the Mythologizing Function of Isaiah 7.14 in Matthew 1.23." In *Biblical Interpretation in Early Christian Gospels*. Vol. 2, *The Gospel of Matthew*, edited by Thomas R. Hatina, 14–29. LNTS 310. London: T&T Clark, 2008.

Bane, Paul. "I Am a Pharisee!," *Mindful Christianity Today*, Feb. 17, 2016. http://www.mindfulchristianitytoday.com/i-am-a-pharisee.

Barclay, John M.G. *Paul and the Gift*. Grand Rapids, MI: Eerdmans, 2015.

Barthélemy, Dominique. "Redécouverte d'un chaînon manquant de l'histoire de la Septante." *Revue Biblique* 60 (1953): 18–29.

Becker, Adam H. and Annette Yoshiko Reed, eds. *The Ways That Never Parted: Jews and Christians in Late Antiquity and the Early Middle Ages*. Texte und Studien zum Antiken Judentum 95. Tübingen: Mohr Siebeck, 2003.

Beckstrom, Brian A. F. "Blessed are the Undocumented? A Reflection on Matthew 5:1-12." *Journal of Lutheran Ethics* 10, no. 12 (December 2010), http://www.elca.org/JLE/Articles/240?_ga=2.108093954.1687925305.1494876105-200062273.1494873747.

BeDuhn, Jason. *Augustine's Manichaean Dilemma*. Vol. 2, *Making a "Catholic" Self, 388–401 C.E.* Philadelphia: University of Pennsylvania Press, 2013.

Blomberg, Craig L. "Matthew." In *Commentary on the New Testament Use of the Old Testament*, edited by Gregory K. Beale and Donald A. Carson, 1–109. Grand Rapids, MI: Baker Academic, 2007.

Boccaccini, Gabriele, and Carlos A. Segovia, eds. *Paul the Jew: Rereading the Apostle as a Figure of Second Temple Judaism*. Minneapolis: Fortress, 2016.

Boyarin, Daniel. "The Gospel of the Memra: Jewish Binitarianism and the Prologue to John." *Harvard Theological Review* 94 (2001): 243–84.

Brooke, George J. "Aspects of Education in the Sectarian Scrolls from the Qumran Caves." In *Jewish Education from Antiquity to the Middle Ages: Studies in Honour of Philip S. Alexander*, edited by George J. Brooke and Renate Smithuis, 11–42. AJEC 100. Leiden: Brill, 2017.

———. "Aspects of Matthew's Use of Scripture in Light of the Dead Sea Scrolls." In *A Teacher for All Generations: Essays in Honor of James C. VanderKam*, edited by Eric F. Mason, Kelley Coblentz Bautch, Angela Kim Harkins, and Daniel A. Machiela, 821–38. Vol. 2. JSJSup 153. Leiden: Brill, 2012.

———. "4Q341: An Exercise for Spelling and for Spells?" In *Writing and Ancient Near Eastern Society: Papers in Honour of Alan R. Millard*, edited by Piotr Bienowski, Christopher B. Mee, and Elizabeth A. Slater, 271–82. LHBOTS 426. London: T&T Clark, 2005.

———. "Reading, Searching Blessing: A Functional Approach to Scriptural Interpretation in the יחד." In *The Temple in Text and Tradition: A Festschrift in Honour of Robert Hayward*, edited by R. Timothy McLay, 140–56. LSTS 83. London: Bloomsbury, 2015.

———. "Shared Exegetical Traditions between the Scrolls and the New Testament." In *The Oxford Handbook of the Dead Sea Scrolls*, edited by Timothy H. Lim and John J. Collins, 565–91. Oxford: Oxford University Press, 2010.

Brown, Peter. *Augustine of Hippo: A Biography*. Berkeley: University of California Press, 2000.

Cadbury, Henry J. *The Peril of Modernizing Jesus*. New York: Macmillan, 1937.

Camus, Albert. *The Myth of Sisyphus, and Other Essays*. Translated by Justin O'Brien. New York: Vintage Books, 1955.

Carroll, James. "Pope Francis and the Renunciation of Jewish Conversation." *The New Yorker*, December 16, 2015, http://www.newyorker.com/news/news-desk/pope-francis-and-the-renunciation-of-jewish-conversion.

Chadwick, Henry. *Augustine. A Very Short Introduction*. Oxford: Oxford University Press, 1986.

Cohn, Yehudah B. *Tangled Up in Text: Tefillin and the Ancient World*. Brown Judaic Studies 351. Providence, RI: Brown University Press, 2008.

Collins, John J. *Beyond the Qumran Community: The Sectarian Movement of the Dead Sea Scrolls*. Grand Rapids, MI: Eerdmans, 2010.

Crane, Susan E. "Bible Study on Women in Ministry," http://www.abc-usa.org/wp-content/uploads/2012/07/BIBLE-STUDY-ON-WOMEN-IN-MINISTRY-for-ABWIM-Resource-List.pdf. Originally published as "Mentoring Women in Ministry: 'Follow Me, as I Follow Christ!'" *American Baptist Women in Ministry Sunday Celebration*, March 19, 2006.

———. *Junia: A Bible Study and Storytelling Resource for the Church*. Valley Forge, PA: Interim Ministries-ABC/American Baptist Women in Ministry, n.d., http://www.abc-usa.org/wp-content/uploads/2012/07/Junia.pdf.

Cunningham, Philip A. "Is the Pope Anti-Jewish? No, but Here Is Why His Critics Think So." *Commonweal* 144, no. 9 (May 8, 2017), https://www.commonwealmagazine.org/pope-'anti-jewish'.

Cunningham, Philip A., Joseph Sievers, Mary Boys, and Hans Herman Hendrix, eds. *Christ Jesus and the Jewish People Today: New Explorations of Theological Interrelationship*. Grand Rapids, MI: Eerdmans, 2011.

Dahl, Nils A. *Studies in Paul: Theology for the Early Christian Mission*. Minneapolis: Augsburg, 1977. Reprinted by Wipf and Stock, 2002.

Donaldson, Terence L. "Jewish Christianity, Israel's Stumbling and the *Sonderweg* Reading of Paul." *Journal for the Study of the New Testament* 29 (2006): 27–54.

———. "Paul within Judaism: A Critical Evaluation from a 'New Perspective' Perspective." In Nanos and Zetterholm, *Paul within Judaism*, 277–302.

Doupe, Andrew. "Partnerships between Churches and People Living with HIV/AIDS Organizations." World Council of Churches, January 1, 2005, https://www.oikoumene.org/en/resources/documents/wcc-programmes/justice-diakonia-and-responsibility-for-creation/health-and-healing/hivaids/wcc-statements-and-studies/partnerships-between-churches-and-people-living-with-hivaids-organizations.

Drawnel, Henryk. "Priestly Education in the 'Aramaic Levi Document (Visions of Levi)' and 'Aramaic Astronomical Book' (4Q208–211)." *Revue de Qumrân* 22 (2006): 547–74.

Dunn, James D.G. "The Justice of God: A Renewed Perspective on Justification by Faith (The Henton Davies Lecture, Regents Park College, Oxford, January 1991)." *Journal of Theological Studies* 43 (1992): 1–22.

———. "The New Perspective on Paul." *Bulletin of the John Rylands Library* 65 (1983): 95–122.

———. *The New Perspective on Paul: Collected Essays*. WUNT 185. Tübingen: Mohr Siebeck, 2005. Revised edition, Grand Rapids, MI: Eerdmans, 2008.

———. "The New Perspective: What, Whence, and Whither?" In *The New Perspective on Paul: Collected Essays*, 1–97. Tübingen: Mohr Siebeck, 2005.

———. *The Theology of the Apostle Paul*. Grand Rapids, MI: Eerdmans, 1998.

Eisenbaum, Pamela. "Paul, Polemics, and the Problem of Essentialism." *Biblical Interpretation* 13 (2005): 224–38.

———. *Paul Was Not a Christian: The Original Message of a Misunderstood Apostle*. New York: HarperOne, 2009.

Erikson, Erik H. *Young Man Luther: A Study in Psychoanalysis and History*. New York: Norton, 1958.

Fitzmyer, Joseph A. "Saint Paul and the Law." *Jurist* 27 (1967): 18–36.

Francis (Pope) Homilies: "The Christian Includes; Pharisees Exclude." *America Magazine*, November 5, 2015, https://www.americamagazine.org/issue/pope-francis-christian-includes-pharisees-exclude.

Frankel, Jonathan and Ezra Mendelsohn, eds. *The Protestant-Jewish Conundrum*. Studies in Contemporary Jewry 24. Oxford: Oxford University Press, 2010.

Fredriksen, Paula. *Augustine and the Jews: A Christian Defense of Jews and Judaism*. New Haven, CT: Yale University Press, 2010.

———. "Beyond the Body/Soul Dichotomy: Augustine on Paul against the Manichees and the Pelagians." *Recherches augustiniennes* 23 (1988): 87–114.

———. "The Confessions as Autobiography." In *A Companion to Augustine*, edited by Mark Vessey, 87–98. Malden, MA: Wiley–Blackwell, 2012.

———. "Jesus the Jewish Christ." *Studia Theologica—Nordic Journal of Theology* 66 (2012): 3–19.

———. "Judaizing the Nations: The Ritual Demands of Paul's Gospel." *New Testament Studies* 56 (2010): 232–52.

———. "Mandatory Retirement: Ideas in the Study of Christian Origins Whose Time Has Come to Go." *Studies in Religion/Sciences Religieuses* 35 (2006): 231–46.

———. "Paul and Augustine: Conversion Narratives, Orthodox Traditions, and the Retrospective Self." *Journal of Theological Studies* 37 (1986): 3–34.

———. *Paul: The Pagans' Apostle*. New Haven, CT: Yale University Press, 2017.

———. *Sin: The Early History of an Idea*. Princeton, NJ: Princeton University Press, 2012.

Fridrichsen, Anton. *Fyrahanda sädesåker: En kommentar till Evangeliebokens högmässotexter*. Edited by Birger Gerhardsson. Stockholm: Svenska kyrkans diakonistyrelses bokförlag, 1958.

Frymer-Kensky, Tikva, David Novak, Peter Ochs, David Fox Sandmel, and Michael Signer, eds. *Christianity in Jewish Terms*. Boulder, CO: Westview Press, 2000.

Gager, John G. *The Origins of Anti-Semitism: Attitudes toward Judaism in Pagan and Christian Antiquity*. New York: Oxford University Press, 1983.

———. "Paul, the Apostle of Judaism." In *Jesus, Judaism, and Christian Anti-Judaism: Reading the New Testament after the Holocaust*, edited by Paula Fredriksen and Adele Reinhartz, 56–76. Louisville, KY: John Knox Press, 2002.

———. *Reinventing Paul*. New York: Oxford University Press, 2000.

———. "Some Notes on Paul's Conversion." *New Testament Studies* 27 (1981): 697–704.

García Martínez, Florentino, and Eibert J. C. Tigchelaar. *The Dead Sea Scrolls Study Edition*. Leiden: Brill; Grand Rapids, MI: Eerdmans, 2000.

Gaston, Lloyd. *Paul and the Torah*. Vancouver: University of British Columbia Press, 1987.

Gayer, Asaf, Daniel Stökl Ben Ezra, and Jonathan Ben-Dov. "A New Join of Two Fragments of 4QcryptA Serekh haEdah and Its Implications." *Dead Sea Discoveries* 23 (2016): 139–54.

Gerhardsson, Birger. *Evangeliernas förhistoria: Nyutgåva med tillägg*. Lund: Novapress, 1991.

———. *Fridrichsen, Odeberg, Aulén, Nygren: Fyra teologer*. Lund: Novapress, 1994.

———. *Memory and Manuscript: Oral Tradition and Written Transmission in Rabbinic Judaism and Early Christianity*, with *Tradition and Transmission in Early Christianity*. Grand Rapids, MI: Eerdmans, 1998. Originally published 1961 and 1964.

———. *The Reliability of the Gospel Tradition*. Foreword by Donald A. Hagner. Peabody, MA: Hendrickson, 2001.

Gundry, Robert H. *The Use of the Old Testament in St. Matthew's Gospel with Special Reference to the Messianic Hope*. NovTSup 18. Leiden: Brill, 1967.

Hageman, Alice. "Foreward/Forward!" In Hageman, *Sexist Religion and Women in the Church*, 11–13.

———. *Sexist Religion and Women in the Church: No More Silence!* In collaboration with the Women's Caucus of Harvard Divinity School. New York: Association Press, 1974.

Harper, Steve. "Commentary: The Ordination of Women," http://www.umc.org/what-we-believe/commentary-the-ordination-of-women.

Harrington, Daniel. "Tribute to Bishop Krister Stendahl." *Studies in Christian-Jewish Relations* 4 (2009): 1–7.

Hatina, Thomas R. "From History to Myth and Back Again: The Historicizing Function of Scripture in Matthew 2." In *Biblical Interpretation in Early Christian Gospels*. Vol. 2, *The Gospel of Matthew*, edited by Thomas R. Hatina, 98–118. LNTS 310. London: T&T Clark, 2008.

Hays, Richard B. *Echoes of Scripture in the Gospels*. Waco, TX: Baylor University Press, 2016.

Heschel, Susannah. "Memorial to Krister Stendahl." Unpublished text.

Hezser, Catherine. *Jewish Literacy in Roman Palestine*. TSAJ 81. Tübingen: Mohr Siebeck, 2001.

———. "Private and Public Education." In *Jewish Daily Life in Roman Palestine*, edited by Catherine Hezser, 465–81. Oxford: Oxford University Press, 2010.

Hodge, Caroline Johnson. *If Sons, Then Heirs: A Study of Kinship and Ethnicity in the Letters of Paul*. Oxford: Oxford University Press, 2007.

———. "The Question of Identity: Gentiles as Gentiles—but Also Not—in Pauline Communities." In Nanos and Zetterholm, *Paul within Judaism*, 153–73.

Homosexuella och samhället: Betänkande av utredningen om homosexuellas situation i samhället. Statens offentliga utredningar 1984:63. Stockholm: Liber, 1984.

Howard, George. "On the 'Faith of Christ.'" *Harvard Theological Review* 60 (1967): 459–65.

Hvalvik, Reidar. "A 'Sonderweg' for Israel: A Critical Examination of a Current Interpretation of Romans 11.25–27." *Journal for the Study of the New Testament* 38 (1990): 87–107.

Ilan, Tal. "Post-Biblical and Rabbinic Women." In *Jewish Women: A Comprehensive Historical Encyclopedia*, edited by Paula E. Hyman and Dalia Ofer. Jerusalem: Shalvi Publishing, 2006. CD-ROM, https://jwa.org/encyclopedia/article/post-biblical-and-rabbinic-women.

Jeggle-Merz, Birgit, and Michael Durst, eds. *Juden und Christen im Dialog*. Theologische Berichte, Band 36. Fribourg, CH.: Paulusverlag, 2016.

Johnson-DeBaufre, Melanie, and Laura Salah Nasrallah. "Beyond the Heroic Paul: Toward a Feminist and Decolonizing Approach to the Letters of Paul." In *The Colonized Apostle: Paul through Postcolonial Eyes*, edited by Christopher Stanley, 161–73. Minneapolis: Fortress, 2011.

Jones, Ivor. "Matthew." In *Early Christian Thought in Its Jewish Context*, edited by John Barclay and John Sweet, 59–69. Cambridge: Cambridge University Press, 1996.

Jonson, Jonas. *Jag är bara Nathan Söderblom satt till tjänst: En biografi*. Stockholm: Verbum, 2014.

Joyce, James. *A Portrait of the Artist as a Young Man*. Mineola, NY: Dover, 1994.

Joyner, Will. "Krister Stendahl, 1921–2008." *Harvard Divinity School—News and Events*, April 16, 2008. hds.harvard.edu/news/2011/02/07/krister-stendahl-1921-2008#.

Käsemann, Ernst. "Justification and Salvation History in the Epistle to the Romans." In *Perspectives on Paul*. Translated by Margaret Kohl, 60–78. Philadelphia: Fortress, 1971.

Kinzer, Mark. *Searching Her Own Mystery: Nostra Aetate, the Jewish People, and the Identity of the Church*. Eugene, OR: Cascade Books, 2015.

Klassen, Pamela E., and John W. Marshall. "Saint as Cipher: Paul, Badiou, and the Politics of Ritual Repudiation." *History of Religions* 51 (2012): 344–63.

Kobia, Samuel. "…And who is my neighbor?" World Council of Churches, June 14, 2009, https://www.oikoumene.org/en/resources/documents/general-secretary/sermons/and-who-is-my-neighbour.

Koester, Helmut. "Tribute to Bishop Krister Stendahl." *Studies in Christian-Jewish Relations* 4 (2009): 1–7.

Kooij, Arie van der. "Scholars and Officials in Early Judaism: The Sôfer of Jesus Ben Sira." In *Septuagint, Sages, and Scripture: Studies in Honour of Johann Cook*, edited by Randall X. Gauthier, Gideon R. Kotzé, and Gert J. Steyn, 190–204. VTSup 172. Leiden: Brill, 2016.

Köstlin, Julius. *The Life of Martin Luther*. Translated by John G. Morris. Philadelphia: Lutheran Publication Society, 1883.

"Krister Stendahl, 86, was HDS Dean from 1968–1979." *Harvard Gazette* (April 17, 2008). https://news.harvard.edu/gazette/story/2008/04/krister-stendahl-86-was-hds-dean-from-1968-1979.

Kümmel, Werner Georg. *Römer sieben und das Bild des Menschen im Neuen Testament. Zwei Studien*. Theologische Bücherei 53. Munich: Kaiser, 1974. Originally published 1929 by J.C. Hinrichs.

Landau, Yehezkel. "An Interview with Krister Stendahl." *Harvard Divinity Bulletin* 35 (2007): 29–31. https://bulletin.hds.harvard.edu/articles/winter2007/interview-krister-stendahl.

Langer, Ruth, *Cursing the Christians? A History of the Birkat ha-Minim*. New York: Oxford University Press, 2012.

Lemaire, André. "Lire, écrire, étudier à Qoumrân et ailleurs." In *Qoumrân et le Judaïsme du tournant de notre ère: Actes de la Table Ronde, Collège de France, 16 novembre 2004*, edited by André Lemaire and Simon G. Mimouni, 63–79. Collection de la REJ 40. Louvain: Peeters, 2006.

Levine, Amy-Jill. *The Misunderstood Jew: The Church and the Scandal of the Jewish Jesus*. New York: HarperOne, 2006.

———. "*Nostra Aetate, Omnia Mutantur*: The Times They are a Changing." In *Righting Relations after the Holocaust and Vatican II: Essays in Honor of John Pawlikowski, OSM*, edited by Elena G. Procario-Foley and Robert A. Cathey. Mahwah, NJ: Paulist Press, 2018.

———. "Quit Picking on the Pharisees!," *Sojourners*, March 2015.

———. *Short Stories by Jesus: The Enigmatic Parables of a Controversial Rabbi*. New York: HarperOne, 2014.

Lönning, Inge. *Antisemittismen som juridisk, intellektuell og moralsk utfordring: En betenkning om rettssaken mot Radio Islam og debatten om professor Jan Bergmans vitneprov i retten*. Uppsala: University of Uppsala Faculty of Theology, 1994.

Luz, Ulrich. *Matthew 1—7: A Commentary*. Minneapolis: Augsburg Fortress, 1989.

Lyonnet, Stanislas. "Augustin et Rom 5,12 avant la controverse pélagienne: A propos d'un texte de saint Augustin sur le baptême des enfants." *Nouvelle Revue Théologique* 89 (1967): 842–49.

———. "Rom 5,12 chez S. Augustin: Note sur l'elaboration de la doctrine augustinienne du peche originel." In *L'Homme devant Dieu: Mélanges offerts au père Henri de Lubac*. Vol. 1, *Exégèse et patristique*, 327–39. Paris: Auber, 1963.

Maier, Johann. "Early Jewish Biblical Interpretation in the Qumran Literature." In *Hebrew Bible/Old Testament: The History of Its Interpretation*. Vol. 1, *From the Beginnings to the Middle Ages (Until 1300)*, edited by Magne Sæbø, 108–29. Göttingen: Vandenhoeck & Ruprecht, 1996.

Malm, Olof B. *Bilder och blad från Ekumeniska mötet i Stockholm 1925*. Stockholm: Svenska kyrkans diakonistyrelses bokförlag, 1925.

Marchal, Joseph A. "Responsibilities to the Publics of Biblical Studies and Critical Rhetorical Engagements for a Safer World." In *Secularism and Biblical Studies*, edited by Roland Boer, 101–15. Oakville, CT: Equinox, 2010.

———. "To What End(s)? Biblical Studies and Critical Rhetorical Engagement(s) for a 'Safer' World." *SBL Forum* (June 2006). http://sbl-site.org/Article.aspx?ArticleID=550.

Markus, Robert A. *Conversion and Disenchantment in Augustine's Spiritual Career*. Villanova, PA: Villanova University Press, 1989.

Marshall, John W. "Misunderstanding the New Paul: Marcion's Transformation of the *Sonderzeit* Paul." *Journal of Early Christian Studies* 20 (2012): 1–29.

Martin, A. W. Bill Jr. "Commentary: Preaching Tips for New Clergy," http://www.umc.org/news-and-media/commentary-preaching-tips-for-new-clergy.

Maxwell, Paul C. "Analyzing the Apostle Paul's 'Robust Conscience': Identifying and Engaging the Psychological Concerns of Krister

Stendahl's Inceptive Article." *Westminster Theological Journal* 75 (2013): 145–64.

McClaren, Brian. "Beyond Fire and Brimstone." *Sojourners*, Feb. 14, 2014, http://sojo.net/magazine/2014/02/beyond-fire-and-brimstone.

Medley, A. Roy. "BWA Assembly Blog 5 – 'But Now,'" http://www.abc-usa.org/2014/07/10/bwa-assembly-blog-5-but-now-a-message-by-dr-medley.

Menken, Marten J.J. *Matthew's Bible: The Old Testament Text of the Evangelist*. BETL 173. Louvain: Peeters, 2004.

Meyers, Eric M. "Khirbet Qumran and its Environs." In *The Oxford Handbook of the Dead Sea Scrolls*, edited by Timothy H. Lim and John J. Collins, 21–45. Oxford: Oxford University Press, 2010.

Miler, Jean. *Les citations d'accomplissement dans l'évangile de Matthieu: Quand Dieu se rend présent en toute humanité*. Analecta Biblica 140. Rome: Editrice Pontificio Instituto Biblico, 1999.

Moore, Joy J. "Commentary: Women in Ministry," http://www.umc.org/what-we-believe/commentary-women-in-ministry.

Munck, Johannes. *Paulus und die Heilsgeschichte*. Copenhagen: Munksgaard, 1954. Translated by Frank Clarke as *Paul and the Salvation of Mankind*. Richmond, VA: John Knox Press, 1959.

Nanos, Mark D. *The Mystery of Romans: The Jewish Context of Paul's Letter*. Minneapolis: Fortress, 1996.

Nanos, Mark D., and Magnus Zetterholm, eds. *Paul within Judaism: Restoring the First-Century Context to the Apostle*. Minneapolis: Fortress, 2015.

Nasrallah, Laura. "A Conversation with John Stendahl." YouTube video, 48:16. Part of HarvardX course, "Early Christianity: The Letters of Paul." Posted by Harvard Divinity School, January 14, 2014. https://www.youtube.com/watch?v=8qYPcZ8WvSU.

Nitzan, Bilhah. *Qumran Prayer and Religious Poetry*. Translated by Jonathan Chipman. STDJ 12. Leiden: Brill, 1994.

O'Donnell, James J. *Augustine: Confessions*. 3 vols. Oxford: Clarendon Press, 1992.

Orton, David E. *The Understanding Scribe: Matthew and the Apocalyptic Ideal*. JSNTSup 25. Sheffield, UK: Sheffield Academic Press, 1989.

Overman, J. Andrew. "Problems with Pluralism in the Second Temple Judaism: Matthew, James, and the Didache in Their Jewish-Roman Milieu." In *Matthew, James and Didache: Three Related Documents in Their Jewish and Christian Settings*, edited by Huub van de Sandt and Jürgen K. Zangenberg, 259–70. SymS 45. Atlanta: Society of Biblical Literature, 2008.

Rindge, Matthew S. "Mark's Gospel, Social Outcasts, and Modern Slavery." *Journal of Lutheran Ethics* 10, no. 6 (June 2010), http://www.elca.org/JLE/articles/291?_ga=2.105837763.1352928997.1494874071-200062273.1494873747.

Robinson, V. Gene. *In the Eye of the Storm: Swept to the Center by God.* New York: Seabury, 2008.

Rodriguez, Rafael and Matthew Thiessen, eds. *The So-Called Jew in Paul's Letter to the Romans.* Minneapolis: Fortress, 2016.

Rosner, Jennifer M. "Messianic Jews and Jewish-Christian Dialogue." In *Introduction to Messianic Judaism: Its Ecclesial Context and Biblical Foundations*, edited by David J. Rudolph and Joel Willitts, 145–58. Grand Rapids, MI: Zondervan, 2013.

Rothfuchs, Wilhelm. *Die Erfüllungszitate des Matthäus-Evangeliums: Eine biblisch-theologische Untersuchung.* BWANT 88. Stuttgart: W. Kohlhammer, 1969.

Runesson, Anders. "Inventing Christian Identity: Paul, Ignatius, and Theodosius I." In *Exploring Early Christian Identity*, edited by Bengt Holmberg, 59–92. WUNT 1, 226. Tübingen: Mohr Siebeck, 2008.

Ryrie, Alec. *Protestants: The Faith That Made the Modern World.* New York: Viking, 2017.

Sage, Athanase. "Péché originel: La naissance d'un dogme." *Revue des études augustiniennes et patristiques* 13 (1967): 211–48.

Sanders, E.P. *Paul: A Brief Insight.* New York: Sterling, 2009.

———. *Paul, the Law, and the Jewish People.* Philadelphia: Fortress, 1983.

———. *Paul and Palestinian Judaism: A Comparison of Patterns of Religion.* Philadelphia: Fortress, 1977.

———. "Paul's Attitude toward the Jewish People." *Union Seminary Quarterly Review* 33 (1978): 175–87.

Schmitz, Matthew. "Rabbi Objects to Pope Francis's Anti-Jewish Rhetoric." *First Things*, March 16, 2017, https://www.firstthings.com/blogs/firstthoughts/2017/03/rabbi-objects-to-pope-franciss-anti-jewish-rhetoric.

Schüssler Fiorenza, Elisabeth and Kent Harold Richards, eds. *Transforming Graduate Biblical Studies: Ethos and Transformation.* Atlanta: Society of Biblical Literature, 2010.

Schweitzer, Albert. *Paul and His Interpreters: A Critical History.* Translated by W. Montgomery. London: A&C Black, 1912.

Second Vatican Council. *Declaration on the Relation of the Church to Non-Christian Religions: Nostra Aetate.* Proclaimed by Pope Paul VI, October 28, 1965. http://www.vatican.va/archive/hist_councils/ii_vatican_council/documents/vat-ii_decl_19651028_nostra-aetate_en.html.

Segal, Alan F. *Paul the Convert: The Apostolate and Apostasy of Saul the Pharisee.* New Haven, CT: Yale University Press, 1990.

Smith, Morton. "A Comparison of Early Christian and Early Rabbinic Tradition." *Journal of Biblical Literature* 82 (1963): 169–76.

Soares Prabhu, George M. *The Formula Quotations in the Infancy Narrative of Matthew: An Enquiry into the Tradition History of Mt 1–2.* Analecta Biblica 63. Rome: Biblical Institute Press, 1976.

Spencer, Aida Besancon. *Beyond the Curse: Women Called to Ministry.* Nashville: T. Nelson, 1985.

Stanley, David. "Some Reflections on the Introspective Conscience from New Testament Data." In *Ecumenical Dialogue at Harvard: The Roman Catholic-Protestant Colloquium,* edited by Samuel H. Miller and G. Ernest Wright, 257–61. Cambridge, MA: Belknap Press, 1964.

Stendahl, Brita K. *The Force of Tradition: A Case Study of Women Priests in Sweden.* Philadelphia: Fortress, 1985. Translated by Ingela Åstrand as *Traditionens makt: Kvinnan och prästämbetet i Svenska kyrkan.* Stockholm: Petra, 1985.

———. *Sabbatical Reflections: The Ten Commandments in a New Day.* Philadelphia: Fortress, 1980. Translated by Astrid Lundgren as *Sabbatsår: Tio Guds bud i vår tid.* Stockholm: Legenda, 1986.

———. *Søren Kierkegaard.* Boston: Twayne, 1976. Translated by Hans-Erik Johannesson as *Søren Kierkegaard.* Stockholm: Atlantis, 1980.

Stendahl, Krister. "Ancient Scripture in the Modern World." In *Scripture in the Jewish and Christian Traditions: Authority, Interpretation, Relevance,* edited by Frederick E. Greenspahn, 201–14. Nashville: Abingdon Press, 1982.

———. "Ännu ser vi en gåtfull spegelbild: Teologi som vet sin begränsning." In *Samtal om religionsteologi,* edited by Kajsa Ahlstrand and Håkan Sandvik. Tro & Tanke 2001:3, 67–72. Uppsala: Svenska kyrkans forskningsråd, 2001.

———. "The Apostle Paul and the Introspective Conscience of the West." In *Paul among Jews and Gentiles,* 78–96. Philadelphia: Fortress, 1976. Originally published in *Harvard Theological Review* 56 (1963): 199–215.

———. *Bibelns mening*. Stockholm: Sveriges kristliga studentrörelses bokförlag, 1952.

———. "Bibelsynen och kvinnan." In *Kvinnan—Samhället—Kyrkan*, 138–67. Stockholm: Svenska kyrkans diakonistyrelses bokförlag, 1958.

———. *The Bible and the Role of Women: A Case Study in Hermeneutics*. Translated by Emilie T. Sander. Philadelphia: Fortress Press, 1966.

———. "Biblical Studies in the University." In *The Study of Religion in Colleges and Universities*, edited by Paul Ramsey and John F. Wilson, 23–39. Princeton, NJ: Princeton University Press, 1970.

———. "Biblical and Theological Basis for Christians Concerned about the Family." Unpublished manuscript for speech delivered at The Family Life Conference sponsored by the Committee on Social and Specialized Ministries of the Episcopal Church's Church in Society Office, Denver, CO, November 13–16, 1978. Harvard Divinity School Archives.

———. "Biblical Theology, Contemporary." In *The Interpreter's Dictionary of the Bible*, edited by George Arthur Buttrick, 1:418–32. New York: Abingdon, 1962. Reprinted as "Biblical Theology: A Program," in *Meanings*, 11–44.

———. "Can Bishops Tell the Truth as They See It?" In *Christianity in the 21st Century*, edited by Deborah A. Brown, 181–90. New York: Crossroad, 2000.

———. "The Charismatic Movement and the New Testament." In *What the Spirit is Saying to the Churches*, edited by Theodore Runyon, 17–28. New York: Hawthorn Books, 1975.

———. *Energy for Life: Reflections on the Theme "Come, Holy Spirit—Renew the Whole Creation."* Geneva: WCC Publications, 1990.

———. "Enrichment or Threat? When the Eves Come Marching In." In Hageman, *Sexist Religion and Women in the Church*, 17–28.

———. *Final Account: Paul's Letter to the Romans*. Minneapolis: Fortress, 1995.

———. *Holy Week*. Proclamation: Aids for Interpreting the Lessons of the Church Year, Series A. Philadelphia: Fortress, 1974.

———. "Kvinnan i Bibeln och kyrkan." In *Handlingar rörande prästmötet i Stockholm den 2, 3 och 4 juni 1975*, 56–73. Stockholm: Diocese of Stockholm, 1975.

———. *Meanings: The Bible as Document and as Guide*. Philadelphia: Fortress, 1984; 2nd ed. Minneapolis: Fortress, 2008.

———. *Meningar*. Translated by Sixten Carlsson. Stockholm: Verbum, 1986.

———. "Om Maria: Min tros moder." *Växjö stifts hembygdskalender* 82 (1991): 30–32.

———. *Paul among Jews and Gentiles and Other Essays*. Minneapolis: Fortress, 1976.

———. "Paulus och samvetet." *Svensk exegetisk årsbok* 25 (1960): 62–77.

———. "*Quis et Unde?* An Analysis of Matthew 1–2." In *Judentum, Urchristentum, Kirche: Festschrift für Joachim Jeremias*, edited by Walther Eltester, 94–105. Berlin: Töpelmann, 1960. Reprinted in *The Interpretation of Matthew*, edited by Graham Stanton, 56–66. Philadelphia: Fortress, 1983.

———. *The Roots of Violence: Creating Peace through Spiritual Reconciliation*. Brewster, MA: Paraclete Press, 2016.

———. *The School of St. Matthew and Its Use of the Old Testament*. ASNU 20. Uppsala: Almqvist & Wiksell, 1954. Reprinted with a new preface. Philadelphia: Fortress Press, 1968.

———. *The Scrolls and the New Testament*. New York: Harper, 1957.

———. "Teologi till vänster." *Vår Lösen* 57:3 (1966): 128–133.

———. "Text and Multiculturalism." Lecture delivered at Hässelby Castle, Stockholm, May 23, 2004.

———. "Vad jag har lärt mig om judendomen mellan 1951 och 1991." *Tro möter tro: Med KJ–information* 1, no. 2 (1991): 16–20.

———. *What the Spirit Is Saying to the Churches: Essays*. New York: Hawthorn Books, 1975.

———. "Why I Love the Bible: Beyond Distinctions of Intellect and Spirit, an Ever-Transforming Affair of the Heart." *Harvard Divinity Bulletin* 35 (2007): 22–31. https://bulletin.hds.harvard.edu/articles/winter2007/why-i-love-bible.

———. "Working Paper and Notes: The Apostle Paul and the Introspective Conscience of the West." *Journal for the Scientific Study of Religion* 1 (1962): 261–63.

Stendahl, Krister, and Lars Gyllensten. "Angelägen teologi: Teologi om viktiga ting. Samtal mellan Krister Stendahl och Lars Gyllensten." *Vår Lösen* 67, no. 7 (1976): 349–54.

Stendahl Papers. Harvard Divinity School Archives.

———. Sigtunastiftelsen Library and Archives.

Stolzfus, Michael. "Christian Eye for the Queer Guy." *Journal of Lutheran Ethics* 5, no. 8 (August 2005), http://www.elca.org/JLE/Articles/646?_ga=2.124910158.515167279.1494874790-200062273.1494873747.

Stowers, Stanley K. A *Rereading of Romans: Justice, Jews, and Gentiles*. New Haven, CT: Yale University Press, 1994.

Stravinskas, Peter M. J. "Papal Anti-Judaism?" *The Catholic Report*, March 14, 2017, http://www.catholicworldreport.com/Item/5495/papal_anti judaism.aspx.

Taylor, Joan E. "4Q341: A Writing Exercise Remembered." In *Is There a Text in This Cave? Studies in the Textuality of the Dead Sea Scrolls in Honour of George J. Brooke*, edited by Ariel Feldman, Maria Cioată, and Charlotte Hempel, 133–51. STDJ 119. Leiden: Brill, 2017.

Thompson, Francis. "The Hound of Heaven." In *The Oxford Book of English Mystical Verse*, edited by D. H. S. Nicholson and A. H. E. Lee. Oxford: Clarendon, 1917. http://www.bartleby.com/236/239.html.

Tigchelaar, Eibert J.C. "Assessing Emanuel Tov's 'Qumran Scribal Practice.'" In *The Dead Sea Scrolls: Transmission of Traditions and Production of Texts*, edited by Sarianna Metso, Hindy Najman, and Eileen Schuller, 173–208. STDJ 92. Leiden: Brill, 2010.

Tov, Emanuel. *Scribal Practices and Approaches Reflected in the Texts Found in the Judean Desert*. STDJ 54. Leiden: Brill, 2004.

Ulrich, Eugene C. "The Qumran Biblical Scrolls: The Scriptures of Late Second Temple Judaism." In *The Dead Sea Scrolls in Their Historical Context*, edited by Timothy H. Lim, with A. Graeme Auld, Larry W. Hurtado, and Alison Jack, 67–88. Edinburgh: T&T Clark, 2000.

VanderKam, James C. "To What End? Functions of Scriptural Interpretation in Qumran Texts." In *Studies in the Hebrew Bible, Qumran, and the Septuagint Presented to Eugene Ulrich*, edited by Peter W. Flint, Emanuel Tov, and James C. VanderKam, 302–20. VTSup 101. Leiden: Brill, 2006.

Van Marter, Jerry L. "Empirical Hermeneutics: Dutch Scholar Employs Intercultural Contextual Bible Study to Explore how Study of Scripture Produces Transformation." Presbyterian News Service, June 4, 2014, http://www.pcusa.org/news/2013/6/4/empirical-hermeneutics.

Westerholm, Stephen. "Justification by Faith Is the Answer: What Is the Question?" *Concordia Theological Quarterly* 70 (2006): 197–217.

———. "The 'New Perspective' at Twenty-Five." In *Justification and Variegated Nomism*. Vol. 2, *The Paradoxes of Paul*, edited by D. A. Carson, Peter T. O'Brien, and Mark A. Seifrid, 1–38. Tübingen: Mohr Siebeck, 2001.

———. *Perspectives Old and New on Paul: The "Lutheran" Paul and His Critics*. Grand Rapids, MI: Eerdmans, 2004.

Williams, George H. *Calm Rising through Change and through Storm: The Contours of Religion and Commitment in an Age of Upheaval and Globalization*. Vol. 3 of *Divinings: Religion at Harvard from Its Origins in New England Ecclesiastical History to the 175th Anniversary of the Harvard Divinity School, 1636–1992*. Newton, MA: Boston Theological Institute, 2014.

Witherington, Ben. *Paul's Narrative Thought World: The Tapestry of Tragedy and Triumph*. Louisville, KY: Westminster John Knox Press, 1994.

Wolters, Al. "The Tetragrammaton in the Psalms Scroll." *Textus* 18 (1995): 87–99.

Wrede, William. *Paul*. Translated by Edward Lummis. London: Philip Green, 1907. Reprint, Eugene, OR: Wipf and Stock, 2001.

———. *Paulus*. Tübingen: J.C.B. Mohr, 1904.

Wright, N.T. "Justification: The Biblical Basis and Its Relevance for Contemporary Evangelicalism." In *The Great Acquittal: Justification by Faith and Current Christian Thought*, edited by Gavin Reid, 1–35. London: Collins, 1980.

———. "The Letter to the Galatians: Exegesis and Theology." In *Between Two Horizons: Spanning New Testament Studies and Systematic Theology*, edited by Joel B. Green and Max Turner, 205–36. Grand Rapids, MI: Eerdmans, 2000.

———. "New Perspectives on Paul." In *Justification in Perspective: Historical Developments and Contemporary Challenges*, edited by Bruce McCormack, 243–64. Grand Rapids, MI: Baker Academic, 2006.

———. *Paul and the Faithfulness of God.* 2 vols. Minneapolis: Fortress, 2013.

———. "Paul in Current Anglophone Scholarship." *Expository Times* 123, no. 8 (2012): 367–81.

———. *Paul: In Fresh Perspective*. Minneapolis: Fortress, 2005.

———. "The Paul of History and the Apostle of Faith." *Tyndale Bulletin* 29 (1978): 61–88.

———. *What Saint Paul Really Said: Was Paul of Tarsus the Real Founder of Christianity?* Grand Rapids, MI: Eerdmans, 1997.

Young, Paul. "The Love Shack." *Christianity Today*, March 4, 2013, http://www.christianitytoday.com/ct/2013/march/love-shack.html.

Zetterholm, Magnus. *Approaches to Paul: A Student's Guide to Recent Scholarship*. Minneapolis: Fortress, 2009.

———. "Paul within Judaism: The State of the Questions." In Nanos and Zetterholm, *Paul within Judaism*, 31–51.

NAME INDEX

OTHER VOLUMES IN THIS SERIES

Clemens Thoma and Michael Wyschogrod, eds., *Understanding Scripture: Explorations of Jewish and Christian Traditions of Interpretation* (1987; e-book only)

Bernard J. Lee, *The Galilean Jewishness of Jesus: Retrieving the Origins of Christianity (Conversation on the Road Not Taken*, vol. 1) (1988; e-book only)

Clemens Thoma and Michael Wyschogrod, eds., *Parable and Story in Judaism and Christianity* (1989)

Eugene J. Fisher, ed., *Interwoven Destinies: Jews and Christians through the Ages* (1992; e-book only)

George M. Smiga, *Pain and Polemic: Anti-Judaism in the Gospels* (1992; e-book only)

Anthony J. Kenny, *Catholics, Jews, and the State of Israel* (1993; e-book only)

Eugene J. Fisher, ed., *Visions of the Other: Jewish and Christian Theologians Assess the Dialogue* (1994; e-book only)

Vincent Martin, *A House Divided: The Parting of the Ways between Synagogue and Church* (1995; e-book only)

Leon Klenicki and Geoffrey Wigoder, *A Dictionary of the Jewish-Christian Dialogue* (1995; e-book only)

Frank E. Eakin Jr., *What Price Prejudice? Christian Antisemitism in America* (1998)

Philip A. Cunningham and Arthur F. Starr, eds., *Sharing Shalom: A Process for Local Interfaith Dialogue between Christians and Jews* (1999)

Ekkehard Schuster and Reinhold Boschert-Kimmig, *Hope against Hope: Johann Baptist Metz and Elie Wiesel Speak Out on the Holocaust* (1999)

Mary C. Boys, *Has God Only One Blessing? Judaism as a Source of Christian Self-Understanding* (2000)

Johannes Reuchlin; translated and edited by Peter Wortsman, *Recommendation Whether to Confiscate, Destroy and Burn All Jewish Books: A Classic Treatise against Anti-Semitism* (2000)

Other Volumes in This Series

Avery Dulles and Leon Klenicki, *The Holocaust, Never to Be Forgotten: Reflections on the Holy See's Document* We Remember (2001)

Philip A. Cunningham, *A Story of Shalom: The Calling of Christians and Jews by a Covenanting God* (2001; e-book only)

Philip A. Cunningham, *Sharing the Scriptures: The Word Set Free*, volume 1 (2003)

Dina Wardi, *Auschwitz: Contemporary Jewish and Christian Encounters* (2003)

Michael Lotker, *A Christian's Guide to Judaism* (2004)

Edward H. Flannery, *The Anguish of the Jews: Twenty-Three Centuries of Antisemitism*, revised and updated ed. (2004)

Lawrence Boadt, CSP, and Kevin di Camillo, eds., *John Paul II in the Holy Land: In His Own Words; With Christian and Jewish Perspectives by Yehezkel Landau and Michael McGarry, CSP* (2005)

James K. Aitken and Edward Kessler, eds., *Challenges in Jewish-Christian Relations* (2006)

Steven C. Boguslawski, OP, *Thomas Aquinas on the Jews: Insights into His Commentary on Romans 9—11* (2008)

George M. Smiga, *The Gospel of John Set Free: Preaching without Anti-Judaism* (2008)

Daniel J. Harrington, SJ, *The Synoptic Gospels Set Free: Preaching without Anti-Judaism* (2009)

Richard C. Lux, *The Jewish People, the Holy Land, and the State of Israel: A Catholic View* (2009)

Cardinal Jean-Marie Lustiger, edited by Jean Duchesne, *Cardinal Jean-Marie Lustiger on Christians and Jews* (2010)

Pope Benedict XVI, *Pope Benedict XVI in the Holy Land* (2010)

Thomas G. Casey and Justin Taylor, eds., *Paul's Jewish Matrix* (2011)

Franklin Sherman, ed., *Bridges—Documents of the Christian-Jewish Dialogue*. Volume 1, *The Road to Reconciliation (1945–1985)* (2011)

Eugene J. Fisher, eds., Memoria Futuri: *Catholic-Jewish Dialogue Yesterday, Today, and Tomorrow; Texts and Addresses of Cardinal William H. Keeler* (2012)

Mary C. Boys, *Redeeming Our Sacred Story: The Death of Jesus and Relations between Jews and Christians* (2013)

Celia M. Deutsch, Eugene J. Fisher, and James Rudin, eds., *Toward the Future: Essays on Catholic-Jewish Relations in Memory of Rabbi León Klenicki* (2013)

Franklin Sherman, ed., *Bridges—Documents of the Christian-Jewish Dialogue*. Volume 2, *Building a New Relationship (1986–2013)* (2014)

Other Volumes in This Series

Ronald Kronish, ed., *Coexistence and Reconciliation in Israel: Voices for Interreligious Dialogue* (2015)

Elena G. Procario-Foley and Robert A. Cathey, eds., *Righting Relations after the Holocaust and Vatican II: Essays in Honor of John Pawlikowski, OSM* (2018)

Paula Fredriksen and Jesper Svartvik, eds., *Krister Among the Jews and Gentiles* (2018)

Carol Rittner, Stephen D. Smith, and Irena Steinfeldt. *The Holocaust and the Christian World: Reflections on the Past, Challenges for the Future*, 2nd ed. (2019)

STIMULUS BOOKS are developed by the Stimulus Foundation, a not-for-profit organization, and are published by Paulist Press. The Foundation wishes to further the publication of scholarly books on Jewish and Christian topics that are of importance to Judaism and Christianity.

The Stimulus Foundation was established by an erstwhile refugee from Nazi Germany who intends to contribute with these publications to the improvement of communication between Jews and Christians.

Books for publication in this Series will be selected by a committee of the Foundation, and offers of manuscripts and works in progress should be addressed to:

The Stimulus Foundation
c/o Paulist Press
997 Macarthur Boulevard
Mahwah, NJ 07430
www.paulistpress.com